VINA
BAY

Archangel

Bakharitza

N. Dvina River

Kholmogory

Pinega

Priluka

Trufanagora

Viskagora

Pinega River

Kuzomen
Ostrov
Leunova

Karpogora

Dvina River

Siskoe

Emetskoe

nova

Obozerskaya

Tiogra

Bolshie
Ozerki

Seletskoe

VERST 445

Shred
Makharenga

Emtsa

Emtsa R.

Kodish

Onega River

Avda

Bereznik

Dvina River

Kurgoman

Kochmas

Malo Bereznik

Maximofskaya

Kitsa

Toulgas

Plesetskaya

Vistafka

Seltso

Shagovari

Fedorova

Vaga R.

Shenkursk

TO VOLOGDA

Ust-Padenga

Visorka Gora

Nijni Gora

40   41   42   43   44

WITHDRAWN

THE
POLAR
BEAR
EXPEDITION

THE
POLAR
BEAR
EXPEDITION

THE HEROES OF AMERICA'S
FORGOTTEN INVASION OF RUSSIA
1918–1919

JAMES CARL NELSON

WM

WILLIAM MORROW
An Imprint of HarperCollins*Publishers*

HarperCollins books may be purchased for educational, business, or sales promotional use. For information, please email the Special Markets Department at SPsales@harpercollins.com.

FIRST EDITION

Endpaper map by Nick Springer, copyright © 2018 Springer Cartographics LLC.

Library of Congress Cataloging-in-Publication Data

Names: Nelson, James Carl, author.
Title: The Polar Bear Expedition : the heroes of America's forgotten invasion of Russia, 1918–1919 / James Carl Nelson.
Other titles: America's forgotten invasion of Russia
Description: New York, NY : William Morrow, [2019] | Includes bibliographical references.
Identifiers: LCCN 2018037597 | ISBN 9780062852779 (hardcover) | ISBN 9780062852786 (pbk.)
Subjects: LCSH: Polar Bear Expedition (1918-1919) | United States. Army. Infantry Regiment, 339th—History. | Soldiers—Michigan—History—20th century. | Michigan—History, Military—20th century. | World War, 1914-1918—Regimental histories—United States. | Soviet Union—History—Allied intervention, 1918-1920.
Classification: LCC DK265.42.U5 N45 2019 | DDC 947.084/1—dc23 LC record available at https://lccn.loc.gov/2018037597

ISBN 978-0-06-285277-9

19 20 21 22 23   RS/LSC   10 9 8 7 6 5 4 3 2 1

CONTENTS

THE POLAR BEARS

Anyone interested in the American experience in World War 1 is familiar with Belleau Wood, Cantigny, Soissons, and the Meuse-Argonne. It's not as likely that they've heard of Vistafka, Kodish, Onega, Pinega, Obozerskaya, Ust Padenga . . .

Nijni Gora.

Those places, and more, are where American soldiers found themselves in a deadly, day-to-day struggle with Bolshevik fighters in far northern Russia in the spring, fall, and winter of 1918–1919. They're battlefields on which more than two hundred of them were killed in action or died from disease, wounds, and accidents, while handfuls of others were taken prisoner or went forever missing.

When the men of the 339th Infantry Regiment, the First Battalion of the 310th Engineers, the 337th Field Hospital, and the 337th Ambulance Company finally returned home in July 1919—long after the Great War had ended—some of them paraded, while others went on to their mostly anonymous lives. They would come to refer to themselves as "The Polar Bears," veterans of a most unusual conflict.

Inquiries about their war and their experience were met by "specious pleas in evasive avoidance," one former Polar Bear, Lt. John Cudahy, would write, "for the enterprise will always remain a depraved one with status of a freebooters' excursion."

There were in fact two American forces sent to Russia in 1918—the "American Expeditionary Force, Siberia," based out of Vladivostok, and the "American Expeditionary Force, North Russia," out of Archangel, near the White Sea, one thousand miles north of Moscow. *The Polar Bear Expedition* focuses on the latter, the so-called North Russia Campaign, and shines a new light on America's intervention in the Russian Civil War and the heroic men who suffered in the intense cold of an Arctic winter, each one determinedly holding his piece of frozen ground for himself and the man next to him—while fighting and dying and wondering with increasing bitterness just why he had been sent into Russia, and why he, why all of them, had remained there for months after World War 1 had concluded.

Their "excursion"—invasion, if you will—constituted a major forgotten act in the long history of U.S.-Russian relations. The two nations' history began with the appointment of an American minister to St. Petersburg in 1790 and the subsequent establishment of trade between the two countries. Eighteen sixty-seven saw the Russian sale of Alaska to the United States. Through the nineteenth century, one writer notes, "there were no real conflicts between the vital interests of the Russian and American states," and relations remained more or less friendly until the revolution that in late 1917 brought the Bolsheviks to power—and led to the U.S. decision to join their European allies in an attempted intervention in northern Russia.

After the Americans left northern Russia in 1919, a rapprochement between the two countries was established, followed by the odd and tenuous alignment of World War 2, and thence the mistrust and enmity and jockeying for hegemony that marked the Cold War. While there was some easing of tensions following the dissolution of the Soviet Union in the late 1980s and early 1990s, relations between the two world powers have once more become strained, this time over allegations that Russia tried to sway our 2016 national elections—just as we almost unwittingly sought to interfere in the Russian Civil War one hundred years ago.

And so as the drama and mistrust continue between the two powers, this book takes a timely look back to where that drama began; it seems the past will always be prologue when it comes to the United States and Russia.

THE
POLAR
BEAR
EXPEDITION

PROLOGUE

They've been expecting it for weeks—hell, months. And so the men of Company A of the 339th Infantry Regiment—the Polar Bears, they would come to call themselves—have stood night and day in forty-below-zero temperatures. They stamp their feet and try not to touch bare skin on the frozen barrels of their weapons lest their flesh be ripped off; they peer through the deep, ebony night from their dark, log-lined dugouts into the frigid tundra toward the south and east across the ice-choked river and watch for it, wait for it, and wonder how many will come and how they will perform when they do—and they wonder, too, if and how they will ever get out of this place, this frozen Hades, this last place on earth at the top of the world.

And then early on this morning they do come, a horde of them, dim forms in the distance spread out across the Vaga River, some on skis and others on snowshoes and all of them armed, like ghost warriors traversing the River Styx—hundreds of them to their mere handful of forty-six.

Bolos, the men call them.

Bolsheviks.

Now a shell, flung from upriver, arcing and piercing the barely gray of dawn, flies over the village. Lt. Harry Mead awakens with a start, quickly dons his fur hat and overcoat and boots, and races to the far outpost, where this scant group of half-frozen men stands guard against not only the enemy but the tide of history.

The sergeant hands him his field glass and he squints through the misty, blowing snow, the only sounds the sharp snapping of frozen tree branches and the dull booming of the river ice cracking. He sees them now, coming on several hundred yards in the distance, and he quickly understands that the company is probably doomed.

Now a grayish form enters his view, much closer, and he peels the glass from his eye. Steam comes from his mouth as the thin outpost is now about to be overrun by a nearer group of the enemy, who have snuck closer and rise like dervishes from their concealment in the deep snow.

Lt. Harry Mead, late of Valparaiso, Indiana, and Detroit, Michigan, stranded more than two hundred miles from his regiment's base at Archangel, Russia, doesn't have to speak as the mass of Bolos descends on his small detachment. His men are already furiously firing their machine guns and rifles at this grisly apparition, all while more artillery shells spew over and land amid them. But Mead yells the words anyway, as if by rote, as if it's not too late, as if any one of them has a chance.

"Fire!" Mead orders his men. "For God's sakes, fire!"

CHAPTER ONE

THE MARCH TO INTERVENTION

The preliminaries began on March 9, 1918, with millions of high-explosive and gas shells raining across the front between the northern French cities of Ypres and St. Quentin; the smothering of the British-held territory continued through that week and beyond, and was topped off with a continuous salvo from 6,700 pieces of German artillery, which began at 4:40 A.M. on March 21.

Five hours later, heavy mortars began raining death and destruction on the British Fifth Army, and five minutes later the advance of three German armies, sixty-nine divisions in all, poured from their trenches and headed east, with the aim of splitting the junction of British and French forces on the southern end of the Somme front and sending the Brits in a panic for the protection of the Channel ports.

There was an urgency to the assault, and for good reason. With the signing of the Treaty of Brest-Litovsk on March 3, Russia had officially taken itself out of the war and relieved the pressure on Germany's Eastern Front. After years of fighting a two-front war, German forces were now consolidated. Meanwhile, the United States, which had declared war on Germany nearly a year before, had yet to send enough men across the Atlantic to tip the balance in the Allies' favor on the Western Front. But the Yanks were coming. During that spring of 1918, therefore, Germany had a small and unique window in which to act while the numbers favored them, and so the handpicked assault troops went forward in great and deadly haste.

Above the attackers, 326 fighter aircraft soared into the morning, their opposition just 261 British planes. Following barrages, small teams of storm troopers appeared out of the deep fog and, ignoring the British strong points, cut swaths through the trenches with light machine guns, automatic weapons, and flamethrowers.

By the end of the first day of what would be a months-long offensive, the Germans had pushed more than four miles through the British and were still advancing. In their wake, they left the bodies of an untold number of defenders, thousands of wounded, and 21,000 prisoners. By March 23, three huge guns made by the arms manufacturer Krupp had been hauled forward and began sending shells into Paris, seventy-two miles away. Two hundred Parisians would be killed on that day alone.

Those unlucky Parisians would be but grains of sand in an ocean of war that had enveloped France since August 1914, when a gray tide of Germans had pushed across the border with Belgium and by early September had very nearly taken Paris. The flood was checked on the Marne River east of the French capital in early September, but the war—it would eventually become known as the Great War—had only begun. The Germans intended to stay, and by the end of 1914 a dizzying series of parallel zigzagging trenches—German, French, and, to the north, those of France's British allies—scarred the French soil from Switzerland to the North Sea as all sides settled into a deadlock.

Over the ensuing months and years, incredibly costly attempts would be made on all sides to break that deadlock, only to fall victim to a new generation of powerful killing tools, chief among them the machine gun, long-range artillery, and gas. The men, meanwhile, lived like troglodytes in the trenches, sloshing about in knee-high water and dodging rats that fed on the dead, and poking their heads above ground only to watch for a coming enemy attack across the scarred ground pocked by shell holes and barbed wire and mud.

And the attacks did come, from all sides. At Loos in the fall of 1915, more than eighty percent of an attacking force of 10,000 Brits were killed or wounded, cut down in rows by machine guns as they advanced. In a single day—July 1, 1916—at the Somme more than 20,000 British soldiers were killed and another 25,000 wounded, this although more than 200,000 artillery rounds had been fired at the German lines prior to the attack. Between July 1916 and the following November, the British would take six miles of ground, losing almost 100,000 men in the effort; the Germans, meanwhile, lost more than 160,000 men over the same period and same ground.

The French fared no better. An April 1917 offensive at the Aisne River was launched with the hope of capturing six miles of territory, employing newfangled tanks in battle for the first time. But the advance quickly ground down, and by the time it was called off, 100,000 French had become casualties. By then, the French had lost so many men—almost 1.4 million French soldiers would die by the end of 1918, a number dwarfed only by the 1.8 million Germans killed in the war— that there were open revolts in the ranks. Fifty French soldiers— poilus—were subsequently tried, found guilty of mutiny, and shot by firing squads, while hundreds of others were imprisoned.

The stalemate continued, but there was hope for all.

The United States, prodded by German U-boat attacks on its shipping, had finally cast off its isolationism and on April 6, 1917, declared war on Germany. With hardly more than 100,000 American men in uniform and the Allies asking for 1 million men, it would take some time for the United States to get up to speed militarily, and there were great concerns among the French and British, who were just holding on on the Western Front, that all would be lost before American boys could arrive in numbers great enough to tilt the balance of power Over There.

As for the Germans? By design, they faced a two-front war, as Russia by treaty was obligated to strike to the west should France be attacked. German military architects had planned to invade and take France at the war's outset while the Russians slowly mobilized, then turn east and contend with Russia. Those designs obviously went kaput as the German Army became bogged down on the Western Front.

Russian forces did indeed quickly move west into East Prussia, only to be checked at the Masurian Lakes in August 1914. Unlike in the west, the Eastern Front would thereafter remain fluid, as fighting raged from Lithuania south through Poland, the Ukraine, and Romania, the Germans and their Austro-Hungarian allies and the Russians trading blows, victories, and terrible losses.

But for the Germans, a ray of hope emerged in 1917. While twelve million Russian soldiers had kept eighty German divisions pinned across the Eastern Front, the collapse of Czar Nicholas's regime in March 1917, and a subsequent disastrous Russian offensive the following June, led to the dissolution of the army.

Many disgruntled Russian soldiers, sick of war and hardships, simply stopped fighting, and in some cases murdered their officers. Much of the army then began drifting away, and many soldiers threw down their weapons and headed home. While Alexander Kerensky's Provisional Government had supported continuing the fight against Germany and its allies, and the Allies—including the United States—had quickly recognized his government in the belief that Russia would keep its huge army in the fight, all such hope was dashed when the Bolsheviks assumed power in November 1917. On November 8, Bolshevik leader Vladimir Lenin, who with the help of Germany had been spirited back into Russia from exile the previous April, issued a Decree for Peace at a Congress of Soviets, asking all warring nations to lay down their arms and negotiate an end to the war. On the same day, he issued a Decree of the Land, announcing that all private ownership of land would be abolished.

Soon after, armistice negotiations began with the German high command, which was eager to end the conflict on the Eastern Front as soon as possible so it could transfer troops to the west for a planned March 1918 offensive. The Germans intended to win the war in the west before the Americans could arrive in numbers large enough to make the difference.

Lenin, too, was eager to quit the fight so his government could focus on the increasing troubles at home, where the economy was in chaos and armed forces loyal to the deposed czar—the so-called Whites—were attempting to undo the Revolution.

After achieving an armistice with Russia on December 15, Germany indeed began moving men west, and according to some estimates one million German soldiers were transferred to France between mid-December and the ultimate March 3, 1918, signing of the Brest-Litovsk Treaty, which besides costing Russia one-quarter of its peoples and farmable land took Russia out of the war once and for all.

For the Allies, the treaty between Germany and Russia was a disaster—one that was only compounded when Germany unleashed its long-planned, huge offensive on March 21. With the Eastern Front gone, more and more German soldiers would be joining the drive on the west, and it seemed all but certain that the Allies would be pushed into the sea. "Things look very bad," British prime minister David Lloyd George said during the early days of that offensive. "I fear it means disaster."

Adding to the despair and nervousness of the Allies was the discovery in April 1918 that 55,000 German troops had been sent to Finland, which borders Russia on the northeast and whose eastern boundary is just 150 miles from the Russian port of Murmansk. The port was ice-free in winter, and there were worries that the Germans could easily seize Murmansk, where millions of dollars' worth of Allied war materiel meant for the Russian Army had been off-loaded, and build a submarine base from which attacks on Allied shipping could be made.

Though there was little or no evidence such plans were being laid, the besieged Allies' minds ran rampant with all of the ruinous possibilities Russia's leaving the war could bring them—and by April, a British force of 150 marines had landed at Murmansk, which was followed by another contingent of 370 men at the end of May.

The Bolsheviks had their own concerns about Murmansk and what appeared to be the threatening force of Germans, but Leon Trotsky, Lenin's minister of war, turned a blind eye to the British landings, and both he and Lenin appeared happy to let someone else deal with the threat on the Kola Peninsula while they were consumed with more pressing matters.

The Allies, too, had more pressing matters that spring of 1918. The great German drive had continued east through April, but by some miracle the target city of Amiens had held, and north of that city French colonials had managed to break the German tide around the villages of Montdidier and Cantigny.

But, even as the American First Division was making its country's first large-scale assault of the war at Cantigny on May 28, a new German push south of the Aisne that had launched the day before threatened the envelopment of Paris, which by June 1 was only thirty-five miles away from where the German military architect Erich Ludendorff's storm troopers were surging to the Marne River.

Elements of the American Third Division held the line at the river in the first days of June, and after Ludendorff ordered a southeasterly advance toward Paris, the river of gray uniforms found themselves being stymied by United States Marines at Belleau Wood. Three weeks of savage fighting would leave the marines in possession of the field and the wood, which by the end of June sported little more than a jumble of splintered trees, shell holes, and the detritus—dead bodies, rifles, shattered equipment—of battle.

The great German tide was stemmed for the time being, but the anxiety among the Allies remained at a boiling point—and to some, the only available option to win the war was intervention in Russia and the reestablishment of the Eastern Front. Winston Churchill, the British minister of munitions, was adamant about a Russian solution, saying "the sacrifices of the peoples and the armies" would be in vain if the Allies could not "reconstitute the fighting front in the East."

The British had attempted to gain support for Russian intervention from the Allied Supreme War Council in early April, and appealed for American help in an intervention not only in the Murmansk-Archangel area to the far north, but at Vladivostok in the far east, where another huge pile of Allied materiel lay, about which there were concerns that they could fall into the hands of the Germans and be transported west along the Trans-Siberian Railroad.

The British appealed over and over to President Woodrow Wilson to approve the sending of troops to Russia, and while he did agree to send a single American ship—the *Olympia*—to Murmansk, he repeatedly refused to send in the army.

Wilson, who had made the evacuation of "all Russian territory" by alien forces one of his famous Fourteen Points, had the backing of his most influential advisors, among them Secretary of War Newton Baker, Secretary of State Robert Lansing, and Gen. Peyton C. March, who would call the idea of an intervention in northern Russia "nonsense from the beginning."

Not so the British and, to a lesser degree, the French. On May 26, the British war cabinet approved sending 1,000 troops to the Murmansk area to protect it from any German designs, and also agreed to send another contingent of 560 men east from Murmansk to Archangel in the summer.

This force, it was hoped, would be able to connect with and train locals in northern Russia who were opposed to the Bolsheviks—and also, it was further hoped, link up with a large army of veteran soldiers who were then fighting their way east and through Bolshevik opposition along the Trans-Siberian Railroad.

Known as the "Czech Legion," these 40,000 to 70,000 men had mostly begun the war as conscripts of the Austro-Hungarian Empire, Germany's main ally. They were well-trained and able fighters, but ethnically related more to their Slavic cousins the Russians. In dribs and drabs, or sometimes as entire units, they had managed to surrender to the Russians and so wound up fighting in the Russian Army.

Though the Czechs at that time had no country but were simply part of the Austro-Hungarian Empire, back home Czech nationalist leaders Thomas Masaryk and Eduard Benes were pressing for the creation of an independent republic and had successfully persuaded the Provisional Government for the creation of a "Czech Corps" within the Russian Army.

When the armistice between Russia and Germany was signed, how-ever, the Czechs, like their Russian cousins, were put out of the war. Masaryk suggested to the Allies that the corps be moved to the Western Front—and the suggestion was approved. Now the problem became one of how to move this well-organized force of men from the Ukraine to Vladivostok, and thence to France.

The Bolsheviks initially approved of the movement, and before long trains crammed with the still well-armed Czech Legionnaires were rolling east toward Siberia. But as they did, British and French military minds began to consider whether some, or most, of this seasoned group of fighters could be turned around and help with the intervention in the north of Russia—and with a re-creation of the Eastern Front.

As the Czechs rolled on, they ran into local Bolsheviks who de-manded payment, usually in the form of weapons. Germany, too, de-manded that the Bolsheviks prohibit the Czech movement, wanting to keep them away from the Western Front.

In May 1918 an incident occurred that led to the Czechs turning against the Reds when a legionnaire was killed in the city of Chelya-binsk by a piece of heavy iron that had been thrown by a Hungar-ian former prisoner who was headed west. The offender was quickly dragged from his train and hanged by the Czechs, which led to a series of recriminations. Finally, the Czechs stormed the train station and then the local armory.

A few days later, the Czechs were ordered to disarm; they instead gathered together and pronounced themselves the Congress of the Czechoslovak Revolutionary Army. They also split their force, with one contingent continuing eastward across Siberia toward the Asia-Pacific port of Vladivostok while the other turned north toward Ekaterinburg in the Ural Mountains, where its advance that July would lead the Bol-sheviks to execute the deposed former czar Nicholas and his family out of fears the Romanovs might be rescued from their exile and returned to power.

In the United States, this "lost legion" of Czechs became the object of intense interest in the newspapers; "Czech Successes Alarm Soviets," the *Detroit Free Press* reported on June 25, 1918. "Czechs Capture Kazan Control Lower Volga," the *New York Times* relayed on July 16. President Wilson himself had much interest and sympathy for the plight of the Czechs, who were scattered along the Trans-Siberian railroad from Vladivostok in the east to the Ural Mountains to the west.

The situation with the Czechs slowly caused Wilson to reconsider the continuing Allied pleas for help in the intervention, and while the president and many of his advisors never bought the idea that re-creating an Eastern Front was feasible, Wilson saw in the Czechs a possible justification for the United States to intervene militarily, both in far eastern Siberia and in north Russia: the guarding of Allied stores, and the rescue of the Czechs.

Anti-Bolshevists in Siberia assured the president that American intervention in Russia's vast Asia-Pacific region would be welcome, and one official—Charles Turner Williams, who had spent time in Russia—told Wilson that an armed intervention by American and Japanese soldiers there would "result in bringing to the cause of the allies thousands of Russian soldiers, officer[s] and leaders who are only waiting for some such display of force to take sides against the present impossible Bolsheviki."

In European Russia's north, as well, there were pleas for intervention. America's ambassador to Russia, David Francis, was rabidly anti-Red, and had warned after the November 1917 Revolution that any Bolshevik success would be "a menace to all orderly governments, ours not excepted." Sending American troops, he said, would provide support to "millions of sensible Russians" who "only need encouragement to organize" against the Bolsheviks.

"Russia is awaking from the orgy or dream of the last seven months realizing this fallacy Bolshevism and the failure Lenin's 'experiment in government' to use his own words," Francis wrote in a cable to the secretary of state on June 22, 1918.

"Workmen and peasants have turned against [the] Soviet government as they see paralysis of industry and are facing famine. Weakness of Soviet government is demonstrated by the success of Czecho-Slovaks who have overcome whatever resistance offered and have been welcomed by every city because they have carefully abstained from interference in internal affairs while overturning unpopular local Soviets and installing whatever government citizens desired."

With those words Francis pushed aside the exact *opposite* argument that the vice consul in Archangel, Felix Cole, had made in a long cable to the ambassador on June 1. Cole had had his ear to the ground in the north of Russia since 1916, and he saw nothing but peril in intervening. "Intervention cannot reckon on active support from Russians," Cole wrote. "All the fight is out of Russia."

The average Russian, Cole added, supported the Bolsheviks, and an intervention would only alienate them. And he pointed to history—one had to look no further than Napoleon Bonaparte's disastrous experience in Russia one hundred years before—as another sound reason to stay away.

Napoleon during the latter half of 1812 crossed into Russia with an army estimated to have contained between 500,000 and almost 700,000 men. Most of this "Grande Armée" reached Moscow in September 1812 only to find it deserted and stripped of food and other supplies; leaving Moscow in October, the force retraced its steps over the same route it had picked clean on its five-hundred-mile advance. "General Winter" soon added temperatures of twenty below and colder to the misery of the troops. Estimates vary wildly, but it's safe to say that only 40,000 to 70,000 men survived the round-trip.

"Every foreign invasion that has gone deep into Russia has been swallowed up," Cole wrote. "The Germans know this and have only taken the nearest and most fruitful regions, avoiding the unproductive north." Cole would add, presciently, "If we intervene, going farther into Russia as we succeed, we shall be swallowed up."

Cole also said that any intervention would, in effect, put the United States on the wrong side of history, writing that the U.S. "shall have sold our birthright in Russia for a mess of pottage. The birthright is the future friendship and economic cooperation with a great and free democracy controlling untold riches. The pottage will be the recovery of a few thousand tons of materials [*sic*] that we once gave to Russia after deciding we could ourselves do without them."

Not wanting Cole's pessimism to sway Wilson's coming decision on intervention, Francis was careful to mail Cole's passionate arguments to Washington instead of cabling them.

Cole's well-thought-out thesis would not arrive in the U.S. until July 19; meanwhile, even while Wilson and his cabinet continued to argue that no resources should be spared on the Western Front and believed that that was where the war would be won, the Allied Supreme War Council on June 3, 1918, recommended the occupation of Murmansk and Archangel to counter any German threats, and decided that the British should be in command of any expedition.

British foreign secretary Alfred Balfour pressed Wilson to send a brigade—two regiments—"and a few guns" to Murmansk, and he discounted any fears that the soldiers would see any real action. He, like many in the Allied governments, regarded Trotsky and Lenin and their Bolshevik cronies as little more than thugs, and few could imagine that the Red government would last very long.

"It is not necessary that the troops should be completely trained," Balfour said, "as we anticipate that military operations in this region will only be of irregular character."

Slowly, Wilson's opposition to intervention was eroding, and a plan of action, with the Czechs at the center, began to emerge. Secretary of State Robert Lansing argued that "furnishing protection and assistance to the Czecho-Slovaks, who are so loyal to our cause," would differ from "sending an army into Siberia to restore order and save the Russians from themselves."

On the evening of July 16, the sixty-one-year-old Wilson, admittedly "sweating blood" over the issue of intervention, sat down and poured out his agonized, sometimes contradictory assent to sending American troops into Russia.

In his aide-mémoire, he would vow that the "whole heart of the people of the United States is in the winning of the war" and they wished "to cooperate in every practicable way with the allied governments, and to cooperate ungrudgingly."

He would go on to assert that the United States could not "consent to break or slacken the force of its present effort by diverting any part of its military force to other points or objectives." An intervention in Russia, he continued, "would add to the present sad confusion in Russia rather than cure it, injure her rather than help her, and that it would be of no advantage in the prosecution of our main design, to win the war against Germany."

But then, while opposing any intervention he vexingly allowed that he *did* support "military action" in Russia to aid the Czechs—and went on to write:

"Whether from Vladivostok or from Murmansk or Archangel, the only legitimate object for which American or allied troops can be employed . . . is to guard military stores which may be subsequently needed by Russian forces and to render such aid as may be acceptable to the Russians in the organization of their own self defense [*sic*] . . . For helping the Czecho-Slovaks there is immediate necessity and sufficient justification."

Carefully worded, the aide-mémoire went to great lengths to deny that any American military presence, whether in the east or in the north, would constitute an organized "military intervention." Such presences, instead, were simply "modest and experimental" missions.

American troops in the European north, who would operate as the American Expeditionary Force, North Russia, Wilson added, would simply guard materiel. The soldiers sent across the Pacific to Vladivostok, the American Expeditionary Force, Siberia, would similarly guard stores, and also help the Czechs who were moving west along the Trans-Siberian Railroad in an attempt to link with their brethren heading east.

As one author notes, the "rambling, misguided document" would result in American troops being sent into Russia without "a clear understanding of their purpose." It also ignored the actual stated British and French aim of the intervention in northern Russia: a drive to connect with a Czech army that was supposedly coming west, and the subsequent reestablishment of the Eastern Front.

As Felix Cole had prophesized, that strategy would result in the swallowing up of the American force sent to northern Russia, and the loss of more than two hundred American lives, some of whose bodies remain under the taiga and hidden in the deep forests of northern Russia.

CHAPTER TWO

OVER WHERE

No one saw it coming, not one of them. Not Harry Costello or Joel Moore or Godfrey Anderson; not Harry Mead, nor Charlie Ryan, nor Robert Boyd, nor Thurman Kissick nor Clyde Clark nor Clifford Ballard nor Glen Weeks, nor Herbert Schroeder nor any of the men of the U.S. Army's 339th Infantry Regiment as they labored at Michigan's Camp Custer in the spring and summer of 1918 while their futures were being decided in Wilson's White House and the stuffy environs of London's 10 Downing Street and the Allied Supreme Council at Versailles, outside Paris.

Organized in August 1917, the 339th—one of four regiments that made up the Eighty-Fifth Division—consisted mostly of draftees from Michigan, and there were so many from the area around Detroit that the regiment called itself "Detroit's Own."

One man of the 339th would describe the mélange of troops as "factory workers, farmers, office help, school teachers. Some who could neither read nor write, from Kentucky or Tennessee. Some from Europe who had been in the U.S. for a month or years. A few who had been in some trouble, and had joined the Army to stay out of jail." Among them, too, were Slavic-speaking immigrants, Russians, Poles, and others from eastern Europe; they could not know that as they trained at Camp Custer their language skills would one day come in very handy.

To a man, all believed and hoped that one day they would steam for Europe and fight on the Western Front; their more immediate realities entailed learning what they could of the ways of the military under the guidance of U.S. Army regulars.

One of these young draftees was Godfrey Anderson, the twenty-two-year-old son of Swedish immigrants Fred and Sophia. Enjoying school and reading, the boyish-looking Anderson grew up on the family's Sparta, Michigan, farm but elected to attend the larger high school in Grand Rapids. He played football and baseball before graduating in 1913 and then returning home, where he remained for the next five years.

But world events, chiefly the world war then raging, would make their way to the Anderson stead in Kent County, as they did to the homes of some four million American men in 1917 and 1918. In March 1918, Godfrey registered for the draft; he would be ordered to report to Camp Custer on May 28, the day on which the U.S. First Division was storming the German-held village of Cantigny.

He was soon marching, drilling, being inoculated for a variety of diseases, and being lectured about the dangers of venereal disease; he and the other green recruits were soon also being put in their places by the camp's non-commissioned officers—one of whom, "a red headed foul-mouthed sergeant," Godfrey would recall—read them the riot act as they prepared to drill in full uniform and equipment one day.

"He began by delivering a violent diatribe, mostly consisting of threats, cursing, and obscenities, his voice at times rising almost to a shriek as he belabored us with vituperation and insult, referring to us repeatedly as bastards and sons of bitches," a shocked Godfrey would recall.

"What seemed incomprehensible was that an officer—a lieutenant— stood right behind him, impassive and preoccupied, making no slightest effort to temper this vile ranting."

That officer could have been Harry Costello, a tough, diminutive Irishman from what was called Dublin Hill in Meriden, Connecticut. Standing just five foot seven and weighing less than 140 pounds, and already sporting in his midtwenties the battered face of a punch-drunk prizefighter, Harry was the son of Irish immigrant Patrick, an iron molder, and Katherine, also an immigrant from the Emerald Isle.

Despite his size, Harry starred in football while at Meriden High School, and in 1910 he was recruited by then football powerhouse Georgetown University. Playing quarterback, he earned the nickname "Nine Point Harry" after almost single-handedly defeating the University of Virginia three years in a row. "After his fourth year, Virginia broke off athletic relations with Georgetown," the *Washington Times* would report.

"If ever a varsity eleven had an evil genius, Virginia has one in Harry Costello, the most brilliant individual football player in this section of the country, and his spells and devilish incantations brought [Georgetown's] third successive triumph over the Orange and Blue, 16 to 13," the *Times* would also report after the 1912 tilt.

"As fleet as the wind itself," another paper would gush in 1911, "he has indomitable pluck and nerve and an eye that is sharp as the hunter's . . . It is related of this young hero that once when he was supposed to be in bed with a broken rib or some similar ailment, he suddenly appeared on the football field . . . and insisted on getting in the lineup.

"He had escaped from his room by dropping his football togs out the window and going out after them as he knew that his relatives would never permit him to play if they knew his plans. That is only one instance of his grit."

Even the legendary Jim Thorpe got into the act, saying that the best football player he ever played against was the "tough Irishman from Georgetown." By 1913, Harry had been named captain of the Georgetown squad.

After graduating in 1914, Harry headed back home, and played professional football for the "Yosts" in Bridgeport, but in his first game broke a rib. In 1915, at the age of just twenty-five, he was hired to coach the University of Detroit football squad, and also worked as a sportswriter for the *Detroit Free Press*, continuing an interest in newspapering that he had indulged with the *Washington Times* while still a student at Georgetown.

The lure of football was too much, however. By 1916, Harry was again prowling the gridiron, this time earning four hundred dollars per game while playing for his former rival Jim Thorpe, who was the player-coach of the famed Canton Bulldogs, which in 1920 would become one of the first franchises in the NFL.

In one game, against the Buffalo All-Stars, Thorpe quickly scored on a forty-six-yard punt return. "Moments later he zipped a pass to Harry Costello for another touchdown," according to the Professional Football Researchers Association. "In the second quarter . . . Big Jim ran for two TDs, tossed a second touchdown pass to Costello, and then reversed the process by scoring a touchdown via a throw from Costello."

Final score: 77–0.

There would be no football for Harry Costello in the fall of 1917, however. The United States had declared war on Germany on April 6; on May 11, Harry married Mary E. Kitchin in Detroit; four days later, he reported for officers' training at Fort Sheridan, outside of Chicago.

The following fall, the newly minted second lieutenant Harry J. Costello arrived at Camp Custer, near Battle Creek, Michigan, to which others fresh from training at Fort Sheridan were also heading. Harry Costello would soon find himself in the Machine Gun Company of the 339th Infantry Regiment.

Among them, too, was Harry Mead, a native of Valparaiso, Indiana, where his family ran a boardinghouse, taking in students of Valparaiso University. Mead also attended the school, and graduated in 1910 in the "Classics Class," and after studying law at the University of Michigan he moved to nearby Detroit and hung out his shingle.

As had Harry Costello, Mead applied to and was accepted by the first officers' training class at Fort Sheridan, and at the age of twenty-eight he began his own journey to Camp Custer—and whatever service with Company A of the 339th Infantry Regiment might hold for him.

Another Fort Sheridan graduate, Joel Roscoe Moore, was considerably older than either Harry. Already thirty-eight, Moore had been born in Hillsdale, Michigan, to father William, a miller, and mother Emma, who cared for Joel and his three younger siblings. He was married in 1903 to Mabel Olmstead. Sadly, they lost their only child, daughter Helen Emily, to acute ileocolitis—inflammation of the bowels—at the age of three months in October 1906, while Moore was attending Albion College in south-central Michigan.

After graduating in 1908, Moore began working on his master's degree in economics at the University of Illinois, and took a position of assistant in the Economics Department, earning the grand sum of $450 for the academic term. He eventually would publish his thesis, the scintillatingly titled work *Taxation of Corporations in Illinois*, in 1914.

Like Harry Costello, the cerebral Moore was also athletic and loved track and football—so much so that in 1910 he took a job at Great Falls High School in Montana, where he taught three history classes and coached the football team. Only fifteen boys turned out—but he would remember that being a luxury compared to other teams.

"Take Fort Benton, for instance," he would tell a reporter in 1947. "It didn't have enough players, so by prior agreement the coach, Culbertson, played one tackle and the town blacksmith at the other, and that blacksmith was a big fellow."

Moore would last only one year in Great Falls. Despite a student petition asking that he be retained for the following school year, the school's teachers' committee hired someone else to take his place.

"The superintendent didn't like me and wouldn't give me a contract," he would recall. Moore and wife Mabel moved on to La Crosse, Wisconsin, where he taught at La Crosse State Teachers College and coached football on the side, until he applied for officers' training. He, too, trained at Fort Sheridan and would soon take over Company M of the 339th Infantry Regiment.

Not everyone at Camp Custer wanted to lead, of course. Donald Eugene Carey, a twenty-five-year-old from Eaton County, Michigan, was, like Moore, older than the average recruit, and with a college degree from Olivet College and experience in teaching, he was offered a chance for officers' training through the auspices of an uncle, a prominent attorney.

But Carey turned him down. "I didn't even want to be a corporal," he later said. "I didn't want the responsibility for the lives of other men." Instead, after being classified 1-A in January 1918 and later taking a physical and being told by the doctor, "Go home, and get ready for war," he bided his time, teaching school in Camden, Michigan, until receiving a telegram that ordered him to report for induction on May 28.

Carey, like Godfrey Anderson, soon enough encountered his own trash-talking drill instructor. "You should have heard the lieutenant bawl out a couple of the Wops in our company," he wrote home on June 5. "He talks two languages: English and profane." But, Carey would add, "I like him and try to do my best."

One other arrival at Camp Custer came from a much more illustrious background and would prove to be one of the most popular men in the 339th Infantry Regiment.

J. Brooks Nichols, who turned thirty-three in the summer of 1918, was the only child of a prominent manufacturer in New York, and attended the Hill School in Pottstown, Pennsylvania. He moved on to Yale, and after graduating in 1908 "entered the oil business in Lexington, Kentucky," one social register would report in 1922.

After a year, Nichols moved to Detroit, and managed the United States Radiator Corporation for three years before becoming restlessly engaged in "various private enterprises of his own," one history of Detroit would say. "His business interests and investments rank him among the capitalists of Detroit and his sound business judgment is manifest in the continued development of those business activities which he controls."

He had been married for nine years to Rosa Sparks Dunlap, by whom he had three children, when duty called in 1917. He then added the Fort Sheridan Officers' Training Camp to the list of organizations to which he already belonged—among them the Detroit Athletic Club, the New York Yacht Club, the University Club in Chicago, and the Grosse Pointe Riding and Hunt Club in Michigan.

It wasn't long before 2nd Lt. J. Brooks Nichols, "several times a millionaire," was rising through the ranks at Camp Custer, jumping to major by April 1918 and lieutenant colonel by war's end. He would in between take command of the 339th's Second Battalion, and later the Third.

"And if ever there was a popular promotion it was that which elevated Major Nichols to his present station," the *Detroit Free Press* would report that April. "Every army man you speak with, even the regulars—which is the acid test of a newer officer's personality and worth—say Major Nichols is a 'fine officer:' than which no finer tribute could be paid a man in the olive drab of his country."

Others arrived at Camp Custer that summer of 1918, and while some had the alleged benefit of months of training, others had but weeks or even days to get some sense of what they had been dragged into.

"Many men arrived here today," Donald Carey, who was himself just a month into training and had been assigned as a private first class to Company E of the 339th, wrote on June 25. "They'll soon be enjoying the pleasures of army life."

Rumors by then abounded through the camp of an impending trip overseas. "Every indication points to a speedy departure," Carey would write. "The canteen closed last night; trains are loaded and coaches awaiting someone—probably our division."

That same month, the Eighty-Fifth Division received several thousand men who had been training at Camp Grant, in Illinois, and Camp Taylor, in Kentucky. By that time, one history of the division says, "the division knew definitely that it was going to France."

Sure enough, on July 14 orders were given to prepare to move. The Eighty-Fifth Division's men packed their few belongings through the morning and afternoon, and that evening boarded a series of trains. Before long, all were headed east toward uncertain futures.

The journey took them through Detroit, thence to Canada, where the Eighty-Fifth Division's men encountered "considerable cheering along the route," Carey remembered. (Canada had been at war since 1914.) At dusk on the second night of moving, they went around Niagara Falls and across a suspension bridge into New York.

The men eventually arrived in Hoboken, New Jersey, where Godfrey Anderson and the other midwestern farm boys gawked at the looming skyline of New York City to the east across the Hudson River. The city was "thickly congested with towers and skyscrapers, stretching off in the distance as far as the eye could reach," Godfrey would write. "I, for my part, stood completely dumbfounded, gaping spellbound at the magnificent scene."

The men were then ferried around the tip of Manhattan, where in the distance they could espy the Statue of Liberty "holding aloft her torch, and beyond the water glittering in the brilliant sunshine," Godfrey would remember. The ferries headed up the East River to the Long Island Rail Road Station, where they again boarded trains for Camp Mills, which was located near Hempstead on Long Island.

On July 21 and July 22, the call to move out came once more, and the division's men reversed and found themselves heading back through Long Island to Brooklyn, and thence by ferry down the East River and back to their embarkation point in Hoboken, where various overseas transports—the *Plattsburg*, the *Northumberland*, the *Anchises*, the *Harrisburg*—plus a convoy of battleships awaited the Eighty-Fifth Division.

"Great adventure begins," one soldier aboard the *Plattsburg*, Clarence Scheu of Company B of the 339th Infantry Regiment, would note in his diary.

Rocking and rolling through a stormy North Atlantic, the ships would take more than ten days to reach Liverpool, England. As they sailed, all thoughts aboard the vessels focused not only on the rough seas, but on the threat of German submarines.

Many men became seasick; sailing on British transports with English crews, even the still-hungry could barely force down the food prepared by the cooks. Rice, meal, potatoes, and tripe were offered to the men aboard Carey's ship, the *Northumberland*, but it was "so unpalatable and sickening that I ate little during the voyage," he would write.

"Execrable" was the term Godfrey Anderson, who was aboard the British ship *Anchises* with the rest of the 337th Field Hospital Company, would say about the food. As well, "the whole mess was spoiled and stank to high heaven."

On or about August 3, the convoy's battleships turned about, and British destroyers took over the watch. As the transports approached the "forbidden zone" off the English coast where enemy submarines would be most likely to roam, "lifeboats are lowered, rafts loosened, everything held in readiness to abandon ship," Clarence Scheu wrote.

One by one, though, the transports left the Irish Sea and entered the mouth of the Mersey River, and soon were at the docks of Liverpool. "We dis-embark, march through city to railroad station, nice reception," wrote Scheu of the English, who, after almost four years of bleeding and suffering, were more than happy to have these Yanks finally pick up some of the burden.

From there, it was once more on the trains, which began rolling across the pastoral English countryside, carrying the thirty-five hundred men of the 339th U.S. Infantry Regiment, Eighty-Fifth Division, each one of whom looked forward to whatever perils and ordeals might await them on the scarred and storied battlefields of France.

CHAPTER THREE

TO RUSSIA. WITH ANGST.

They started getting sick as the ships skirted the coast of Norway. They began dying even as the ships rounded the Kola Peninsula and headed south, toward the Russian coast, in the early days of September 1918. The first body was wrapped in a sheet and dumped overboard while the *Somali* was still coursing through the White Sea. Other men lay in various states of distress, shivering and moaning and ashen, as the medicines that might have helped them had been left back in Newcastle, England.

"All bunks were occupied by soldiers desperately ill, with raging fevers," Godfrey Anderson would write, while "others lay on stretchers, the breathing of all a rasping wheeze."

The influenza had also struck the *Nagoya*, aboard which Lt. Harry Mead and the rest of Company A of the 339th sailed. Making things worse even for those not afflicted was the cold; the voyage had taken the regiment above the Arctic Circle, and yet their baggage and needed cold-winter clothing had been loaded into the ships' cargo holds.

In their postwar book, *The History of the American Expedition Fighting the Bolsheviki*, Mead, Joel Moore, and Company K's Lewis Jahns would write, "This suffering from the cold as they crossed the Arctic circle was a foretaste of what they were to be up against in the long months to come in North Russia."

Far from home, the 339th and its associated engineer and hospital units were also far from France, to which the rest of the Eighty-Fifth Division had sailed, there to be designated a replacement division, and its soldiers meted out to various American divisions preparing to fight in the offensives at St. Mihiel and the Meuse-Argonne in the fall of 1918.

The 339th, however, had been personally plucked by Gen. John Pershing, commander of the American Expeditionary Force, for special duty as the American Expeditionary Force, North Russia (AEFNR). Following Woodrow Wilson's pained and agonized decision to allow American combat forces to enter Russia—supposedly to do nothing more than guard Allied materiel from the predations of Bolsheviks and Germans—the regiment had been ordered to sail from England, and thence to Murmansk, on the Barents Sea. The Twenty-Seventh and Thirty-First U.S. Infantry Regiments, stationed in the Philippines and California, meanwhile, were ordered to Vladivostok as the AEF, Siberia.

Pershing selected the 339th for three reasons: One, it was already in England. Two, its commander, Col. George Evans Stewart, then forty-six, had spent the past twenty-plus years in service, had earned a Medal of Honor in the Philippines in 1899, and had subsequently spent two cold years in Alaska. Three, it was thought, and perhaps rightly so, that men who were mostly from the colder northern states of Michigan and Wisconsin could more easily bear the deep freeze of a Russian winter than those from the southern states.

One of the first inklings of the change in plans had been conveyed to Harry Mead. While in London during the 339th's three-week stay at a camp just outside the city of Aldershot, Mead had run into the globe-trotting self-promoter and quasi-journalist Lowell Thomas, who had boarded with Harry's family while attending Valparaiso University for two years.

As Thomas, just returned from his adventures with British colonel T. E. Lawrence—whom Thomas would almost personally make famous as Lawrence of Arabia—and Mead chatted on a street corner, Mead mentioned that his regiment expected to leave for France soon.

Thomas, who had sources in the British government, set his friend straight, telling Mead that his information was that the 339th was being rerouted to, of all places, northern Russia.

Soon, there were other not-so-subtle hints as to the regiment's future destination. Ernest Shackleton, the famed Antarctic explorer who had recently and only just survived the sinking of his ship *Endurance* in the polar ice and a subsequent harrowing, eight-hundred-mile sea voyage in an open boat to seek rescue for his crew, was brought in to lecture the regiment's men on the conditions in the Arctic.

He had plenty to tell them: Shackleton had been on three separate expeditions to Antarctica, including two attempts on the South Pole: the first with Robert Falcon Scott from 1901 to 1903, the second between 1907 and 1909, when Shackleton and his small party sledge-hauled to within ninety-seven nautical miles of their target. On his third expedition, an attempt to cross the continent between 1914 and 1916, his ship became trapped in the ice and was crushed after ten months of drifting.

The party eventually reached a refuge—tiny Elephant Island—after which Shackleton and five others made their death-defying journey by open boat to the whaling station at South Georgia Island. From there, Shackleton mounted a rescue party and made it back to Elephant Island, where his men were still alive and waiting. He returned to England to find a war on, and served in the British Army until its end.

Their polar briefings done, on August 20 the men of the 339th were told to turn in their Lee-Enfield rifles, and in turn were supplied with Mosin-Nagant 7.62 rifles—"guns made in America, purchased by the Russia of the Czar, and stored near Aldershot awaiting shipment to the Russian Imperial Army which had collapsed," a bemused Harry Costello would write.

Lt. John Cudahy, the scion of a wealthy Wisconsin family who served with the 339th's Company B and would one day serve as President Franklin Roosevelt's ambassador to Poland and later Belgium, characterized the clumsy rifles that had been intended for Russian hands as "long, awkward pieces, with flimsy, bolt mechanism, that frequently jammed."

What's more, the weapons had been sighted "in Russian paces instead of yards. They had a low velocity and were thoroughly unsatisfactory." Still others would joke that the rifles could "shoot around corners." However, the issuing of them had some reasoning; a large cache of ammunition for the weapons was supposed to be available and waiting for the men in Russia.

Gone, too, were the Browning machine guns that Costello and his mates had learned to master. They were instead issued water-cooled Vickers guns, which would freeze and prove troublesome to operate in the deep, deep cold of a Russian winter.

As the regiment made ready to leave southern England, the men received more lectures, this time from the British, whose officers would lead the coming grand adventure.

"Their one great thought was well expressed to me by an enthusiastic staff officer," Costello wrote. "'We'll just rush up there and reestablish the great Russian Army—reorganize the vast forces of the Czar! Russia's former great armies will rise to welcome us.'"

"'One good Allied soldier can outfight twenty Bolsheviks,' was the usual boast of the Commanding Officer in the early days of the fighting," Cudahy would add.

The men of the 339th also received new woolen British clothing and winter supplies—including the "Shackleton boot," which had been designed by the explorer expressly for work in polar regions. However, moving about in the mukluk-type footwear would prove to be a frustrating and slippery task, and on some occasions the men would be reduced to tossing them away and walking through deep snow and over frozen trails in just their wool socks.

Some in the regiment took news of their destination in stride. "Company notified we are going to Russia," Sgt. Gordon Smith of Company D wrote nonchalantly in his diary on August 22. "Turned in Enfield Rifles and draw Russian equipment."

Others were crushed "to have missed the Big Show and be sent instead to an unknown country to fight an unknown enemy for an unknown reason," as Dorothea York, the author of the 1923 book *The Romance of Company "A,"* would put it.

On August 25, the 339th once more boarded trains and headed north, instead of east for France. At Newcastle, the men boarded the transports *Somali, Nagoya,* and the *Tydeus,* while a contingent of Italian troops also bound for the unknown loaded onto the *Czar.*

In the early morning the four ships, plus a convoy of four British warships, slipped their moorings and stole down the Tyne River and toward the North Sea. Aboard the cramped *Somali,* Godfrey Anderson found space in the hold, and "managed to get a fairly good night's sleep."

Aboard the equally cramped *Nagoya,* the men found sleeping places in hammocks below deck. Quickly, conditions deteriorated.

"The ever-present cootie, rats and a number of other species of vermin repellant to man were present in force," wrote York, whose *Romance of Company "A"* was based on the recollections of a number of the unit's veterans.

"The air was fetid with packed humanity and there was no pretense of any system of ventilation . . . The stench from the hatchways was unmistakable warning against venturing below and yet one must go below for food and sleep."

The *Nagoya* in her previous life had been a trade ship in the Asian Pacific, and she was in filthy condition. Before long, it was apparent, too, that she was a carrier of disease; within days of leaving port the dreaded and so-called Spanish influenza, which would kill 21 million people worldwide before running its course, was crawling through her decks, making dozens of men deathly ill.

The flu broke out on the *Somali* as well, as the ship rolled and fought through gray, leaden seas and toward the north. Seasickness also afflicted some, and as the convoy approached and then passed through the Arctic Circle the cold intensified but could not be remedied.

"Our overcoats had been packed in barracks bags and stored deep down in the hold so we could not put on the warmer clothing so badly needed," Godfrey Anderson recalled.

"It is getting colder, men packed like sardines in impoverished hold, a number of men getting sick," Company B's Clarence Scheu would write on August 28 of conditions on the *Nagoya*.

Three days later, Scheu noted the deaths of several men from the flu: "Stormy and colder, sun not visible, see northern lights, hear several men die on board, there sure is a bunch of them getting sick."

One of them was Donald Carey. Though on August 30 he had written a cheery letter home saying that he had "not been sick and have been eating all I want," by September 4 he had to eat his words. "Was weak and ill all day," he wrote. "Despite this I had to help clean our quarters."

Even as the ships carrying the sick and well men of the 339th were rounding the northern coast of Scandinavia with their intended destination being Murmansk, events were playing out that would see the convoy rerouted to the east—and urgently. Unknown to the men, Americans had already gone into action against Bolshevik forces south of the city of Archangel, and a polyglot force of Allies was fighting for its survival in the deep woods and swamps in the Russian interior.

In the first step toward intervention in Russia, Woodrow Wilson had answered the Allies' pleas for help by agreeing to send the 5,800-ton cruiser *Olympia* to Murmansk. The ship, which had been Adm. George Dewey's flagship during the Battle of Manila in the Spanish-American War, was quickly refitted at the Charleston Naval Yard and then sailed for England.

There, it refueled and then picked up the man who was to oversee the Allies' actions in Russia, forty-nine-year-old British general Frederick Poole, who had been designated as the British military's representative in Russia.

On May 24, the *Olympia* heaved to off Murmansk, which had been garrisoned by 130 British marines since March in an effort to meet the supposed German threat to the area. On June 8, an American contingent of 108 men landed in the city; though Murmansk was under control of the Bolsheviks, the landing was not contested, but indeed had been encouraged by Leon Trotsky, who was in a lather over the phantom German threat.

On June 23, a French warship arrived, carrying a token force of soldiers. By the end of June, the Allied force at Murmansk numbered more than 1,600, the largest portion being British veterans, some adorned with one or more wound chevrons earned on the Western Front. Two degress north of the Arctic Circle, Murmansk was bathed in midnight sun.

It wasn't until late July, however, that Poole was ready to strike the Russian mainland, targeting Archangel, a port city some three hundred miles southeast, which had been operating under Bolshevik rule for several months. On July 30, a convoy of ships left Murmansk carrying five hundred French soldiers, one hundred British marines, and a force of fifty American seamen under command of Lt. Henry Floyd aboard the S.S. *Stephens*.

One of the ships carrying the French, the *Amiral Aube*, ran aground in the dense fog off the Kola Peninsula, but at first light the others reached the mouth of the wide Dvina River, which emptied into the White Sea. After reducing two batteries of Bolshevik artillery on Modyuski Island, the flotilla proceeded the twenty-five miles to Archangel.

Anti-Red forces in the city had been planning a coup to coincide with the pending arrival of Poole's force, and even as the ships navigated the river on August 2 a bloodless local revolution put the city in the hands of the new Sovereign Government of Northern Russia.

The Bolsheviks, meanwhile, were in a panic, and they began looting the vast stockpile of Allied materiel, whose protection had been one of the main excuses for the intervention occurring in the first place. By boat and locomotive, they began shipping the stores south; some were moved by boat up the Dvina River, and others were hauled by rail toward the town of Obozerskaya, some one hundred miles south.

The haul was enormous: besides military and hospital equipment and medical supplies, the Bolsheviks made off with food stores, hardware of all kinds, jewelry, boats, and the rolling stock of the railroad. Even as the city was being cleaned out, refugees were flowing in from east, west, and south, as the Bolsheviks invested their villages and homes.

Arriving, too, was the small Allied contingent. Quickly, the American naval force of fifty men was split, with twenty-five sailors being assigned to the railway yard at Bakharitza, across the river from Archangel. There, Ens. Donald M. Hicks and his merry band of bluejackets went searching for adventure—and found it in an abandoned steam engine that still had some kick in it.

The sailors attached flatcars to the wood-burning locomotive and, armed with machine guns and protected by rows of sandbags, were soon rattling south in search of the Bolsheviks and their Allied booty.

Thirty miles down the track, near the village of Tundra, they had their first encounter with the Reds. Halting at a bridge that had been destroyed by the Bolsheviks, the sailors opened fire, but soon realized the sandbags offered scant protection from the enemy's return fire—which was intense.

They found a more secure defensive position and remained there for almost a week before Hicks and another sailor returned to Archangel on August 10 with fifty-four Bolshevik prisoners in tow.

By then, the Allied force had been split. Hicks and the other sailors from the *Olympia* were put under the command of a British lieutenant colonel, Haselden, along with one hundred French soldiers, twenty-seven Poles, and thirty-five Russians, many of them deserters from the Russian Army who became part of the British-trained and -led Slavo-British Allied Legion, or S.B.A.L.

They would comprise Force B, while more British, French, and Russian troops plus the remaining twenty-five American sailors would become Force A. The plan, as devised by the British command, was for Force A to head down the railway to Obozerskaya while Force B would head 120 miles up the Dvina to the village of Siskoe, then head south toward Plesetskaya, a Bolshevik railway base about forty miles south of Obozerskaya.

At its grandest, the plan drawn by General Poole and his staff envisioned the quick taking of Obozerskaya and then a rapid movement toward Vologda, another three hundred miles south along the railway. Another mixed body of troops, called Force C, would steam for Kotlas, three hundred miles to the southeast. From Kotlas, the tiny river army would entrain almost three hundred miles farther to Viatka and make contact with that part of the Czech Legion supposedly moving—or trying to move—west.

The Czechs would then be led another five hundred miles west to Vologda, and so link with the Allied force there. Along the way, Poole's men and the Czechs would rally "100,000 friendly Russians" to their cause, as he conveyed to one American official. From Vologda, one author would write sardonically, these tens of thousands of patriotic Russians and wandering Czechs would move "unopposed" yet *another* five hundred miles west to Petrograd, and from there move east and reconstruct the Eastern Front.

As Cudahy would note, "There was nothing lacking in the imagination of the plans of the Allied High Command, whatever else might be said about them."

In reality, Force C quickly bogged down when confronted with Red gunboats and land batteries at Beresnik, 140 miles upriver from Archangel (as the crow flies). Ens. Donald Hicks and his contingent meanwhile found themselves also being towed forty miles up the wide, shallow, sluggish Dvina—characterized as northern Russia's Mississippi River by many—to Siskoe, and then, with fuzzy maps and virtually no information about the countryside, they followed a road through deep forests, headed southwest for Plesetskaya.

Passing through Emetskoe, and encountering here and there locals who cheered the strange conglomeration of soldiers, Force B made the village of Tiogra on August 15. There, they learned that a group of 250 Red sailors were in the next town to the west, Seletskoe, and had with them seven machine guns, an armored car, and two pieces of field artillery.

Undeterred, Force B advanced and at five P.M. attacked. By ten thirty that evening, the town was clear of Bolsheviks, except for a few prisoners. During the fight, one British officer and five soldiers—one Polish and four French—were killed; one of the *Olympia*'s sailors, George Dewey Perschke, was shot in the arm and became the first casualty the Americans would suffer in the campaign. Many would follow.

Force B then returned to Tiogra for a week's rest. On August 22, new orders fell from the sky—literally. A British plane zoomed over the force and dropped orders for the men to abandon, for now, their move on Plesetskaya and instead turn and attack Obozerskaya from the east, while Force A would assault it from the north.

Before most of Force B left for Obozerskaya on August 27, it was reinforced by fifty-three anti-Red Russians and two machine guns. The Russians were sent south to Seletskoe to guard the flank of the main force, which advanced nineteen miles toward Obozerskaya the first day and another thirteen on August 28. That same day, Force B learned from scouts that a large group of Red sailors was once more headed toward Seletskoe.

An American sailor, Corbin Hardaway, was dispatched on a horse to alert headquarters at Tiogra of the pending attack, and he earned a Navy Cross for "accomplishing a long march successfully under trying conditions, and at times practically within the enemy's lines," as his citation reads.

Hicks and Force B began encountering Bolsheviks as they approached Obozerskaya from the east; the Americans cut their way through the opposition, and were in line and ready to attack as planned at six A.M. on August 31. Rushing the Bolsheviks, they were forced to ground "due to heavy resistance met," as Hicks would later report.

The fighting was intense through the day, and on the night of August 31 Hicks and his sailors took over the front line from the French. Two more seamen were wounded that day, one taking a bullet in the arm and the other spraining his ankle.

The next day, the fighting continued, but before noon it was learned that the Reds behind them had taken Seletskoe—the supposedly anti-Bolshevik Russians there, it was reported, had "fired three shots" and then fled—and were now moving west toward Obozerskaya.

Encountering heavy opposition before Obozerskaya, and now also facing annihilation from the rear, Force B retraced its steps thirteen miles and set up defenses across the road from Tiogra to Obozerskaya. The next day, a small force of French soldiers was sent almost a mile east and ordered to hold at least until five P.M., while the main body of Force B set off across swamps and woods for the railway at Obozerskaya.

Hicks and his sailors, meanwhile, were ordered to hold the original line and then relieve the *poilus* (French soldiers) that night—but at two thirty in the afternoon, the French came back to the main line, where they and the sailors beat back a Bolshevik bayonet charge. The French then took off west, following the rest of Force B.

Ordered to reinforce Hicks and the other seamen at the main defense line that night, the Russians instead plundered the force's supply wagons. Hicks decided to get while the getting was good, and destroyed as much of the remaining supplies and equipment as he could before he and his merry band also took off west, moving cross-country.

Force B was now as good as lost, out of touch with the Allied command as its men waded through swamps and trekked night and day across the heavily forested Russian north, their empty stomachs gnawing at them and their legs giving way from the effort. Finally, on September 5, the main body of Force B emerged at the railway above Obozerskaya, followed by Hicks and the *Olympia* sailors, who emerged from the woods thirteen miles to the north.

There, they received rations from the French and were ordered to escort a trainload of 123 Bolshevik prisoners to Isakagorka, just south of Archangel, to which the sailors finally returned on September 6 after their arduous adventure.

By then, though, they and the rest of Force B were the object of much concern among the Allied command—and their meanderings and disappearance would directly affect the fates of the men of the 339th Infantry Regiment, which was still plowing across the White Sea as the first Americans went into action in the gloomy forests of Russia.

CHAPTER FOUR

WE'RE HERE BECAUSE WE'RE HERE

The trains swayed and jerked and rattled as they knifed deeper, ever deeper, into the heart of northern Russia in the second week of September 1918. All through the night they rolled, while in boxcars the men fitfully tried to sleep, or gave up and sat in the doorways, their legs dangling limply, their minds wandering but always coming back to the strangeness of their predicament, this, their great adventure.

At one point the trains stopped at a remote railway outpost, and those awake saw by torchlights a herd of prisoners taken in the previous days of fighting at Obozerskaya. To the Americans they seemed unsoldierly, an "unheroic spectacle," one soldier would write. "They look like Bolo wild men," one American joked; from that time on, the Bolsheviks would be referred to as just that—Bolos.

The trains, and men, moved on. Somewhere ahead, they had been told, American sailors were fighting for their lives, and so here they were, these men of the Third Battalion, 339th Infantry Regiment, coming to save American lives and thence, according to the possibly psychotic fantasies of their British commanders, roll ever deeper and fight their way to Vologda—nearly three hundred miles—if need be, and then locate the Czechs who were said to be wandering in the wastes of Russia like a lost tribe, and so save Russia, and maybe the world itself.

Their ships—the *Somali* and *Nagoya* and *Tydeus*—had still been steaming for Murmansk when the urgent calls came over the wireless and told their captains to break off and head southeast toward Archangel. And so the ships turned, and in early September 1918 reached the mouth of the Dvina River, and, pulled by tugs, coursed as quickly as they could the twenty-five miles to the city.

"The entire vista was dreary and desolate," Godfrey Anderson would recall, "the sky being heavily overcast and the vast swamps stretching interminably, unrelieved by any woodland, except for a few stunted pine trees."

On September 4 the wharves and log homes and the blue-painted domes on the city's great cathedral came into view. "There were several handsome churches in sight, especially one majestic cathedral with half a dozen bulbous spires that was the most imposing focal point in the entire panorama," Anderson wrote.

The port of Archangel, into which Allied materiel had been flowing to support the czar's great army since 1914, had been reached in 1553 by the English explorer Sir Richard Chancellor, who with three ships under his command was trying to find a northeast passage to India. When the czar, Ivan the Terrible, learned of Chancellor's arrival on the coast, he sent orders for Chancellor to travel overland to Moscow, more than six hundred miles due south, where a trading relationship between Russia and England was soon formed.

The city of Archangel was founded thirty years later, and over the following centuries became the capital of the large Archangel District, a cosmopolitan center peopled not only by Russians of all stripes and ethnicities but seafaring Scandinavians, British, and Germans. Through the port went lumber, furs, flax, and other commodities.

In the seventeenth century prisoners were set to work on improving the town, and a large trading hall and a bazaar were constructed. As well, the Troitski Cathedral, with five domes, was constructed and featured a fourteen-foot-high wooden cross carved by Peter the Great himself. The great cathedral dominated the otherwise flat skyline of Archangel, which consisted mainly of well-fenced homes hewn from the vast forests of the region and stone buildings housing businesses.

The city itself was only a few blocks wide but was splayed along the Dvina River, at which numerous boats docked and loaded and unloaded their wares. A trolley ran along the main avenue, and the city formed a crescent shape, curving along the river south to the suburb of Smolny, and to the north to Solombola.

Across the river on the west bank sat Bakharitza—and it was there that on September 5, 1918, the men of the Third Battalion—Companies I, K, L, and M—debarked. "The dark waters of the Dvina River were beaten into fury by the opposing north wind and ocean tide," Joel Moore et al. would write. "And the lowering clouds of the Arctic sky added their dismal bit to this introduction to the dreadful conflict which these American sons of liberty were to wage with the Bolsheviki during the year's campaign."

Company B's Lt. John Cudahy would write more ominously, "That September day . . . those who looked from the decks breathed in the oppressive air a haunting presentiment of approaching evil."

Even to men from the north woods of Michigan and Wisconsin, the area surrounding Archangel, with its endless marshes and dark, brooding forests of spruce and pine and birch through which few roads ran, was akin to the dark side of the moon.

The terrain, and the redolence of pine wafting through air that already carried a nip to it in September, was somewhat familiar, as was the dull, dungy smell of the muskeg and swamps and the clouds of maniacal mosquitoes that swarm in the north from May to September.

Not as familiar were the mostly simple *moujiks*—peasants—who toiled endlessly to claw a living from the deep woods and oft-frozen ground, and who huddled in their sparse log homes in tiny villages flung hundreds of miles across the Archangel District. Each home had a large stove, the top of which served not only for cooking but as a warm, nightly refuge for an infant or elder.

The men worked at felling and cutting timber, trapping, limited dairying, and raising a few hardy varieties of vegetables and grains while the women tended to children and housekeeping. Independent and superstitious, the people of the area contended with nature just as the average American soldier "had heard of his grandfathers struggling in pioneer days in America," Moore would note.

It took but little time for the Americans to begin their probing of this vast and strange land; the American invasion of northern Russia—the "Polar Bear Expedition"—took shape within hours of the landing at Archangel on September 5, 1918.

Even as Ens. Donald M. Hicks and his ragged band of sailors were emerging from their deep-woods hegira on the railway above Obozerskaya, all safe, if not all quite sound, Capt. Joel Moore, himself under the weather with the flu, and Company M and the rest of the Third Battalion were already chugging to Hicks's aid, unaware that their services as rescuers would not be needed.

The battalion had been assembled shortly after arrival and was ordered to leave immediately for the south "with just the clothes on our back[s] and without a single blanket," Company K's Lt. Charles Ryan would write. The men then boarded two rickety trains and spent "a very uncomfortable night sleeping on ammunition cases with only our overcoats for cover."

On the morning of September 6, the trains were stopped by a blown bridge just north of Obozerskaya. The town had finally been taken by the Allies' Force A on September 4, and while the men of Companies M and K spent the entire day of September 6 lolling in their boxcars, the Third Battalion's commander, Maj. Charles Young, led Companies I and L forward to the town.

At the town's railway station, they were met by a French officer who quickly pointed out the numerous shell holes that pocked the surrounding area. The Frenchman then spoke quickly to a nearby British officer "who was gnawing his mustache," Moore would write.

The Brit managed to overcome his embarrassment at having to point out to Major Young that he was now in a war zone and could come under fire from the Bolos, as evidenced by the shell holes. "The major shouted orders and shooed the platoons off into the woods."

That night the 339th suffered its first battlefield casualty when a nervous doughboy yelled "Halt!" and fired at the same time; an American working a handcar along the tracks was hit in the leg.

The next day, Company K's commander, Capt. Mike Donoghue, was ordered to take his two platoons—the other two had been dropped off farther north to guard a railroad repair shop and wireless station—east to the area around Tiogra, the last known location of Hicks and the bluejackets.

The men drew rations for six days and began their march over "the worst roads in the world," Ryan wrote. The way led through swampy, waterlogged muskeg and black forests of stunted spruce. As they searched for the Bolos, they encountered a different enemy. "The mosquitoes are awful," Ryan wrote. "They have me just eaten alive."

They made twelve miles that day before bivouacking in the open on the swampy ground. The next day, September 8, Company K passed the wreckage left behind by Force B. After stopping at noon, Ryan led a patrol south down a forest track toward the village of Emtsa. But the sodden ground soon proved unpassable, and the men turned around, having waded three miles in water up to their knees.

Company K's two platoons continued to scour the landscape for any sign of the supposedly lost Force B, but before long ran into Bolos. Turning back, they reached Tiogra, which sat on the north bank of the Emtsa River, on September 12, and there they spent the night and the next day until an anti-Bolshevik Russian cavalryman arrived with orders for them to move to Seletskoe farther upriver.

There, they were met by the 380 men of Force D, a detachment under command of a British captain that consisted of French machine gunners, a contingent of Royal Scots and Royal Marines, and a Russian S.B.A.L. (Slavo-British Allied Legion) unit.

On September 15 they came under attack for the first time, and they raced to man the outlying posts that ringed the village. Bolo machine-gun bullets sliced overhead as Ryan held the right flank; on the left, Sgt. Michael Kenney was soon cut off from the main body. Ryan sent a few men, among them Pvt. Glenn Staley, to reinforce Kenney. Staley would quickly go missing amid the pitched battle.

At two P.M., a Bolo aircraft appeared overhead, and after it signaled the location of Company K, the Bolos began heavily shelling the American positions. As Moore et al. would write, "'Guard duty at Archangel' was aiming now to be a real war, on a small scale but intensive."

"This is my first experience under fire and it will certainly leave an impression that will all be remembered," the thirty-year-old Ryan would write. "They are striking all around me, high explosion and shrapnel."

That night, a Bolo soldier crept up to the American lines and tossed a hand grenade into a post manned by Pvt. Alvin Olechowski. He was wounded in the neck, but "I don't think it is very serious," Ryan wrote. Alvin Olechowski would indeed survive.

The next day, September 16, the Bolos opened up "stronger than ever," Ryan wrote. But there was one solace for the novice soldier Charlie Ryan: the French, who had learned their lessons on the battlefields in France. "It is a comfortable feeling to look out and see these cool Verdun veterans," he would write.

That evening, a scout reported that the Bolos had crossed to the American side of the Emtsa River, and a retreat north to Tiogra was ordered. The bridge that spanned the Emtsa below Tiogra was burned to prevent more Bolos from attacking them; the next morning, it would be found that the Bolos had in fact taken off in the opposite direction after assassinating their leader and burning their own bridge farther south.

Charles Ryan's missing man, Pvt. Glenn Staley, was also found by a patrol on September 19. He had been shot, and also bayoneted, and thus became the first Company K man to be killed in this strange conflict.

At Obozerskaya, the supposed guard duty had also turned into a real war. The destroyed bridge north of the village had been repaired and a "ferocious-looking" armored train, bristling with machine guns and naval artillery pieces, had been brought up, Moore et al. would write. An airfield was being improved, fighting units—Poles, French, Brits, Russians—were being assembled, and orders had been issued by the British that patrols were to be "aggressive" and mindful that they were to fight an "offensive war, not a defensive one."

Here, an area which would become known, appropriately, as the railroad front, President Woodrow Wilson's pledge that Americans sent to Russia would be there to "guard military stores" and were *not* to take sides in the civil war then raging between Whites and Reds had been quickly ignored.

From the very moment the *Olympia* had arrived in May, Americans had been swept up by circumstances, usurped by the British military command with the tacit approval of both the American ambassador, David Francis, and their own commander, Col. George Stewart, and raced out to fight Bolos. As the Bolos slowly pushed back against the foreign invaders, the fighting could only continue, as it did on September 11.

That morning, Lt. Gerald Danley of the 339th Infantry Regiment's Company I reported that a Bolo railroad gun was three miles south of Obozerskaya and coming on fast. The British colonel in command of Force A disputed Danley's account, saying the gun in question was in fact the smoke pipe at a sawmill. Still, he dispatched a patrol from Company L, which was followed by two platoons of Company M on the armored train.

As the men moved south, the "smokestack" suddenly belched fire, and a shell twisted and turned over the patrol and landed on the reserve trenches they had just passed through. In a clearing by a telegraph station at Verst 466—distances were measured in Russia in "versts," which were about the length of a kilometer—Company M's Cpl. Frank O'Connor's squad, on the left flank and walking point, came under fire, and promptly returned it.

Sgt. Walter Dundon took three squads to support the left, while Lt. James Donovan pushed through the woods on the right and attacked the enemy's flank five hundred yards beyond the clearing. It was the battalion's first engagement with the Bolos, and a success. Patrols were pushed farther south to Verst 464, and the ground consolidated. A prisoner told them they had faced two hundred Bolos; a promised three hundred more Reds had failed to arrive. "We liked the place," Moore wrote. "We never did intend to give it back to the Bolo."

On the evening of September 15, even as Company K was fighting not far to the east at Seletskoe, a plane flew over the position at the railway. Battalion commander Young declared it to be Allied; when it came down near Verst 464 he raced toward it, yelling, "Don't fire! We are Americans!" Fire from a Lewis gun quickly answered him, and Young went to ground.

From then on, whenever the Third Battalion's men encountered Bolos, a cheer of "Don't fire—we are Americans!" would ring along the line with sardonic hilarity.

The next day, the Bolos launched a "savage counter-attack" on the front being held by Company L and two platoons from Company I. Out of ammunition and being pressed hard, Lt. Gordon Reese of Company I led his platoon forward in a driving rainstorm "and gave the Bolshevik soldiers a sample of the fighting spirit of the Americans," Moore et al. would write. The Reds retreated.

Two Company I men were killed, as was one from Company L.

Back at Obozerskaya, a newly dug American graveyard was already growing.

CHAPTER FIVE

ARCHANGEL

Thirty-year-old Pvt. Clyde Clark of Lansing, Michigan, had not had an easy life. Stocky and of medium height, he was a bricklayer and laborer by trade, and he had caught the eye of laundry worker Bessie Madden and married her in June 1913, when he was twenty-five and she twenty-two. Two years later, they welcomed a daughter, Thelma; but the marriage soured not long after, and in August 1916 Bessie filed for divorce. A judge granted her wish, and as well gave her custody of their little girl. Then, he watched as Bessie married Clare Ballard in April 1917.

When Clyde registered for the draft on June 18, 1917, he could list no regular employer but did mention he was supporting his daughter and paying alimony to a "divorced wife." Just a little more than a year later, on June 27, 1918, the draftee Clyde Clark would indeed find regular employment, though it was with the Eighty-Fifth Division, within which he was assigned to Company L, 339th Infantry Regiment.

Just three weeks later, Clyde found himself boarding the *Harrisburg* at the Hoboken docks; on September 5, he found himself in Bakharitza, Russia, sick with influenza, in his delirium perhaps wondering just how his fate had brought him to this state. Within two weeks, Clyde Clark was dead, just one of sixty-five members of the 339th who would die before September was out, before they'd fired a weapon, before they could figure out what exactly they were doing so very far from home.

While Clyde Clark and the others lay in their death throes, chaos reigned around them. Archangel, with a peacetime population of about 50,000, had swelled to 100,000 people with the various refugees who had flooded in as the Bolsheviks tried to consolidate power in the provinces. Because the same Bolsheviks had looted everything and anything of use or value prior to the landing of the Allies, "there was nothing left," Company I's Lt. Albert May of Omaha, Nebraska, would write.

"All that was left was the weather-beaten hulk of a devastated city . . . Business had practically ceased. A few shops were open but offered scarcely anything for sale. There was no food except fish or fish products.

"The people virtually were starving—living mostly on fish, black straw bread and tea. There was no coin money. Paper money of the wall paper variety and multitudinous makes, from old Nicholi prints and Kerensky issues to the provincial greenbacks of Archangel, was plentiful, but it would buy nothing, as there was nothing to buy."

The city teemed with exotic characters, the mélange of nationalities and types and persuasions stunning and bemusing the now-worldly New Englander Harry Costello of the 339th's Machine Gun Company and favorite son of Meriden, Connecticut, and Georgetown University.

"The long-haired Pole is a character to study," he would write to his father that winter. "The Eskimo shuffles along with his winter garments muffling him from the cold winds of the White sea. The Chinese passes by. Like all other sons of China, he seems to be frozen and his sphinx-like countenance tells you that he is interested in nothing.

"The Laplander, the Finn, the Norwegian, the Englishman, the Dane, the Lithuanian and Cossack, the Russian peasant, the American, the Frenchman, the Serb, and the Canadian pass by. There are others, but I must give up the task of trying to enumerate them all, as this mixture here in Archangel is too difficult to list."

Since the August 1918 arrival of General Poole and his initial force, and the subsequent headlong retreat of the Bolsheviks, Archangel had been governed by an entity that called itself the Sovereign Government of Northern Russia.

The architect of the new government was a dashing Russian naval officer, Georgi Chaplin. He would place at its head a bearded, passionate, and energetic Russian named Nicholas Chaikovsky, who had spent the years from 1875 to 1879 in the United States, where he lived in Independence, Kansas, and tried, but failed, to organize a new religious sect. "He is an able writer, a fine character and a valuable man," the U.S. ambassador, David Francis, would write.

He and his fellow ministers were, alas, also socialists. Chaplin, an ardent anti-Bolshevist, used the opportunity of the landing of the 339th Infantry Regiment to quietly effect another revolution: during the night of September 4–5, he had Chaikovsky and his government kidnapped and sent by steamer to a monastery on Solovetsky Island thirty miles west of Archangel.

The kidnappings had gone on under the nose of Francis, who only learned of them from General Poole on September 5. Confronting Chaplin the next morning during a review of newly landed American troops, Francis protested, and was told, "The ministers were in General Poole's way."

Chaplin had planned to issue a proclamation explaining to the people that the Sovereign Government had been deposed and that he was in command. "Chaplin's manner indicated that he was proud of the deed, and expected commendation," Francis wrote.

Francis, though, convened a meeting of the Allied ambassadors the same day and convinced Poole not to allow Chaplin—who served on Poole's staff—to read the proclamation before the ambassadors could have their say.

"The Allied Ambassadors immediately decided to bring back the kidnapped ministers and sent for Chaplin," Francis added. They told Chaplin not to issue the proclamation, and informed him as well that the ministers had been sent for. "I told him that I considered his act a flagrant usurpation of power, and an insult to the Allied Ambassadors," Francis wrote.

There was one problem: the ship then bringing the ministers to exile had no radio communications. The ambassadors had to send a message to Kem, a station on the Murman Railroad, "to get a boat over there and get these ministers when they landed there and bring them back to Archangel," Francis wrote.

In the meantime, the deposing of Chaikovsky's government had alarmed the locals, who suspected it to be a power grab by the Allies. A general strike was called, and some thirty thousand Archangel residents walked out on their jobs.

"Rumors were rampant that the Allies were in Russia to get a slice of it; to enforce payment of loans made by the Allies to the old imperial government," Albert May would write in 1919.

The Allies had vowed not to interfere in Russian internal affairs, but as soon as the Americans arrived a coup had taken place, followed by the imposition of martial law. What were locals to think?

"Naturally the Russians—the 'ignorant Russians'—didn't warm up to the British or the Allies as they were supposed to do," May would write. "The British were 'running the show,' as the saying goes, and, as the Americans were directly under the British command, naturally the Russians also mistrusted the Americans."

Among those who struck as a protest against the kidnapping of the Archangel government were the workers who ran the city's streetcars. In an attempt to display goodwill, the 339th stepped in, as Maj. J. Brooks Nichols, commander of the Second Battalion, soon sent out a call for any Americans who could man the cars.

"For twenty-four hours or perhaps thirty hours, Americans were conducting the street cars, or acting as motormen, and at every stopping place, which in Archangel is every two or three blocks, there were two or three American soldiers to keep the crowds from overloading the cars," Francis wrote. "That was because no fares were being charged."

As the ministers, meanwhile, were being transported back to their places in the city's government, Francis, seeing in the general strike a threat to law and order, saw fit to issue his own proclamation. In it, he warned the populace of Archangel that if the locals tried to revolt against the Allies, the soldiers would be recalled from the interior and "kill Russians" if need be. The threat of revolution receded.

Equally pressing during those first days of intervention was the condition of the dozens of Americans who were ill with influenza, or who soon became sick after landing at Archangel.

Godfrey Anderson, working in the 337th Field Hospital, would write that a Red Cross hospital established in Archangel opened on September 10 and was immediately filled. Another, cruder facility across the Dvina at Bakharitza was soon overflowing with the sick, forcing the use of several barracks and an "old sailor's home" in Archangel to handle the overflow.

At the makeshift Bakharitza hospital, the patients were placed on bare stretchers with just a thin blanket to cover them against the cold night air. Soon overflowing with flu-ridden men, the place resembled a scene from Dante's *Inferno*.

Men lay in their death throes everywhere, hacking and gasping and moaning and dripping with sweat as fevers burned through them. Then, there would be "an abrupt silence, and the staring eyes became fixed and vacant," Anderson wrote.

The only available water was located in a "swamp" outside the barracks and was "yellow like tea and of course had to be boiled," Anderson added, and the only medicine on hand were "cathartics"—purgatives.

One sick soldier, "delirious and far gone," got the idea that the medical staff had oranges and were keeping them from him. He kept demanding his oranges, and then issued an ultimatum: "Either give me those oranges before I count three or I'll let 'er rip!"

"Then 'one-two-three' and let her rip he did, and he lay befouled in his own vile and foul smelling [sic] excrescence," Anderson wrote. "And immediately after he gasped out his last breath."

Another soldier, Headquarters Company's Pvt. Jesse Jackson, from

Detroit, moaned and agonized through the night while on his stretcher, apparently haunted by some painful recollection of the past. "Oh God, oh God, oh God," the soldier repeated over and over for hours.

"When I came back on duty the next night the stretcher was vacated," Anderson remembered.

Men died; their bodies were simply lifted by two attendants and laid in the hallway, to be retrieved later for burial in the new and quickly filling American cemetery in Archangel.

Clyde Clark would be one of these unfortunates. Clyde Clark of Lansing, Michigan, would never see his daughter Thelma grow up, and never understand why he had been sent to the top of the earth to die (not so unusual—very few of the men ever did know).

And Clyde Clark, of Lansing, Michigan, would never know that his former betrothed, Bessie Madden, the mother of his daughter and the recipient since their divorce of part of his hard-earned wages, would also die just four months later from the raging flu that took the lives of millions worldwide that fall and winter, passing at the age of twenty-eight on January 21, 1919.

—※—

CHAPTER SIX

UPRIVER

They had spent the previous night in a swamp, a "vile morass," one of them would later say, huddling in a drizzling rain on the night of September 19–20, 1918, while the Bolos probed the woods with artillery fire. They had no rations, nor overcoats to stem the late-September chill night air, and the first light of morning brought no relief, nor succor, just an increase in the dropping of those shells, many of them, they would later learn, made in the good old U. S. of A.

The Bolos had machine guns in front of the village of Seltso—on the Dvina River two hundred miles southeast of Archangel—as well as one-pound "pom-poms," and during the night they placed a battery of three-inch guns at their flank on the Dvina River. They also had more artillery on rafts in the Dvina. That night it was decided that Company B of the 339th Infantry Regiment should attack on September 20, or face extermination by the array of Bolo artillery.

In the morning, a patrol was ordered out. Lt. Walter Dressing led the way, feeling for the enemy line. Soon the men ran into a Bolo outpost, and were scattered by severe machine-gun fire. After regrouping in the tongue of woods that had been their night home, they discovered one of the men was missing. Lieutenant Dressing would spend thirty minutes vainly beating the bush in search of Cpl. Herbert Schroeder, a twenty-two-year-old linotype assembler from Detroit.

But the grandly named Herbert Schroeder was to remain a casualty of the plan devised by the British and French architects of the intervention and zealously put into motion by the British general Frederick Poole, "a gunner, a short stocky man of about fifty" on whose coat hung "a long row of war medals," his eventual replacement in Archangel, Gen. Edmund Ironside, would write.

Poole had served "in most parts of the Empire," including South Africa, Somaliland, and posts in East and West Africa. He retired from the service in 1914 but quickly returned when the Great War erupted the same year. After serving in the artillery on the Western Front he had been named chief of the British Artillery Mission in Russia, Ironside noted.

Poole seemed to be laboring under the impression that he would at some point receive enough reinforcements to brush aside the supposedly hapless Bolsheviks and then move on Petrograd (St. Petersburg) and even Moscow.

During that autumn of 1918, Poole was laying groundwork to do just that—at least in his own mind. Ignoring the reality that he had a force of just 4,600 Americans and some 2,000 British, French, Canadians, and Polish, and a handful of Russians in the Slavo-British Allied Legion, he dreamed big; and it was because of those grand dreams— call them hallucinations, if you will—that Americans would die, or melt into oblivion, as had Cpl. Herbert Schroeder.

The push on the railway front was one part of the strategy, and Poole and the Allied planners seemed to believe that a single battalion of the 339th could break through the Bolshevik lines and storm south nearly three hundred miles to Vologda before winter set in. There, the one thousand men of the Third Battalion would make contact with the ephemeral Czech Legion and a would-be army of Whites and move to the west to reestablish the Eastern Front.

Those Czechs and Whites would be coming west toward Vologda because of the other underpinning element of Poole's plan: the First Battalion's three-hundred-mile push up the wide and lazy Dvina River to Kotlas, where a spur of the Trans-Siberian Railroad would be reached, and contact would be made somewhere farther east with the Czechs. Poole, ever optimistic, was certain the river force could reach Kotlas before winter set in.

General Poole would discount much too much the Bolshevik armies on the railroad and the Red soldiers and gunboats that stood in the Allies' way on what would come to be called the river front. Still, obeying the fevered obsessions and optimism of the British command that September of 1918, the First Battalion—Companies A, B, C, and D—of the 339th U.S. Infantry Regiment would dutifully debark from Archangel on September 7 and board a flotilla of large river barges. And so began the long slog.

Among them were men in the throes or first stages of the flu, who had to be assisted onto the boats and into the holds, where they would fitfully attempt to sleep in a mixture of coal dust and the grime that develops from delivering cattle, produce, flax, "and a thousand-and-one other things," Moore et al. would write.

They shoved off at six P.M., headed up the wide Dvina, two miles wide at some points and always shallow. But few of the men would even see the river and many never reached their destination.

"Suffering Sea Cooks, what a rotten hole they have dumped us into now, coal dust 2 inches thick, damp, filthy dungeon, we are sleeping on bottom of scow, no light, ventilation, or anything," Pvt. Clarence Scheu of Company B would note in his diary.

Even as they went, men died. "C company man dies overnight, military funeral in a little Russian village," Scheu wrote on September 9 of the death of Pvt. Joseph Gresser. He followed with this the next day, about Pvt. Carl Jordan: "One B. company man died overnight, we stop and bury him in the nearest village, this is not a very promising beginning for our small force."

On September 11, four days out, Scheu would note the passing of Pvt. John Wetershof. "Another B. company man dies, quite a few of the boys have not yet recuperated from the influenza that attacked them aboard the Nagoya, the fellows have not had proper medical attention so far, still going on."

The barges had no heat, and men had to sleep—and in some instances die—on the bare wooden floors. At times, one soldier would write, the "antic caravel seemed more a funeral procession than an aggressive expedition of war."

Supplies of medicine had been left up to their British overseers, and Henry Katz, a member of the 339th's medical detachment, told the men that there was hardly any medicine to give them. "What medicine that was taken there was the little that the medical officers had in their private bags," Company B's Sgt. Simon Davis would write.

They moved, thirty-five miles a day, into the vast interior of Russia's north, past marshes and tundra and almost impenetrable forests of pine, birch, and other species. The land, Company I's Lt. Albert May would write, "is one vast expanse of forest and swamp—and swamp of the variety that sucked up those lost legions in Russia in the Manchurian [Masurian] lakes region in the early days of the war.

"Except along the streams, the country was very sparsely populated. Here and there one finds [a] small clearing, inhabited by a few wood cutters or trappers or a few peasants. It is indeed a forest primeval, with untapped treasures beyond the dreams of man."

Passing by the villages of Siskoe, Emetskoe, and Morjagorskaya, the flotilla on September 12 finally arrived at Beresnik, which would be the base for the river front. They were almost 150 miles from Archangel, in hostile territory and facing the great unknown.

Many of them were also deathly ill. Henry Katz would write that forty men, sick with influenza, were taken from the barges at Beresnik and placed in a small British hospital. "Accomadations [sic] very poor," Katz wrote. "They were not prepared to receive more than 10 or 15 men."

Harry Costello would claim that though the British had a hospital boat at Beresnik, the sick Americans were not allowed on board but instead "were placed in a vacant outhouse." That, he wrote, was where Pvt. Orville Stocken of Company A died on September 13, and also where Lt. Marcus Casey of Company C passed on September 16.

When Stocken died, "he had received no medical aid whatever,"

Costello added. "It is true that a British doctor looked at the dying soldier, but what could he do? For, although Beresnik had been a British base since August, all the medical supplies had long been exhausted."

Other sick swelled the base, and more died, including Company A's Pvt. Harry Surran on September 16. Lt. Edward Saari while scouting to the south with a platoon of Company A's men came across a group of Royal Scots, twenty-one of whom had the flu. "These men had been sick and nearly dead for days without any aid," Costello wrote. "Their officers failed to look after them."

On September 13, Companies C and D moved upriver, while Company A relieved a detachment of Royal Scots and took up defense of Beresnik. On the fourteenth, C Company skirmished with some Bolos at the village of Shedrova, which was taken by the Americans the next day.

The Bolos continued to retreat in the face of the American advance. But at Chamova, the next village upriver, the men came under fire from Russian gunboats; a British monitor following the push came up and, from three miles distant, landed a salvo and sank the Russian boat.

On the eighteenth, Companies A, B, and C of the First Battalion made their way south to Toulgas, where they paused for the night and sent scouting parties to the south. The next day, the column moved south toward Seltso, and Company D reached the tiny village of Yakovlevskaya at about one P.M. Seltso sat just to the south, across a mile-long marsh that was fed by an arm of the Dvina.

Here, "'D' Company gallantly deployed and wading the swamp approached within one thousand five hundred yards of the enemy, who suddenly opened up with machine guns, rifles, and Russian pom pom," Moore et al. wrote.

Here as well, the Bolos made a stand. Stymied, the American company's men went to ground, and later retreated to Yakovlevskaya, where the men dug a trench behind a fence and tried to sleep. "It rained constantly and we were soaked to the skin by morning," Company D's Pvt. Frank Douma would write.

Company C arrived and took up a position in a slightly elevated wood that jutted into the swampy ground of the marsh, and at dark Company B followed. The men dug in as best they could in the sodden earth and waited for orders from battalion commander Maj. James Corbly.

And here Cpl. Herbert Schroder and the men of Companies B and C spent an awful night, without food, without cover, as the rain pelted down and the Bolo artillery searched out their position.

"Bolo artillery opens up heavily, we spend night on hill, no shelter during bombardment, rain falling steadily, temporarily our position bad, cornered up, no eats and no sleep for 24 hours, everyone tired but anxious to vacate this position," Clarence Scheu would write.

The Bolo gunboats pounded Company D in Yakovlevskaya the next morning, the twentieth, while two platoons from Company B probed the Bolo lines. "We run into a nest of machine guns, we retire," Scheu wrote.

Pvt. Bill Henkelman of Company B would remember brewing tea and sharing a can of "bully beef" with his friend, Cpl. Morris Foley, before setting off on the patrol. "I say to Foley, 'Hey Maurice [*sic*], let's save enough for after while,'" Henkelman recalled.

"Maurice, on the last of the can says, 'There might be no after while.'"

The two platoons formed a skirmish line but encountered trouble on the right, where the men ran into entrenchments. Henkelman's recollection of what happened next has a hallucinatory feel.

"Kudzba got a bullet through the brain. His gun pitched forward and he fell backwards and lay still. I hit the dirt. Rapid fire began. Pellets of death cut off weed tops. Kudzba's head was all bloody and his face was in a rivulet of water . . .

"Then Cpl. Foley was hit and John VanDerMeer killed. Lt. Smith was shot in the side. We retreated, I helping the lieutenant." (Lt. Albert Smith would in fact earn a Distinguished Service Cross for continuing to direct his men during the assault while "fearlessly exposing himself to fire throughout the action," his DSC citation reads.)

Corbly, finally on the scene, ordered a full-scale assault on Seltso. Russian artillery also finally made it up through the muck and mire, and at 4:45 P.M. laid barrages on Seltso and the Red gunboats. At five P.M., the three American companies advanced over the open ground of the marsh, and within an hour had the village, which had been mostly evacuated by the Bolos.

"We wheeled," Henkelman would say, "then after our shell fire routed them, we went over the top again and jumped over Bolo dead and captured the village."

Henkelman saw the disturbing sight of his dead friend, Morris Foley, after volunteers went and collected the dead and wounded. "Foley had half his neck and face gone, yet had taken off one legging before he died," Henkelman would say. "I just wondered, so there was no 'After while' for him. Two of us carry him on a litter and I, in rear, looking at old pal, collapsed and passed out."

Like Henkelman, other semitraumatized soldiers wondered at what had just occurred, and wondered as well why they weren't lying dead like some of their pals. Covered in mud and ashen-faced after their ordeal, they could only shake hands and congratulate each other for still being alive.

Company C's Pvt. Edwin Arkins came upon a dead body and noted in his diary, "The sight of the first casualty I'll never forget; the lower part of face a bloody mass; the eye lids swollen and blue and the head resting on the inside of the upturned helmet."

Continuing, Arkins came across a wounded Bolo gunner with a shattered leg. "As sergeant and I stop beside him, he utters one word, 'Comrade' in German. Sergeant suggests we put bayonet through him for fear he [will] rise up and shoot at us." Arkins suggested that they instead just take the wounded man's rifle. "This we do and advance into village," Arkins wrote.

Amazingly, the action at Seltso incurred just thirteen casualties—four men killed in action, eight wounded, and one—Herbert Schroeder— missing in action. That night, the survivors occupied the Bolos' works, and their spirits were somewhat lifted by a generous gift from a British major downriver.

"Everyone was tired, wet, muddy, and cold, not sleeping very well as we knew the enemy was only a short way off," Company B commander Robert Boyd would write. "At midnight the British major sent up a gallon of rum which made a swallow for each man. It did a wonderful lot of good."

As would happen repeatedly during the 339th's Russian ordeal, after taking Seltso they had to briefly relinquish it. Red gunboats continued to prowl the Dvina, and the merry band in Seltso came under their fire. As well, a large force of Bolos was rumored to be in their front and preparing an attack.

They retreated to Yakovlevskaya once more, but the rumored attack never came off. One last advance, this to the village of Pouchuga beyond Seltso, was ordered. After several days, the vicinity of Pouchuga was reached. By then, the doughboys were worn out and out of smokes, as well, and those with the nicotine habit had been reduced to rolling cigarettes out of tea leaves. "A more miserable looking and feeling outfit can scarce be imagined," Moore et al. would write.

Halting in a "suburb" of Pouchuga, the men fell out and found billets in the homes of Russian peasants, each man so tired that he stopped in the first place where there was room to spread a blanket. But there was to be no rest for the weary; Corbly came up late that night and ordered an advance on the main village.

The men rose and staggered on, fighting not just exhaustion now but the muddy ground as well. Robert Boyd would remember one soldier in particular having great difficulty.

"We were ploughing along through the mud when from my place at the head of the column I heard a splash," Boyd would say. "I went back to investigate and there was Babcock floundering in a ditch with sides too slippery to crawl up.

"The column was marching stolidly past, each man with but one thought, to pull his boot out of the mud and put it a little farther on. We finally got Babcock up to terra firma, he explained that it had looked like good walking, nice and smooth, and he had gone down to try it."

Boyd would add: "I cautioned him that he should never try to take a bath while in military formation, and he seemed to think the advice was sound."

The tired, filthy little column reached the main village of Pouchuga only to find that the Bolos had fled before them. The upper Dvina cleared of Bolos to the satisfaction of the British, the men of Companies B, C, and D were toted out by barge. And when they did they left the graves of their comrades killed at Seltso—and left behind as well the enigma of Cpl. Herbert Schroeder.

"A native told me that the enemy had one prisoner with them when they left the village," Lt. Walter Dressing would report. Another member of Company B talked to a captured female Red officer. The short, slightly built Corporal Schroeder was described to her, and she said the description "answered to that of Schroeder," a newspaper account would relate in 1920.

"The Russian said that the prisoner was taken to Petrograd. Schroeder was an expert lino-typer and it is believed the reds are using him to 'get out' propaganda to be sent to America for distribution."

It had been hoped the First Battalion could reach Kotlas by winter; at Pouchuga, the men had already penetrated as far south as most of the Allies would go, and they were turning back. As they did, Cpl. Herbert Schroeder was well on his way to Kotlas, and thence to Vologda and St. Petersburg, fulfilling in his own small way the grand plans of Gen. Frederick Poole.

CHAPTER SEVEN

THE ROMANCE OF COMPANY A

Pvt. Harry H. Surran would be the object of attention at two funerals. The second was held back in his hometown of Warren, Indiana; the first convened on the banks of the Dvina River in the district of Archangel, in northern Russia, and occurred just two days after he succumbed to influenza, on September 14, 1918.

The funeral, held in a small churchyard just outside of Beresnik, was simple. His mates in Company A, 339th U.S. Infantry Regiment, were the pallbearers, and they carried his thirty-year-old body from a log house in which it had lain in a coffin made from fences. They brought Harry then to a small, four-wheeled cart—such a conveyance, called a droshky, would become familiar in coming months to the Americans—and then moved amid a crowd of some forty soldiers and officers.

At the grave, "with the gorgeous autumn woods on one side and the wide blue river on the other," Company A's chronicler Dorothea York would write, a British chaplain read over Harry. Afterward, a firing squad popped off three volleys, taps was played, "and it was over," York wrote.

For Pvt. Harry Surran and others of the 339th, "the glory of dying in France to lie under a field of poppies," Moore et al. would write, "had come to this drear mystery of dying in Russia under a dread disease in a strange and unlovely place."

And so came to an end the long journey of Harry H. Surran, whose father, John W., had been a newspaper founder, owner, editor, and publisher who had watched despondently as his first wife—Harry's mother, Sarah—"a most estimable lady," as one newspaper would put it, had died of the consumption at their home in March 1894 after suffering with the disease for years.

John Surran had founded the Warren *Weekly News* in 1878 after careers as a teacher and an attorney. In 1881 the newspaper building was destroyed by fire, but he rebuilt and went on with it through the death of his wife and the raising of three children until selling out to Monroe Wiley in 1902. In 1904 he moved west to Missouri with a new wife, Lizzie, and his children: Harry—"a promising youth of 16," the Huntington, Indiana, *Herald* would report—Anne, and Helen.

He planned to farm on eighty acres he bought in Vernon County, and he did for some time, but by 1916 he was working as a printer in Kansas City, where on March 17, 1916, death took him; the cause, ominously, was pneumonia.

Harry by then was working as a farmhand, and not long after became a soldier with Company A and was sent to Beresnik, Russia, where he died and was buried on the banks of the Dvina River by forty of his company mates, some of whom, even as taps was still ringing in their ears, gathered their weapons and once more boarded an old coal hauler, headed this time not down the Dvina but to its sister river, the Vaga, where they would in time become the farthest-flung, and most forlorn, and most exposed, American unit to serve in what John Cudahy would call "this strange, strange war."

The barge carrying Private Surran's former unit headed southeast on the Dvina for about four miles and then left the big river and headed south on the Vaga, a twisting, winding tributary that would take them ever deeper into the heart of Russia, and ever farther from their base at Beresnik.

Aboard were two platoons of Company A, the third commanded

by Lt. Carl McNabb, the fourth by Lt. Harry Mead, late of the Detroit offices of Harry H. Mead, Esq., and the training grounds at Fort Sheridan. Overall command went to Capt. Otto Arthur Odjard, a native of Portland, Oregon, a thirty-two-year-old career army man, and a man who was "more an antique Viking than a city-bred modern," in the words of Cudahy.

The men liked what they saw of the country around the Vaga. The small villages the 339th had passed by on the way to Beresnik were sparsely populated, poor, and unfailingly and even shockingly dirty, with cockroaches roaming the walls and floors of their peasant billets, in which sanitation was an unpracticed art.

In contrast, the villages of the Vaga seemed much wealthier and more promising—especially the river's largest town, Shenkursk, where on September 17 the Americans piled out of their boat and began garrison duty.

Shenkursk, which is about two hundred miles from Archangel (again, as the crow flies), stood high on the east bank of the Vaga, and boasted a monastery and three churches. "There are many comfortable houses of the well-to-do and some of the wealthy and in normal times it was used somewhat as a summer resort," York would write. "It is surrounded by forests where the hunting is excellent."

Compared to the backward, simple *moujiks* who eked out a living in the harsh environs of the Archangel District, Shenkursk was also populated by a more "effete" class, Cudahy would write, its roughly three thousand inhabitants being people who were schooled in Russian literature, better dressed, more soft-spoken, and "accustomed to the niceties, the softer things of life."

Shenkursk had been fortified to a degree with log-and-earth emplacements for both men and machine guns, and when reached by Company A, it held a platoon of American engineers, and in addition to a British headquarters for the region, there were some members of the Slavo-British Allied Legion.

Company A's men quickly took to the town, and the locals were welcoming. "The little barishna especially cast soft eyes on these amazing young strangers and evinced great willingness to teach their language and dances to such apt and interesting students," York wrote.

The interest was mutual, but the happy interlude with the opposite sex was not to last. Just a few days after arriving in Shenkursk, the Americans were told they were being replaced by British soldiers, and were ordered to move farther south down the Vaga. It was the last week of summer 1918.

On September 19, Captain Odjard and Harry Mead led forty-five men seventeen miles to a cluster of villages called Ust Padenga, and encountered no Bolos during their eighteen-hour round-trip through swamp and forest. Two days later, two platoons of Company A began journeying south on the gunboat *Tolstoy* with the intent of attacking any Bolos they could turn up.

Helping them would be thirty Russian S.B.A.L.s and a detachment of irregular Russians called "partisan troops," local civilians who were anti-Bolshevik. This force was moving by land toward the area of Ust Padenga even as the *Tolstoy* ferried the Americans upriver. In theory, the parallel movements would see the land force flush the Bolos, who would then be cut off farther south by a landing of the Americans.

Just ten miles above Ust Padenga, the boat was spotted by the Bolos. Having the advantage of American rifles, they began firing from a bluff and wounded four of Company A's men. The *Tolstoy* fired back with its twelve-pound artillery, and then landed. Though in their first fight, the Americans didn't hesitate and charged up the bank. They soon ran into about two hundred men who comprised the Bolos rear guard.

Linking with the S.B.A.L. force, Americans and loyalist Russians drove the Bolos south and through the village of Gora, where the *Tolstoy* had landed. That night, all found billets in the village, and then the offensive was taken up again the next morning, with Captain Odjard leading thirty men through the swamps and deep woods in an attempt to flank the main Bolo party at Rovdinskaya, while Harry Mead led the rest on a frontal attack.

The Bolos gave ground steadily before the assault, and by five P.M.

the Americans had taken the village. They remained there for ten days, constantly patrolling in an attempt to disguise the puny numbers of the Allied force. Fire was exchanged, but the gun on the *Tolstoy* led the Bolos to restrain any imminent urge to attack.

Still, Captain Odjard worried constantly about their perilous situation and isolation, and he feared a Bolo attack might come at any moment.

(His concern was not necessarily shared by his men; one dark night as he made the rounds, he found two sentries deep in conversation. As Odjard approached, he clued in on the subject matter: it was about what they wanted for their first meal when—if—they got home. Fresh food in the form of a chef's salad, Cpl. Max Troutner told his companion. "Wouldn't I like some now.")

In early October, the First and Second Platoons, under command of Lts. Hugh McPhail and Edward Saari, came in from Shenkursk and relieved their comrades at Rovdinskaya. They brought with them more reinforcements—Russian civilians, S.B.A.L. recruits, and two sections of Canadian artillerymen that had only recently landed at Archangel.

On October 8, Americans and Russians, now under command of a Colonel Delatorsky, moved three miles south and attacked a Bolo force at the village of Nijni Puya. It was no mere skirmish. The Bolos numbered between four hundred and seven hundred. The seamen "presented a warm reception of rifle and machine gun fire," Dorothea York would write.

The Americans advanced in the center while the Russian mercenaries took the left flank and the S.B.A.L.s the right. Pushing through a swamp, the line emerged at a swale a quarter mile wide, at the other side of which the Bolos were positioned.

The advancing line went to ground—except for the S.B.A.L.s, who had taken refuge behind a church. Odjard ordered McPhail, toward the right of the American line, to roust them. He found them "having a dandy coffee klatch," each one smoking cigarettes and drinking tea, McPhail remembered. They had a machine gun, but seemed disinterested in using it, so McPhail set it up and gave instructions on how to sight and operate it, "and told them to get on the ball."

The S.B.A.L.s enfiladed the enemy line, and Company A and the Russians then advanced and routed the Bolos, who retreated, leaving some fifty dead and hundreds of wounded behind them.

Company A suffered three casualties: two men wounded by gunfire and one man, Pvt. Max Ostrow, who was struck in the ankle by an errant artillery shell fragment. The Allied force returned the same night to Rovdinskaya, to which the Third and Fourth Platoons returned as well on October 11, making the company whole again for the first time since landing at Archangel.

In addition to the Bolo threat, Russia's famed "General Winter" was showing his face; ominously, it snowed for the first time on October 15, temperatures were dropping, and the Americans had no winter clothing. Unbeknownst to them, the Bolsheviks to their front would over the next months grow from a rag-tag, piecemeal, and polyglot army into a real fighting force.

Their situation, though they might not yet have known it, was beyond perilous.

To make matters even worse, food, too, was becoming scarce, and the Americans' tobacco was almost out. "Got a little tobacco yesterday for a change," Odjard would write to a friend in the States on October 20.

"Coffee thus far is unheard of, but often thought of. One of my men remarked to me the other day that if he had a cigarette, the latest Detroit Free Press and 15 minutes' quiet he would gladly serve the remainder of this emergency without compensation or hope of other reward."

Despite the privations, there was one more task for Company A to perform. Odjard led a small, mixed patrol south on October 22, and reached the vicinity of Navolok, about eight miles away from Rovdinskaya, more than two hundred miles south of Archangel—and still one hundred miles from Kotlas and any hope of connecting with the Czech Legion. He then returned to Rovdinskaya.

It would be the farthest any Americans penetrated into Russia during their strange war. At one A.M. on October 24, as Company A's men lay shivering in a cold, sodden marsh, orders came to withdraw to Ust Padenga, on the west bank of the Vaga twelve miles south of Shenkursk.

The men spent the rest of the night scrounging the area for horses and transport. At six A.M., Company A about-faced and headed north in a long and bizarre cavalcade of three hundred two-wheeled Russian carts, "floundering, miring, and slipping in the sticky, muddy roads," Moore et al. wrote.

"Following in their rear, came the tired, worn and exhausted troops— unshaven, unkempt and with tattered clothing . . . The god of war, had he witnessed this strange sight that morning, must have recalled a similar sight a hundred years and more prior to that, at Moscow, when the army of the great Napoleon was scattered to the winds by the cavalry and infantry of the Russian hordes."

Late that autumn night, the column reached Ust Padenga. There, all supposed, they would simply wait out the coming winter before resuming military operations in the spring.

CHAPTER EIGHT

THE STRANGEST FIGHTING MISSION EVER UNDERTAKEN

On November 26, 1899, while serving as a first lieutenant in the Nineteenth Infantry Regiment of the United States Army on the island of Panay in the Philippines, George Evans Stewart, while leading a crossing of a river in the face of the enemy, saved an enlisted man who was drowning.

His heroism would earn him a Medal of Honor.

George Evans Stewart was twenty-seven at the time of his brave and selfless act. At the age of forty-six, he was sent into Russia in command of the 339th U.S. Infantry Regiment . . .

And, in effect, disappeared.

"No one could predict that at the time that this medal would be the last decoration that Stewart would receive from his country, that he would finish out a lackluster military career in obscurity, conscience-plagued and shunned by the men who had served under him," one writer would observe.

While two-thirds of his regiment scattered to the railway front and the Dvina and Vaga Rivers to fight Bolsheviks under British command, Col. George Stewart and his staff occupied what had been known simply as the Technical Institute, a large, three-story building on the Dvina riverfront that boasted electric lighting and steam heat—exotic features in a city of mostly primitive log homes.

It was from there that he would venture out to visit his troops only rarely, and it was from the vast distances at which his soldiers found themselves that he would become an object of derision as he hid, as it were, in the comfort of steam heat while they froze and died in the obscure wastes of northern Russia through the winter and spring of 1919.

His reputation took a hit early on with the widely reported story of how, instead of remaining at the railway front an extra ten or twenty minutes so he could attend the funerals of three of the first Americans to die in action there, he had left for the comforts of Archangel.

That story would morph into the rumor Harry Costello would relate, that Colonel Stewart had sat in a house "reading a magazine" while an American soldier, one of the first to be killed, "was being buried outside the house or within a few rods of it."

John Cudahy, in his postwar diatribe *Archangel*, would be more blunt. Stewart, he would write, "never saw any part of his regiment in action. For a long time I believe he had not even a vague notion regarding the location of his British dissipated troops."

A rare trip to the river front by Stewart "was marked principally by his losing one of his mittens," Company B's Capt. Robert Boyd would say. "He searched everywhere, and half insinuated that Capt. Dean, my adjutant, a British officer, had taken it."

Costello, as bitter and vituperative in his own postwar book as Cudahy, would also write that on a visit to the front, Stewart, an engineer by trade, had mistaken a Vickers machine gun for a Lewis machine gun. Stewart then picked up a Very pistol—used for firing flares—and asked Maj. J. Brooks Nichols: "What kind of a cannon do you call this?"

"Major Nichols was forced, in the presence of the enlisted men, to give his superior all the information about the Very pistol, even to the detail of pulling the trigger," Costello wrote. "This officer was a colonel."

Costello in turn lionized the 339th's original and popular commander, Col. John Craig, who had been replaced by Stewart shortly before the regiment left Camp Custer. "John Craig would have made our campaign in Russia one that would have demanded of the whole world that it turn its eyes to Russia and the 339th," he wrote in his highly critical postwar book *Why Did We Go to Russia?*

"Col. Craig would not have stood supinely by while his outfit was stolen . . . He was a FIGHTER and not one who would sit calmly back in Archangel and blame the war department because they sent him orders to place himself at the disposal of the British . . . Can anyone tell us that John Craig would have been 'lolling' back in Archangel and his men scattered to the four winds? I should say not!"

In Stewart's defense, it should be noted that the American authorities had acquiesced to putting American troops under British command, and Stewart, one writer would say, was "basically powerless . . . To visit his troops invariably placed Stewart in a humiliating position, since his men were serving under the British flag and under British officers."

As a result, Moore et al. would write, the average soldier "came to look upon American Headquarters in Archangel as of very trifling importance in the strange game that he was up against."

Stewart had no say in strategy, few orders to write, no lines of communication or supply to see to. Even the medical service was overseen by the British. And so George Evans Stewart upon landing at Archangel in northern Russia watched as his men traveled off to "the strangest fighting mission ever undertaken by an American force" and tried in vain to keep track of his widely dispersed forces, Moore et al. added.

His Third Battalion was far down the railroad, with orders to take Vologda three hundred miles to the south. His First Battalion was struggling far up the Dvina River on its own vain mission to reach Kotlas by winter. So from the beginning until the end, "he lost touch with his battalion and company commanders" (none of whom, it should be mentioned, he had had much time to get to know in any case).

Dan Steele, a lieutenant with Company F, would write that the interruption of the American chain of command was intentional on the part of the regiment's British handlers.

"Their technique in organization was marvelous," Steele wrote. "They managed to provide a British officer, senior in rank, to any American officer in command of troops at a given point, and thus extend their command of the expedition as a whole to the command of individual units.

"Their regulations conveniently allowed temporary promotion without pay or allowances, so that a quartermaster shavetail could be made a major overnight to outrank an American captain whose company might be doing most of the job."

Harry Costello would write that while cooperation between the British and their American subordinates could be dicey at the front, it was "conspicuous by its absence" in Archangel.

"There was a continual divergence in everything, instead of a getting together," he wrote. "Many American officers had little or no respect for the majority of the British officers, all statements to the contrary notwithstanding."

The average enlisted man also chafed under British authority; they also blanched at eating English "bully beef," and fumed as they sucked on inferior British cigarettes. As well, as in any war, the men on the front line were derisive toward the "ration eaters" and "ration stealers" back at Archangel, no matter their nationality.

In Archangel, there were indeed teas and luncheons and dinners and dances, among them "eight hundred English officers who had nothing to do and all winter to do it in, proceeded to enjoy themselves, as did the two thousand batmen who attended them," as Dorothea York would write. And yet others in Archangel that fall, meanwhile, had plenty of things to do, chief among them the men of the 339th's Second Battalion, which had been tasked with overseeing the city while their comrades left to battle the Bolos.

Company E's PFC Donald Carey would write home of pulling twenty-four-hour shifts of guard duty at the wharves of Bakharitza and Smolny barracks; he also watched as the battalion's soldiers stole liquor, English cigarettes, and anything else that wasn't nailed down. They drank the liquor, and sold or bartered the smokes to the city's downtrodden residents.

Cpl. Fred Kooyers, also with Company E, in his diary made a running count of the debauchery—his own and others'—and pilfering that went on among the men of the Second Battalion. Assigned to be a prison guard on October 8, Kooyers would write, he and his mates found and got into some British officers' supply of champagne, "which made the guard a good job for that day." The same day, a Russian was caught "going through the boys barracks bags they beat him up then threw him in the river," Kooyers wrote.

Five days later, Kooyers was assigned to be a guard at the Y.M.C.A. canteen. That night, Kooyers and his mates pilfered thirty-six cases of Scotch, ten cases of Gordon's gin, twenty fruitcakes, twenty-two cases of canned fruits—and forty thousand cigarettes. "Our officers and all were drunk the next day," Kooyers wrote.

Several days later, Kooyers and some pals received passes to leave their barracks and go across the river to Archangel. They tried to get into the Paris Café, a swinging night spot. "An M.P. met us at the door and told us that those rooms were only for the officers and their girls, so we had to hunt another place to spend our time in Archangel," he wrote.

Archangel, in fact, had quickly become a nexus for "get-rich" schemes, one source notes. From the Red Cross to the Y.M.C.A. to cooks and the quartermaster staff, it seemed everyone had his hand in the till— including the Brits at the front, who somehow managed to get their rations of whiskey while medical and other supplies never got through.

The men on the river front, Costello would write, "knew that there had been loaded into the boats before they left England, thousands upon thousands of cases of Scotch whiskey, and it wasn't stretching the imagination for them to wonder, if there was transport room for this whiskey, why medical supplies were left behind."

The regiment's Supply Company came under severe suspicion as well; some of its members "suddenly grew very wealthy," York would write. Colonel Stewart knew of all of this and yet let it go on, the soldiers on the front charged.

"Somehow the doughboy felt that the very limited and much complained about service of his own American Supply Unit, that [*sic*] lived for the most part on the fat of the land in Bakaritza [*sic*], should have been corrected by his commanding officer who sat in American Headquarters," Moore et al. would write.

But at least one of the gougers and pilferers was caught: a sergeant with Headquarters Company, who had stolen and resold sugar from the warehouses at great profit. After being nabbed, he committed suicide. In his barracks bag was an astonishing $89,000 in American currency.

Amid the strife, amid the outright criminal activity, good work was being done in Archangel and Bakharitza. Despite the privations, some flu cases were getting better with the aid of the medical detachment, and the epidemic gradually passed.

The young medic Godfrey Anderson was put to work cleaning an old building that would become a hospital. Helping him each day was a group of Russian prisoners, probably of the political variety, half starved, scabrous, and "miserable looking," he would write.

Some good was being done by the 310th Engineers, also; they built twenty-eight new barracks, laid three thousand feet of water pipes, and wired thirty-two buildings and four streets with electricity. They also improved the city's water and power plants, and in some cases operated the sawmills that were pervasive on the waterfront.

While one company of engineers went out to the fronts to build blockhouses and fortifications, the other laid duckboards across muddy streets, built warehouses, dug latrines, and generally improved the city's conditions and cleanliness.

"There is a perfect oodle of work to be done and it is a real pleasure to me to help do it," Sgt. Rodger Clark of the engineers' Company C would write home.

CHAPTER NINE

THE BRIDGE

Floundering. Tripping. Falling.

Failing.

Capt. Joel Roscoe Moore of Company M is lost, consumed by the darkest midnight of north Russia, wandering through its swamps and woods. He is the blind leading the blind, not only his men but two platoons of Company I, slipping and sliding in "treacherous mire," attempting to launch a flank attack on the Bolos but in fact getting nowhere except desperate.

Just eight years ago, he had coached the Great Falls High School Bison to a championship game, only to lose to Butte, 12 to zip, in a driving snowstorm on Thanksgiving Day.

Now, he was attempting to guide his new team, the boys of Company M, 339th Infantry Regiment, to victory at the railway front. But the effort quickly turned into a fourth-and-long predicament.

It had seemed like such a grand game plan the previous day, September 28, 1918.

With the optimism and accompanying shortsightedness that typified the British approach to the north Russia adventure, General Poole had ordered a push from Obozerskaya toward the village of Plesetskaya,

forty miles down the railway track, at which the Bolos were based in
that part of the country and from which they were sending troops to
fight the Allies.

Moore was told to lead his company south from Verst 464 to the
dug-in Bolo position at Verst 455. A separate force, two platoons from
Company I, would do the same. All would first head east through the
woods to a north–south road that had been laid out in the time of Peter
the Great, overnight in the woods opposite and behind the Bolo camp,
and then strike at six A.M. on the twenty-ninth.

At the same time, a French company would advance south down the
track to Verst 461, bringing with it a Stokes mortar squad from Headquarters Company that would rush in "and assist in consolidating the
positions gained." The remaining two platoons of Company I, meanwhile, would pull their own night march to Verst 458.

"You Americans can do it somehow, you know," the British commander, Colonel Sutherland, summed up. "Ten Americans are as good
as a hundred Bolos, aren't they?"

Righty-o, sir. What could go wrong?

"No Russian guide could be provided," Moore would write. "No one
had been over the proposed route of march." There had also been a
delay in getting ready; they had not entered the woods until it was late
afternoon; it was dark long before they reached a broad path in the
forest through which they were to travel.

And after turning south and walking and stumbling for hours
through the deep night, the only light available the spare, pale twin-
kling of the stars above, they emerged from the cutting and were confronted, Moore would write, by a "great marsh" that blocked their way.

The "tantalizing optical illusion" drew them toward what seemed to
be firm ground, but in fact was not.

"But ever the same, or worse, treacherous mire," Moore would recall.
"We cannot stand a moment in a spot. We must flounder on. The column has to spread. Distress comes from every side. Men are down and
groggy. Someone who is responsible for that body of men"—Moore—
"sweats blood and swears hatred to the muddler who is to blame."

Then came the news: Moore had lost contact with three squads from Company M and both platoons of Company I.

He returned for his men and found them at a crossroad where they were disoriented and "fearing to take a choice." Moore told Cpl. Edward Henning to use the dim stars above to navigate south, and they moved again. Not far away, they could hear the steam engine of the Bolo train, panting and hissing like a wild animal.

There was only one problem in reaching it: the uncharted marsh lay in their way, and it proved to be impassable. Moore decided to return north, and perhaps join the now-raging battle at Verst 461. But when he and his force finally emerged from the woods, they found they were back at their starting point on the railway.

If it was any consolation to Moore—and it wasn't—the two platoons from Company I that had left with his company also became lost and had to return to the Allied line. The two Company I platoons under Lt. Albert May reached their objective at Verst 458, and when the attack was launched they were able to drive the Bolos on their left from their entrenchments.

After enduring that all-night misadventure in the swamps and woods, Moore was determined to do *something* to aid the attack. While many of his men fell out in exhaustion, Moore called for volunteers for an ad hoc platoon, aiming to lead it forward to the bridge at Verst 461, which had been taken by the French that morning.

Quickly, Sgts. Jacob Kantrowitz, Charles Riha, and Norman Zapfe volunteered. Others were willing but were deemed too far gone. Fifty-eight men who were in the best shape for the patrol were chosen.

The situation was becoming critical. Before Moore and his men could reach the bridge, the Bolos counterattacked and split the force of American mortarmen and Harry Costello's "valiant machine guns" on the left from the French, who were holding in the woods to the right.

"Early in the game we came under the machine gun fire of the enemy who was spraying our reserve positions with indirect machine gun fire preparatory to delivering his counter-attack upon the French and

Americans who had pushed into his first line positions and were caught in a trap," Moore wrote.

As Moore and his men advanced, Lt. James Donovan was wounded by a machine-gun bullet, which hit him in the left side and curled around one of his ribs, just barely missing a vertebra before lodging below his right shoulder.

Moore would recall "that grim-faint feeling [we] had when the Bolos charged with their devilish yell and won back their trenches and we saw the French and Americans come running back along the railway side."

The Bolos regained their trenches, but not the bridge. Moore and his single platoon, plus the mortarmen, were able to hold their enemy at bay and "inflicted such losses upon the enemy that he did not attempt to retake the bridge that day." During the fighting, Company M's Sgt. Matthew Grahek wormed his way forward through heavy Bolo fire to rescue a wounded enlisted man. Grahek was awarded a Distinguished Service Cross for his heroics.

Moore and his men endured Bolo shelling, but suffered eight wounded—two mortally—when the British commander, Colonel Sutherland, ordered the hard-won front then being held by the Americans to be shelled.

Sutherland had the "panicky idea" that the Reds were going to cross the bridge and ordered bursts of shrapnel to be fired over it. As the shrapnel cut up Moore's platoon, Captain Alliez, the French officer in command of the attack, and Harry Costello warned Sutherland of his mistaken order to fire.

Notified that he was killing his own troops, Sutherland "first asked on one telephone for another quart of whisky and later called up his artillery officer and ordered the deadly fire to lengthen range," a furious Moore would recall, adding that an American soldier attached to Sutherland's headquarters, Company M's Homer Steinhauer, had witnessed Sutherland's actions.

Before the order to fire could be rescinded, nine men had been wounded and another was shell-shocked. Two of the wounded would die, Pvt. Schliomo Dyment succumbing to his wounds on the field, and Pvt. Matthei Neimi passing while en route to the hospital at Obozerskaya.

Sutherland was ready to quit the battle, withdraw the Allied troops, and head back to the officers' club in Archangel. But by then the Third Battalion's commander, Charles Young—who had made the astonishing leap from sergeant to major at Camp Custer, a fact perhaps more indicative of the green state of the 339th than Young's talents for command—had been relieved midbattle and replaced by former Second Battalion commander Maj. J. Brooks Nichols, who refused Sutherland's order to withdraw.

"From the day he arrived on the scene with us," Harry Costello would write, "Major Nichols proved himself one of the most energetic, resourceful and competent military leaders of the whole campaign."

Nichols, who would spend the next months at the front working and sleeping in a railway car, consulted with Alliez, received reports from the front, and ordered the position held. After two more days of holding on, it was the Bolos who went home empty-handed.

The cost of gaining roughly three miles of ground: eight French killed, wounded, or missing. The Americans lost four killed, fourteen more wounded, and five missing.

But "the Reds never did get back the important bridge," Moore wrote.

The Bolos had, however, awoken to a growing danger.

While the Reds fought Whites that early fall throughout Russia, the scant Allied force—no more than nine thousand men at its largest—in the faraway Archangel District had not loomed in importance. But Leon Trotsky, who had implicitly sanctioned the original Allied landing at Murmansk, now frothed at the impertinence of the British and Americans and came to understand that they were trying to undo Lenin's historic revolution.

The Allies, he now saw, were a threat. He resolved to drive them into the White Sea.

CHAPTER TEN

ONEGA

Clifford Fuller Phillips was a Republican, a Mason, a "live wire," and a partner with Frank Hebenstreit in the law firm Phillips and Hebenstreit of Falls City, Nebraska.

The son of J. Thomas Phillips, an expert plasterer and general contractor, and Mary Tice Phillips, Clifford grew up in Beatrice, Nebraska, and while in the local high school was a member of various debate organizations, among them the Crabtree Forensic Club and the I.F. Debating Club.

Naturally, given his interest in oratory and debate, Clifford graduated with a law degree from the University of Michigan in 1914. On March 26, 1915, Clifford Fuller Phillips married Kathryn Justesen, of Council Bluffs, Iowa.

Kathryn gave birth to daughter Ellen Jane on August 26, 1916. A little more than two years later, after having earned a commission as a first lieutenant from the officers' school at Fort Snelling, Minnesota, Clifford Fuller Phillips found himself prowling the Onega River Valley in northern Russia, in command of the First Platoon of Company H, 339th Infantry Regiment, as it sought to push back the Bolos and protect the right flank of the Third Battalion, which was holding the railway front.

Twenty-eight-year-old Clifford Phillips hadn't had much time to enjoy the dubious pleasures of Archangel. In mid-September 1918 orders had come for him and Lt. Howard Pellegrom to place their platoons, the first and third, respectively, aboard the transport *Michal Kace* and head northwest through the White Sea for Onega Bay and thence to the village of Onega, at the mouth of the Onega River about seventy-five miles from Archangel as the crow flies.

When they landed, they found the village devoid of Bolos. Another detachment of sailors from the *Olympia* had attacked the village and driven the enemy south up the river valley toward Chekuevo. Three days after landing at Onega, the British commander of the area, Lt. Col. W. J. Clark, ordered Pellegrom to lead his platoon to Chekuevo, take the village, and occupy it.

Clifford Phillips and his platoon, meanwhile, drilled in Onega until they, too, were ordered to Chekuevo; when Phillips and his men arrived by steamer at about six P.M. on September 23, he took command of 115 Americans and 93 Russians.

At five A.M. the following morning, Lt. Clifford Phillips, late of Phillips and Hebenstreit, father, husband, and small-town Republican, found himself fighting for his life when 350 Bolos swarmed like angry bees and attacked the two platoons of Company H from three sides.

At Chekuevo, the main Bolo force was launched at the Americans guarding the left bank, while a smaller force of about seventy-five Reds aimed for the Russians on the right bank. "The enemy moving down the right bank of the river succeeded in driving back the Russian outpost and placed a machine gun on our flank," Company H captain Richard Ballensinger would recall.

The force on the left bank, meanwhile, drove in that outpost and put a machine gun on that side of the river. As this occurred, a group of about eighty Bolos attempted to get behind the defenders, using a swamp for cover.

"For a time the advantage seemed decidedly with the Bolsheviki, the Americans being forced to give ground on the main position, while the enemy placed another gun where it constituted a serious menace, and smaller parties were working in the rear," Lt. Harry Ketcham of Company H would recall.

The firing on all sides—"mostly at long range," Ballensinger would write—went on for four hours before the locations of the Bolo machine gunners were pinpointed and put out of action by the Americans' own Lewis guns.

Among the dead that morning was the Bolo leader, named Shiskin; when he died, his men became demoralized "and retreated in disorder," Ballensinger wrote. They were followed by a strong patrol of Americans, who chased them five miles up the valley, and recovered the two machine guns, five thousand rounds of ammunition, and a trove of clothing and equipment.

Besides Shiskin, two other Bolos had been killed, and seven wounded. Among the Americans, there were two men wounded—Pvt. William Schultz and PFC Kasmir Wilczewski.

Company H had done good work in its first fight under fire, Ketcham would write. "They were outnumbered three to one, and occupied a position in which all the advantages were on the side of the enemy, who were familiar with the ground."

Company H had a week to recuperate and consolidate before new orders came from the British command. These orders were intended to augment what was supposed to have been the general push at Obozerskaya on the railway front on September 29, when Joel Moore and Companies M and I attempted to ram through the Bolos, only to flounder about, lost, and then gain three miles of railway track in the ensuing days.

The Americans at Chekuevo were about forty miles west of the railway at Obozerskaya, and the high command anticipated great success from the push; it also expected the Bolos at Obozerskaya to flee west toward the Onega River and thence to the Murmansk-Petrograd Railroad under the onslaught.

The Americans, with a contingent of Cossacks, were to move south and cross the front of the Bolos heading west, and stop them from crossing the Onega. They were also ordered to make contact with the railroad force at Obozerskaya via a telegraph line that might or might not be in working order, and find out just how far south the Allied line on the railroad had been pushed.

The orders, as always, were daunting. The party had no signal men; the telegraph wires were old and could be broken in numerous places in any case. There was no telling as well just where the Bolos, who were supposedly fleeing west, could be located.

All told, it was, once again, "'a little job, you know,' for those one hundred and fifteen Americans, veterans of two weeks in the wilds of North Russia," Moore wrote.

Opposing them in the Onega River Valley would be a strong Red force of five hundred to seven hundred men. The Bolsheviks, Harry Ketcham would note, were not fleeing, but were instead massing for an attack of their own.

Yet Clifford Fuller Phillips was game. His first move would be to attack the Bolo force at Kaska, about ten miles upriver, at daybreak on October 1, after moving laboriously in the dark through the woods and swampland surrounding the village.

Two squads, one each from the First and Third Platoons of Company H, plus fifty Russian volunteers, would attack the small village of Wazentia, on the east bank of the Onega across from their target. The Third Platoon would attack Kaska from the west. Phillips would take the remaining squads and eighteen newly arrived Cossacks in on a frontal assault.

The Cossacks, meanwhile, were ordered to remain in reserve and come up on signal. "But as soon as the firing began, the Cossacks retreated to Chekuevo without orders," Ballensinger would write.

The Cossacks may have been onto something. The advance quickly bogged down under heavy machine-gun fire. "It was found impossible to either advance farther or to retire, to try any flanking movement," Ballensinger wrote.

The men instead went to ground, and took up positions on a hillside. None of the attackers had been able to get within three hundred yards of their objective. Phillips ordered all to dig in and stay down, and he and his small band spent the rest of the day beating off Bolo coun-terattacks and waiting for the sun to go down and cover their escape. Finally, at 7:30 P.M., Phillips led his men from the field of battle and back into Chekuevo.

He was a long way from Falls City, Nebraska; a long way from his two-year-old daughter, Ellen Jane; from his wife, Kathryn; from the cozy law offices of Phillips and Hebenstreit. But he was alive; six Americans—two of them reported missing—and at least thirty Bolos couldn't say the same.

Company H spent the coming weeks strengthening the defenses around Chekuevo, and on October 6 were astonished to see a patrol from Company M advancing on the road from Obozerskaya, searching for Bolos.

The Company M boys, led by Cpl. Theodore Messersmith, talked of the amazing numbers of Bolos opposing them at the railway front, and their surprise at their courage, just as Clifford Phillips's men had seen at Kaska.

On October 19, a patrol in force that included both platoons of Company H plus a smattering of Cossacks and Russian volunteers once more deployed southward, moving up the Onega River Valley, only to find that the Bolos had left all of the villages on both sides of the river, including Kaska.

The villages were subsequently garrisoned, while further patrols pushed south and found, ultimately, that the Reds had retreated to Turchasova, about forty miles south of Chekuevo. Phillips now had his force retrace their steps north, where in Kaska they discovered the graves of the two missing Company H men, who had been buried by locals. The bodies were disinterred and reburied with "proper mil-itary honors, and the graves properly marked," Ballensinger would note.

By the time the force reached Chekuevo, the remaining Second and Fourth Platoons of Company H, under the command of Lt. Edmund Collins, had been sent to the village. Over the following months, as win-ter set in with full fury, patrols were sent out and at times exchanged fire with Bolos who were also reconnoitering, and outposts were established at points of concern. But the front largely remained quiet.

Still, as the White Sea froze, the small American force realized its peril. Should they be attacked in force, there would be no steamers to the rescue.

"All through the winter there was in the back of the minds of men in the Onega sector the consciousness that they might at any moment be called upon to make a last-ditch stand against the Bolo for the sake of preventing a flank attack upon their comrades on the railroad," Harry Ketcham remembered.

In the meantime, welcome winter clothing would arrive from Archangel—heavy fur coats and caps, wool socks, leather vests, mitts, snow goggles and sleeping bags and skis and snowshoes and more; all of them the accoutrements a man would need when the temperature pushed sixty below zero and the sun all but disappeared for weeks at a time in the cold subarctic of northern Russia.

"Here old Boreas [the Greeks' god of the north wind] came down upon this devoted company of doughboys," Moore et al. would write. As the days shortened and the thermometer fell, work began on constructing an ice road over which sleighs coming from Archangel could keep them supplied with food, ammunition, and other materiel.

As well, outposts were fortified and manned, and the overriding concern became more about surviving a polar winter than the depredations of the Bolsheviks downriver.

While they could not yet know it, though, their strange, strange war was not over—not nearly.

CHAPTER ELEVEN

STORM CLOUDS

He was still in the trenches when duty called, still dodging German shells, still working as a gunner, still in France, and as a temporary brigadier general still in command of the British Army's Ninety-Ninth Brigade of the Second Division. It wasn't until July 1918, after four years of brutal conflict, his corps had been "blessed" with a short period of open warfare, and his brigade was back on the line from which it had been forced to retreat when the British Fifth Army on the right had been nearly demolished during the spring. After ten long years of staff work, including a posting in South Africa, he was once more enjoying being among the rank and file.

On September 19, 1918, just as thirty-eight-year-old Gen. Edmund Ironside was readying to visit the front, he was summoned to meet with his corps commander, Sir Aylmer Haldane. He had orders for the general to return to Britain at once.

"It was a bad blow," Ironside would write. "I felt it in my bones that the Germans were beaten at last, and I wanted to be in at the death."

At the War Office in London, Ironside—who sported a "marvelous physique, standing 6 feet 6 inches, and weighing in the neighborhood of 250 pounds," one soldier would recall—asked around until finally receiving word that he would be sent to northern Russia to become

Frederick Poole's chief of staff. The next morning, he huddled with Sir Henry Wilson, chief of the Imperial General Staff.

"Your business in North Russia is to hold the fort until the local Russians can take the field," Wilson told Ironside. "You are to prepare for a winter campaign. No joke that!"

On October 1, General Ironside found himself in Archangel, where he was greeted with the news that Poole was departing for a "short leave" to England. Poole, whose usurpation of the Americans and condescending attitude toward the Archangel government had lately resulted in complaints from the U.S. State Department to the British government, had fallen out of favor with the Americans *and* the British. He would not return; Ironside was named the new overall commander of the expedition.

Poole had also surprised Ironside with his belief that the Allied forces would be strengthened considerably at some point, after which they "would take part in a general advance of all the White armies on Petrograd and Moscow." He still believed that the Bolsheviks would not be able to withstand the "avalanche" that one day would fall on them.

After Poole's October 14 departure from Russia, Ironside performed his due diligence, learning what he could about this curious front. He met with British general R. G. Finlayson, an old comrade and friend, who now commanded the river and railway fronts more than one hundred miles from Archangel.

Finlayson told him he had disposed the troops in his command as far forward as he could, thereby making "elbow room" for the numerous recruits who were expected over the winter. In the meantime, his force would consolidate and fortify their forlorn positions amid a populace which, Finlayson acknowledged in the same breath, had "no desire" to fight the Bolos.

Ironside and Finlayson then traveled the railway to Obozerskaya. Work had begun on a string of blockhouses, and Ironside learned the railroad force was "protected" by the forces on the Emtsa River to the east and on the Onega to the west—each thirty miles away across a sea of swamp and mud and deep forests.

The view then prevalent was that, as Finlayson put it, "the Bolsheviks will close down operations for the winter." He would add that he could not imagine "that in the present state of the weather and the roads the enemy will attempt to move this side of Kotlas." The reality would be far different, a fact that was making itself quickly known to Ironside. He noted that the enormous distances along the Allied front made the movements, resupply, and possible eventual withdrawal of troops exceedingly difficult.

As for the state of the troops, the Royal Scots, many of whom had been wounded in fighting on the Western Front, had not impressed. Told by medical officers that they were fit neither for marching nor fighting, the "Category B" men had expected little more than a "cushy holiday" in Russia.

On one occasion they had panicked and run during an assault on a Bolo position, throwing arms and equipment to the side. When they were asked by Finlayson why they had dropped their weapons, "the answer generally received was 'they prevented me from running fast enough,'" Finlayson would say later.

The French, 1,650 Colonial Infantry, were in better shape initially, but as will be seen, they had lost heart when rumors of peace on the Western Front made their way to Archangel. Ironside would report that the French contingent was "in a thoroughly disaffected state. The men, encouraged by some of the younger officers, have openly stated that, if there is an armistice in France, they do not intend to fight."

Ironside also tackled the issue of recruitment. Meeting with Nicholas Chaikovsky, president of the government at Archangel, he tried to make him understand that the Allied mission had always been envisioned as a partnership with the Russian people, and that Chaikovsky's government needed to urgently begin recruiting locals and form "the most effective force it could, so that when the time came they could co-operate with the other White armies in Russia."

According to Ironside's plan, locals would be recruited, trained, and then sent forward to the front and take a place in line with the Allied troops to gain experience. But Chaikovsky had little interest in the idea and, in fact, dismissed the notion that force alone would oust the Bolsheviks.

Ironside's sense of urgency in the grand plan, an early echo of the American strategy of "Vietnamization," found little favor with Chaikovsky's minister of war, Col. Boris Douroff, or his chief of staff, Gen. T. Samarine, both veterans of the old Russian Army that had melted away the previous spring.

They explained to Ironside that the recruitment issue was most "delicate"; though there were some 1,500 veterans of the former army quartered in the local barracks, and three hundred ex-czarist officers in Archangel as well, "it was thought that few of them could be induced to fight again."

The government plan, such as it was, was to find and send "nonreactionary" officers into the hinterlands to explain to village headmen the need for recruits to fight the Bolsheviks. As for any thoughts of conscription, "they rather haughtily told me that conscription was undemocratic," Ironside would write.

As the local government in Archangel dithered, storm clouds were gathering out on the myriad fronts, where the temperatures were already well below zero, the drifting snow was in some places thigh-deep, and the pitifully small Allied force unknowingly now faced an enemy that was itself recruiting, conscripting, and readying for a winter campaign that would itself have the effect of, as Poole had said, an avalanche on the freezing Americans of the 339th Infantry Regiment.

Ironside himself recognized the threat, and the potential peril the Allied troops were in, and in late October ordered a halt to offensive operations. He also began drawing plans for a fortified line of defense eighteen miles below Archangel.

It was too late in the season to withdraw the far-flung columns safely. And so they were to dig in before the ground froze. Should all collapse out there in the snowy wastes of northern Russia, this thirty-six-mile line of blockhouses, interspersed with lakes in the warm months, would serve as a beckoning enclave to the retreating troops now at the Dvina, the Vaga, and at the Kodish and railway fronts, where most movement had been stopped, as the dream of pushing to Kotlas and Vologda had been swept aside by, at last, a sense of reality.

All had already gone too far; all manned their little Fort Apaches in the midst of a hostile wilderness and in the face of growing Bolshevik resistance. For now, there was no way out, and no way forward.

The deep frost of winter was descending; it would freeze exposed fingers and toes and, ultimately, lead to a deepening despair among the men who'd left Hoboken just a few months before to join the fray in France—but had instead found themselves marooned in northern Russia.

CHAPTER TWELVE

FRIENDS AND COMRADES

mericans! The voice, Slavic but with an accent redolent of the East Side of New York, came from the south, across the bridge, startling the assembled Americans and their various Allies—French, Brits, Russians—seeking to take the village of Kodish in the fall of 1918.

"Americans! Can you hear me?" The voice rang out again from somewhere in the midnight black.

A young doughboy, hoping for a shot at the mystery Bolo, answered back: "Where the hell are you?"

The mysterious voice continued:

"Why are you fighting us? We are all working men. You American boys are shedding your blood way up here in Russia and I ask you, For what reason?

"My friends and comrades, you should be back home. You have no war with us. The coworkers of the world are uniting in opposition to capitalism. Why are you being kept here—can you answer that question? No! We don't want to fight you. You are our brother."

Harry Costello heard it. "He spoke for 20 minutes in that strain that night," Costello would remember. "His exceptionally strong and clear voice revealed the trained speaker. His language was simple, and almost eloquent."

The Bolo, whoever he was, asked a lot of good questions.

Few members of the increasingly forlorn 339th U.S. Infantry Regiment had much of an answer to the orator's rhetoric as they stood guard on what had become known as the Kodish front, spending weeks trying to ram south twenty-some miles toward the tantalizing Bolo base at Plesetskaya, which had to be taken if the dream of pushing on to Vologda was ever to be realized.

Following the stand at Seletskoe in mid-September, the retreat of Company K to Tiogra, and the subsequent burning of the bridge over the Emtsa River farther south by the Bolos, engineers had arrived and thrown across a pontoon bridge.

On September 26, 1918, Company K began a new pursuit of the Bolos, this time reinforced by two platoons that had remained near Archangel, the whole of Company L, and forty-eight machine gunners under command of Lt. Clifford Ballard. The next morning, the Bolos were encountered at the half-burned bridge south of Seletskoe, and the men, some on rafts and some using the charred timbers, attempted to cross.

"This proved to be a regular battle," Lt. Charles Ryan would write, "there must be 1,000 of them. I was on the right flank. The left caught it the heaviest."

Company K's Lt. Charles Chappel led his squad toward the Bolo machine guns and attempted to deploy his men to form a continuous firing line. He was soon killed and would receive a posthumous Distinguished Service Cross for his heroism. During the day's fighting, Company K's Sgt. John Agnew and Pvt. John Vojta also fell dead, as did Cpls. Edward Mertens and Edward Kreizinger of Company L and Cpl. Harley Hester of the Machine Gun Company.

At six P.M., as the fighting raged, Ryan was ordered over to reinforce the left flank, which was doing "awful damage." After gaining a foothold on the north bank, the men had to dig in on terrain that was basically a swamp.

That night, "I established a few Cossack posts on our left, and spent the night in the woods, walking around in water up to my knees," Ryan would write.

The next day, the men were ordered by the local British commander,

Colonel Henderson, to build rafts and again try to force a crossing under the direct observation of the Bolos. Company L's Lt. Morland Mc-Murray was to go first, "with me to cover him," Ryan wrote. "Then I do the same trick.

"This will be suicide," Ryan would add, "as they are laying for us."

The crossing was to begin at noon; but just as the men were preparing to launch, Company K's Capt. Michael Donoghue told Ryan and the others to stand down. All readily obeyed the order. In the meantime, carts brought the dead and wounded back to Seletskoe. For the next two weeks, the men on each side of the Emtsa took potshots at each other while enduring incessant rainfall and increasing cold.

"The condition of the men is terrible," Ryan wrote on October 3. "They have been out here for a week with water up to the knees."

Still insistent on making a play for Kodish, and thence Plesetskaya, the high command deployed to the front English marines, two platoons of the 339th's Company D, and gunners with the Sixteenth Brigade of Canadian Field Artillery, all of whom were admired—as well as feared—by the Americans.

The artillerymen had been "seasoned and scarred by four years of barrages and bombardments in France," Company B's John Cudahy would write, and were now "rather keen for the adventure of North Russia while the fighting was on, and thoroughly 'fed up' when there was a lull in the excitement.

"These Canadians, in peace, had probably been kindly disposed farm folk, gathering the rich bronzed harvests of Saskatchewan fields. But four years of war had wrought a transfiguration of many things and no longer did life have its exalted value of peace times."

At the finish of a fight, Cudahy would add, the Canadians "passed among the enemy dead like ghoulish things, stripping bodies of everything valuable, and adorning themselves with enemy boots and picturesque high fur hats, with astounding glee, like school boys on a hilarious holiday . . .

"They were deliberate, unpremeditated murderers . . . Generous hearted, hardy, whole-souled murderers."

On October 7, the sector's British commander, Colonel Henderson, was relieved by Lt. Col. Morgan-Grenville Gavin, an "energetic and keen officer" who soon worked out plans for a new push, according to Moore et al. Gavin instructed the American engineers to devise a ferry system farther upriver, and on October 12 Company L and one platoon of K Company finally crossed to the south bank of the Emtsa and bivouacked in a swamp.

The next morning, this cross-river force, led by Company L's Capt. U. S. Grant Cherry Jr., pushed west along the south side of the Emtsa, aiming for the rear of the Bolo force at Kodish. Meanwhile, Company K's Captain Donoghue led the remainder of his men across the river on rafts farther below and established a beachhead.

On October 13, Company K moved west through the woods at the river's edge, while Cherry's combined force moved on its left flank and the English marines and Canadian gunners poured fire onto suspected Bolo positions in the woods.

"The woods and swamps were so foggy that we couldn't see 20 feet ahead," Ryan would write. Moving forward, "we found Bolsheviks building homes for winter quarters." Two of the Bolos were killed, and twenty captured.

Outside Kodish, the Americans found the main Bolo force well dug in. At five P.M., the Bolsheviks attacked Company K's left flank, which was unprotected because Company L had encountered an impassable swamp. The flank held.

The next morning, Company K was reinforced by one Vickers gun and fifteen English marines, and contact with Company L was made. The combined force now approached Kodish along a forest road, deployed in skirmish lines on both sides.

They soon ran into the Bolos, who were also deployed along both sides of the road for at least one thousand yards, and a sharp firefight ensued. Company K lost two men killed and four wounded before dark, after which the men lay down in the woods and slept on their arms in the rain.

Finally, on October 15, patrols were sent out and reported that the

Bolos had retreated, and the ground was clear before and in Kodish. The Canadian artillery, now following the advance, shelled the village, which the Reds had hastily departed, leaving a store of ammunition behind.

Ryan was not impressed with the hard-won prize. "This is a filthy town," he remembered, "we slept in the cleanest house, it was full of cockroaches, etc."

Company D's Sgt. Gordon Smith would agree, penning in his diary: "We fixed up dugouts, so we could live in them, but my God! how lousy we got in them."

But for the first time in many days, the men were able to dry their shoes, eat some "warm M&V"—canned British rations of meat and vegetables—and sleep under a roof.

True to form, the Canadians went about pilfering the dead of rubles and knives, and even boots, which tempted the cold-footed Americans as well. "In passing let it be stated that many a footsore doughboy helped himself to a dry pair of boots from a dead Red Guard or in winter to a pair of *volenkas*, or warm felt boots," Moore et al. wrote.

There were more days of battle to come. Now having real hope of booting the Reds from their main northern base at Plesetskaya, Donoghue led his men south from Kodish on October 17, only to find the way blocked by Red Guards on the main road.

The Bolos also understood all too well the importance of the base at Plesetskaya, and had no intention of allowing the Allies to pass: the commander of the Northern Army himself had been told by Leon Trotsky to give strict attention to the force at Kodish. The two sides settled into an artillery duel through that day and the next, but on the next night flanking movements by the Americans caused the Reds to retreat from their position.

After two previous attempts to locate the Bolo right flank had come up empty, Company K's Sgt. Cornelius Mahoney went out alone "at great personal risk" and managed to locate a spot from which an attack could be made. A platoon was soon brought up, and its attack scattered the enemy. Patrols found that the way to Plesetskaya appeared to be open (Mahoney would be awarded the DSC).

The Americans advanced south and found the Bolos gone from Avda; meanwhile a combined force of Royal Scots, partisans, and Russian officer trainees, which had forty Lewis guns, cleared the village of Shred Makharenga to the east of Kodish, which only added to the threat to Plesetskaya.

Patrols located the main Red force at Kochmas, just a few miles from the railroad and just nine miles above Plesetskaya. Indications were that the Bolos' morale was low, and that the Reds were preparing to flee. But just at the moment when a vigorous push on Plesetskaya seemed possible, the men were ordered to stand fast.

"Something in the wind today," Ryan would write. "Yesterday the Colonel was strong for going ahead, today we were told to dig in."

That "something" was the orders issued by the new commander, Edmund Ironside, that forward movement on all fronts should end, and the men out on the lines should dig in for the approaching winter. The men on the front grumbled about a great opportunity being lost, not knowing that some of them would get another shot at reaching Plesetskaya in just a few months.

After the pause, the English marines, Company L, and the two platoons from Company D were relieved, and the Canadian batteries were sent to the Dvina front, leaving Company K captain Mike Donoghue with 180 men.

Ominously, the Bolos, perhaps sensing the slackening in the formerly offensive machinations of the Americans, increased their patrols, sending from seventy-five to one hundred well-armed men to probe the American lines. The Americans also sensed a shift in the enemy's posture, and prepared for the worst.

Donoghue deployed his men in outposts along the north–south Avda–Kodish road. Farthest out was the Machine Gun Company's Lt. Clifford Ballard with two guns and forty-six men. Two and a half miles above him in some former Bolo dugouts was Lt. Clarence Gardner of Headquarters Company with a squad of forty men and a Vickers gun.

One verst, or about half a mile, back of Gardner at the clearing at

Kodish were four Vickers guns and forty men who were unable to report to the far front. Though sick or wounded, or both, they were still willing to do whatever they had to in support of the healthy.

On October 29, the Bolos returned to Avda. Hardly as demoralized as reports had had it, they attacked the puny force strung out on the road on November 1, driving in a Cossack post one verst beyond Ballard's station.

For several days, the Reds bombarded Kodish and made raids on Ballard's exposed position. Donoghue sent every soldier who could carry a weapon to strengthen the defenses and patrol the flanks, but the dam finally couldn't hold: on November 4, the Bolos forced Ballard to retreat to a new defense one verst to the north, and it was said that as he and his men retreated they passed through a force of Bolos that lined a road and permitted the Americans to escape.

Gardner, at Verst 12, was reinforced, but the situation remained desperate for all members of the Kodish force as it became clear that the Reds were aiming to flank the Americans, get behind them, and block their only means of retreat—a newly built bridge over the Emtsa.

On November 5, the worst happened. Those holding the far-flung defenses beyond Kodish heard cascades of machine-gun fire coming from the vicinity of Kodish, three miles to their rear.

For three more days, until the afternoon of November 8, the men at Kodish and in the outposts somehow fought off the Bolo assaults. But that afternoon, the new British commander, Colonel Haselden of Force B fame, who had taken over the Kodish front after Lt. Col. Morgan-Grenville Gavin had taken over the railway front from Sutherland, made his way out to visit Ballard's outpost—and found himself, and his American subordinates, finally surrounded by Reds.

Haselden had just gone past Gardner's outpost when he, Ballard, and Gardner and their men were assaulted from all sides by fresh Bolos sent to push the Allies from Kodish and the vicinity. But the machine gunners mowed the attackers down where they massed in anticipation of one final charge, and, seeing their first action, the Bolos finally broke and ran.

"And so the little force was saved," Moore et al. wrote.

Captain Donoghue, back in his field quarters just one verst to the north, heard the yells and cries of the wounded Bolos and was certain that his command was lost. "He had been sure that the howling of the scattered pack had been the fervent yells of a last bayonet charge wiping out the Yankees," Moore et al. recalled.

It was still not over. Ballard and his men were pushed back step by step toward Kodish, still fighting for their lives. Under cover of darkness, the handful of men from Company K, the machine gunners, and the infirm slipped across the bridge over the Emtsa.

There, on the north bank, the healthy took over their old emplacements, and were reinforced by a platoon from Company L and a platoon of replacements from the Eighty-Fifth Division who had just arrived in Russia after performing short duty in France.

Amazingly, the Americans suffered just seven casualties, all wounded. But the terrible week of fighting left many exhausted, not to mention weak from exposure and inadequate rations. These survivors in the middle of November 1918 "looked at their own losses and counted the huge enemy losses . . . and wondered how many such days would whittle them to the point of annihilation," Moore et al. would write.

And there, on the Emtsa River, the mysterious Bolo orator would appear out of the night at the bridge and harangue the Americans and Brits of the "glories of communism, the injustice of soldiers suffering in cold swamps while others sat back in Archangel in soft ease," John Cudahy remembered.

One night the Bolo propagandist brought news—that the world war was over. He also brought some company: a captured Royal Scot and an American prisoner, Company I's PFC George Albers, a twenty-eight-year-old former businessman from Muskegon, Michigan.

These two assured their comrades across the river that they were being well cared for. Their voices, one soldier wrote, "were like those from the grave."

CHAPTER THIRTEEN

VERST 445

Ten past five o'clock in the morning, October 14, 1918. Joel Moore awakes in the dark and fog, weary after yet another night spent in the interminable rain and deepening cold. "No smokes," he would write. "No eats." Nevertheless, Company M assembles, men trying to rub some warmth into their frozen muscles, others stretching cramped limbs.

Ten minutes later, the company is on the march, headed south, once again, to face the Bolos six kilometers down the railway at Verst 455. Lt. Robert Wieczorek's platoon of sixty men leads the way down the track through the dim dawn, while two other platoons try to make their way through the tangle of swamp and woods and brush to forge ahead and get into the Bolos' rear, where engineers are to blow the track behind their locomotive.

But the Bolos' listening posts, and their observation tower on the left, "now stand him in good stead," Moore would write of the Bolos. Wieczorek and his men are spotted as they creep toward the enemy, and quickly come under attack, as do the platoons trying to flank the Bolos.

"By the sounds from Bolo camp they are outnumbering our comrades on the flank," Moore wrote in his history of Company M. "So we must make a rush for the railroad and play our part."

Bolo bugles shrilly rent the morning air as Lt. George Stoner raced up to help Wieczorek and his men. The Bolos, rattled, fired their machine guns and artillery high, and after the first salvo the Americans pressed on. "The enemy in panic leaps to his troop train and dashes away to the south," Moore recalled.

The Bolos left behind two machine guns and gunners, but they were quickly overwhelmed by one of the flanking platoons. The attack was, at least by previous standards, a great success. Only one member of Company M, Pvt. Walter Merrick, was killed, shot through the head by a machine gun. Four more men were wounded.

The Bolos suffered heavily, "hundreds" of casualties being incurred after they took to their troop train and forged south through the fire from the flanking platoons. After moving out of range, the armored locomotive stopped at Verst 450, and shelled the new forward American position as it was being consolidated; an attack by Company I and a company of French pushed them two versts south.

The next day, October 15, Company I went forward alone, and pushed the Bolos south past Verst 448, where the Americans dug in. The Bolos were on the run, but trouble was percolating on the Allied side.

By that mid-October, the French troops had heard of German peace feelers on the Western Front, and were no longer in a mind to fight. The French company had refused to support Company I in its attack on the Bolos at Verst 448, and the previous day, at Verst 455, the French commander had to scatter a meeting of his soldiers, who were discussing their situation.

There had, indeed, been overtures of peace by the Germans. Facing the collapse of their army in France, where the Hindenburg Line had been breached by the British and where the Americans were pushing north through the Meuse-Argonne, the architects of the German war effort, Erich Ludendorff and Paul von Hindenburg, pressed a new chancellor, Prince Max of Baden, to offer an olive branch to the Allies. He did so in an October 5 speech to the German Reichstag, and in a concurrent note sent to President Woodrow Wilson through the Swiss. The note asked for "the immediate conclusion of an armistice on land

and water and in the air," and further asked Wilson to take the lead in setting up a peace conference.

The French and British had rejected any talk of peace while German troops remained on French soil, and Wilson agreed. The world war would slog on for another five weeks—but not at Verst 448, as far as the French soldiers on the railroad front were concerned.

La guerre est finie became their rallying cry, the first instance of troops in northern Russia demanding answers to the question of what, exactly, they were doing there. For many, the answer would never come. Company I, too, would be accused of mutiny before this strange war was out. The seeds of that alleged rebellion may have been laid through their first five weeks at the railroad front.

On October 6, just eight days before jumping off against the Bolos at Verst 450, Company I commander Capt. Horatio Winslow sent a request to the 339th's headquarters asking that his men be given at least ten days' rest before entering battle again.

Winslow cited numerous reasons, one being "an unusual lack of confidence in the ability of the Staff directing operations at this point, owing to the failure of the operations of last Saturday and Sunday," when two platoons had, like Moore's men, become lost in the wilds of Russia.

As well, Winslow said his men had been at Camp Custer "just previous" to leaving for Russia and were untrained, and also were "disorganized by fatigue," had no confidence in the rifles they had been issued ("a result of frequent jams, etc."), and needed some space to build up their "morale."

His plea obviously went unheeded back in Archangel.

The company's Lt. Albert May would concur that morale was low, saying the rifles—and the possible reason for their issuance—were indeed a big problem in the ranks.

The Americans had been issued and had trained with British-made Lee-Enfield rifles, which were modified to take U.S. ammunition and which had an effective range of more than five hundred yards and were relatively easy to keep clean. The American-made Mosin-Nagant 7.62 mm rifles that replaced the Enfields, however, jammed, had a lower velocity—and at the time of issuance had been sighted to account for Russian paces instead of yards.

"When we arrived in Russia," May would write, "this rifle was all we had to fight with, while the enemy was equipped with all the weapons a modern army usually has"—thanks to the shipments of Colts and Brownings and artillery shells from American factories.

All of the issues—the possibility of an armistice on the Western Front, the weapons, the lack of proper supplies, and the burning question of why the hell they were in Russia in the first place—would become topics of conversation, even within Joel Moore's Company M, which through the night of October 16–17 sat around campfires "and talked of the strange campaign, talked of the rumors of German collapse, and speculated on the effect on their war," Moore would write.

And in the morning, the men of Company M arose once more and stretched their limbs and peered south through the deep Russian gloom, where on October 17 they would attempt to push the advance farther down the line to Verst 445.

At 6:25 A.M. on October 17, Moore's men relieved Company I, and stepped off through dripping woods and boggy swamps and toward the Bolo, following a rolling barrage. Lt. George Stoner's platoon soon ran up against a hastily thrown-up Bolo emplacement, and overran it. "Not a man was hit," Moore would write.

Stoner then came across a dugout and tossed a hand grenade at the door. He missed the door by a foot and moved on, and when he returned after the rout of the Bolos he found the dugout contained one red-haired Bolo soldier with a grenade and twenty-seven women and children—one just eight days old.

Stoner's "tender heart near froze with horror [for] an hour afterward," while Sgt. Walter Dundon futilely tried to make the Bolo answer questions in English.

(During the advance, Stoner, wanting to know how far his platoon was advancing, placed one man directly on the railway to watch for "verst poles" that counted distance while the main body moved through the woods on either side. After an hour, Stoner went to the track and asked the soldier if he had seen any verst poles yet. The soldier saluted and replied, "No, but if I do, Lieutenant, I'll shoot 'em.")

Stoner's men continued and came to a broad stream, beyond which was a clearing containing the houses of local woodsmen. Within the houses and the clearing itself were between five hundred and six hundred Bolos, with more reinforcements expected to arrive that very morning.

Moore split his platoons for a three-sided attack, and brought up his reserve platoon and placed it at the stream. He also called up Lt. Woodhull Spitler of the Machine Gun Company and directed him to set up his guns in a clearing to guard the rear.

The attacking platoons, yelling like "Amerikanski devils," then splashed across the brook and emerged from the woods and completely unnerved the Bolo defenders. "The attack was so impetuous that the enemy's fire was wild and his lines broke from cover to cover frantically," Moore added.

Two platoons chased the Bolos through the woods, while another consolidated their newly won and prized ground. "Though many men had their clothes riddled not a man was scratched," Moore wrote.

The pursuit of the Bolo ended when a runner arrived with orders to halt the chase and prepare a new forward line within the clearing. It was the objective set by the British commander, and "it looked like a good place to arrange troop quarters for the near-approaching winter," Moore wrote.

"We were a few versts north of Emtsa, but 'mnoga mnoga versts,' many versts, distant from Vologda, the objective picked by General Poole for this handful of men."

The Bolos attempted several times to regain the ground, on November 4 sending between 800 and 1,000 men to attack Company I, then manning the front with 140 men. They were repulsed and suffered numerous dead, but Company I would lose just one man killed, Pvt. Leo

Ellis, and two wounded. Ellis would be posthumously awarded the Croix de Guerre.

The day's action would bring more awards. Cpl. Clement Grobbel earned a DSC for manning a machine gun in an exposed position, while another corporal, Theodore Sieloff, was awarded a DSC for a similarly heroic effort.

The company's men—perhaps ironically, considering how their own commander had denigrated their abilities—would be praised by the commanding French colonel, G. Lucas, for realizing "that troops with self-control and confidence in their superior officers, and in their arms, have nothing to fear from the enemy, even if he is three times superior in number."

As the front went quiet, French and Americans found time to mingle. Moore would recall one instance, in which an American medic treated a *poilu* suffering from a cold with a remedy of hot water and whiskey.

"Next morning the whole machine gun section of French were on sick call," Moore wrote.

And there was a more touching occurrence one morning when "a big, husky Yank in 'I' Company was brokenly 'parelvooing' [speaking] with a little French gunner." The Frenchman was soon seen draping his arms around the doughboy's neck.

"My son, my son," the Frenchman cried. "My dear sister's son!"

CHAPTER FOURTEEN

ARMISTICE DAY, PART 1

By the day the Great War ended on November 11, 1918, it was impossible not to know that something was up. The enemy had been probing the Allied defenses, firing from the woods, displaying themselves and then ducking away and disappearing; the local peasants were building bomb shelters, obviously aware something was brewing but refusing to say just what. The men of Company B, 339th United States Infantry Regiment, understood their predicament and their peril.

"Things are coming to a head," one of them, Clarence Scheu, would note in his diary. "We don't know how soon, but we are going to manage to be ready."

On November 8, the Bolos had begun a steady shelling of Toulgas by riverboats and land batteries. On November 9, 1918, a patrol captured a Bolo prisoner, who reported an impending attack. The next day, patrols reported a strong force of Bolos moving toward the village, where Company B, some Royal Scots, and two batteries of Canadian artillery—about six hundred troops—had frantically built defenses.

And early on the morning of November 11, even as the armistice ending the Great War was about to be signed in a railway car in the Compiègne Forest not far from Paris, a day that would see throngs celebrating from Paris to London to, soon enough, the United States, PFC Jake Anderson and Pvts. Leo Gasper and Alek Pilarski of

Company B, 339th Infantry Regiment, lay crumpled and dead, their blood oozing into the frozen, deep snow, while their comrades furiously attempted to fight off an enveloping attack—one could hardly call it a surprise—by hundreds of Bolos.

Toulgas, spread north to south for more than a mile on the west bank of the Dvina River, was actually two villages—Upper and Lower Toulgas, so named because of their relative positions on the north-flowing river. Somewhat paradoxically, Upper Toulgas was farthest south (upriver). A broad, cold stream coursed between them, and a wooden bridge connected the two villages. At the bridge was "the inevitable white church, and its gaudy minarets," John Cudahy, who joined Company B as a replacement from the Eighty-Fifth Division that fall, would note.

Beyond Lower Toulgas and to the north sat a clump of log buildings that were being used as a hospital, in which rudimentary first aid could be given but, with no operating equipment or surgeons, little more than that. Three miles separated Upper Toulgas from the hospital.

The men of Company B would soon become intimately familiar with Toulgas; but not yet. Following its September ordeal at Seltso, the unit left the Dvina and traveled by scow to Shenkursk. Compared to the area of the upper Dvina, the lushness and sense of civilization at Shenkursk had had much appeal to the men, and they had hoped to remain there for the winter.

Their stay, though, was brief; a detachment of Royal Scots that had relieved the unit at Seltso was being hard-pressed by the Bolos, and Company B was ordered to reinforce it. "They are in danger of annihilation," the company's Clarence Scheu would write, "the old russian [sic] bear is beginning to show her fangs."

On October 7, the men returned to their barges and the Vaga and headed north, then south up the Dvina. "Hear heavy artillery action in the distance, hope the Scots are holding their own," Scheu would write on October 8.

Two days later the barges let the men off at a small village just north of Seltso, which was still under fire from the Bolo gunboats and where, Scheu would say, "the Bolos dominate us ten to one in men and long range field pieces, with gunboats in addition."

And there would be no help from the British boats; they had been ordered back to Archangel in early October in anticipation of the river freezing (in fact, the entire Dvina did not freeze until after mid-November that year).

The Bolos had a battery of three-inch guns, which they placed at the edge of the woods south of Seltso or floated through the river on rafts, plus two naval pieces. Infantry attacks on the Americans and Scots began just after Company B landed, and continued for several days.

The situation was perilous. A battery of needed Canadian artillery was trying to reach the area but was stopped by enemy gunboats. "All we have is rifles and machine guns, however, we are holding their infantry at bay," Scheu wrote.

Sgt. Silver Parrish awoke "wet and hungry" on October 11, and soon received orders to take his squad through some woods and try a flank attack on a nearby village held by the Bolos.

"There I got into the hottest hell I ever heard of," he would write.

The Bolos allowed his patrol to pass through almost to the village, and then "they gave it to us." Parrish got himself and his men into a ravine, where one of his men, Pvt. Sam Klein, asked him if he ever prayed. Parrish told him no.

"By God, you'd better," Klein replied. Parrish again told him he couldn't. "I'll do it for you," Klein told him, and he did. Parrish and his squad finally slipped away and got back to Seltso; one of his men, Thomas Downs, had an eye shot out, yet "walked through swamps and timber to camp without kicking," Parrish recalled.

Soldiers with the 310th Engineers had done good work fortifying Seltso's log buildings, and they had also been busy constructing blockhouses. Modeled after the simple log homes of the area, they were hewn from tall pine trees, and had loopholes cut into them on all four sides through which a rifle or machine-gun barrel could be stuck. The area surrounding the houses was clear-cut to provide fields of fire, and barbed wire was strewn at the edges of the clearings.

The blockhouses were sturdy; they also made good targets for the artillery of the Bolos, who launched a furious attack on them at about four P.M. on October 14. Cpl. Howard French of the 310th would remember being outside of one of the houses when the Bolos' six-inch naval guns fired their opening salvo and scored a direct hit on the building, inside of which were engineers Charles French, William Ziegenbein, and Myron Assire.

All three, wounded, ran from the house. Howard French got to Assire, who was leaning against the building's outside wall, and tried to drag him to a dugout. Another shell screamed in as he did so, and French was knocked out cold.

When he came to, he found that "most of Assire's head was shot off." Ziegenbein had a hole just beneath his heart "and lived about an hour." Another engineer, Pvt. Charles Doe, had been hit with shrapnel between his right knee and hip and it was "practically shot off."

Three more engineers—Rudolph Pullman, August Lashinsky, and Alfred Lyttle—were also seriously wounded. Pullman had a broken leg, Lashinsky lost his left hand and a part of his left arm, and Lyttle had a punctured lung.

While they were being tended to by British and American medics, Howard French quickly went to work on Charles Doe's dangling, shattered leg. Using a pocket knife, he sliced through the remaining sinews, severed Doe's leg, and then applied a tourniquet.

The battle for Seltso, meanwhile, raged around them. "All hell broke loose, they had discovered [a] listening post and were circling in our rear, hordes of them," Scheu wrote.

Firing from loopholes in the blockhouses and from behind any other available protection that could be found, the Americans poured a furious fire from their rifles and machine guns into the Bolo horde.

"We gave them a good lickin', killing over a hundred and wounding 150," Silver Parrish would write. "Our losses were 4 Americans killed and 7 wounded. The English platoon got 7 wounded. The enemy had to retire even though they did have 2,000 troops. But their gunboats and field pieces made us leave that town."

Indeed, later that night orders came for all to evacuate Seltso, and the Scots quickly slipped out to the north first, followed by Company B's men, who stumbled through the inky black of night under continuing fire from the Bolos.

"We slip out, through swamp, leaving 4th platoon guard our retreat until 3 a.m.," Scheu wrote. "We arrive in Toulgas in morning. Ye Gods, what a night. We lost everything we had except rifles and ammunition. However, we are lucky to have escaped with our hides."

Thomas Downs, shot through an eye, amazed Company B commander Robert Boyd with his unflinching stamina during the retreat.

"One of my men was shot in the eye, losing the eye, and the doctors think the bullet is still in the brain," he would write home. "He was in the field for ten hours and made a march of seven miles thru swamp and tundra which nearly exhausted all the men.

"He was near the head of the column, and always had a cheery answer when asked how he was making it. It was of infinite value as an example to the men." Downs would receive a British Distinguished Conduct Medal for his stoicism.

"There was a disorderly retreat at this time," the engineer Howard French recalled. "It was dark and raining." The resourceful and heroic French scrounged up two Russian ponies and laboriously improvised a travois for his wounded comrades. He then lashed Doe, Lashinsky, and Lyttle on, and they started north for Toulgas, twelve miles away.

Along the way, French heard a hospital ship plying the Dvina, and called over from the bank. A small boat was sent over and the three badly wounded men were taken aboard. French continued slogging toward Toulgas.

Despite the trauma of a battlefield amputation of his leg, Charles Doe survived; Alfred Lyttle lingered for two weeks, first at a hospital in Beresnik and then at the Fifty-Third Stationary Hospital in Archangel.

Shortly after five P.M. on October 30, Lyttle called to Sgt. Charles French "and some of the other boys to him, shook hands with them, and said he guessed it was about over with him," a report would say. "Lyttle opened his eyes, half turned his head, lay back, and that was all."

Toulgas at that point wasn't much better of a sanctuary than Seltso had been. Soon after arrival, its defenders went to work constructing a defense line of dugouts and blockhouses at the southern end of Lower Toulgas, where the stream separated the village from Upper Toulgas, which had been quickly taken by the Bolos. They also constructed more fortifications on the western and northern edges of Lower Toulgas, much like a wagon train circling against the American Indians in the Old West.

"Our position here is problematical," Scheu would note. Patrols brought the information that the Bolos were in Zastrovia, a village fewer than two miles north; the Allied force was confined within "the tall woods circling our right and rear, and the Dwina [sic] river on our left. We are clearing all small trees and bushes for our line of fire."

Eventually the 310th Engineers and working soldiers would build forty-seven blockhouses, dig more than 1,100 yards of trenches, string 7,700 yards of wire, and also put in thirteen dugouts at Toulgas.

As the work to fortify the village went on that October, the small force was constantly harassed and attacked by the Bolos—including on October 22, when the Allies' front and right were assaulted. Canadian batteries, which had finally arrived, quickly went to work, spewing shrapnel into the woods, and a well-placed Lewis gun performed its deadly work well.

"We hold frontal advance and rush men to bolster our right flank, quick work that," Scheu would write. "We took them by surprise at a spot they fully expected our weakest, enemy is repulsed in disorder with heavy losses, our casualties are three."

The sheltering log buildings in Upper Toulgas were becoming a nuisance and a threat; on the night of October 24, the main body of Company B left just enough men to man a defense and crept through the woods to the west of the village, aiming to strike in its rear.

Bolos manning listening points believed a large force was attempting to encircle them, and notified their commanders of the threat. "Upper Toulgas was emptied of the Bolos a half hour before we entered," Scheu wrote.

The company put in place two listening posts of its own and went back to Lower Toulgas. For the next two weeks all was quiet. "All at Toulgas were aware that the lull was ominous," Cudahy would write, and so the work continued on blockhouses and dugouts, as all waited for the proverbial other shoe to drop.

And they had other enemies to confront, Clarence Scheu would write.

"On guard tonight, billets in villages are lousy with cockroaches," Scheu complained one night during this quiet time. "We sleep on floor in russian [*sic*] houses, and believe me, if you haven't already made the acquaintance of dozens of cockroaches visiting you in military formation, you have something to look forward to."

Scheu and his mates also discussed their "possibilities" one evening in the event of a large-scale attack. "Several optimistic," he would report. He was not so sure.

Others also remained optimistic about the possibilities that the small force of Allies could prevail against hundreds—soon to be thousands—of angry Bolos in this godforsaken, isolated, frozen outpost more than 150 miles from Archangel.

On November 10, the Dvina column commander, Brig. Gen. R. G. Finlayson, inspected Toulgas and pronounced everything okay. Some officers told him they were concerned about a possible assault on their rear, but Finlayson was nonplussed.

There was no way, he told them, that a large number of enemy troops could get through the heavy swamps to their west without being noticed.

Luckily for R. G. Finlayson, he headed back down the Dvina on the same day.

CHAPTER FIFTEEN

ARMISTICE DAY, PART 2

L ady Olga was in love.

A former soldier in the Red Army's "Battalion of Death," she had joined the Bolsheviks more out of a longing for adventure than politics; and during her short months with the Bolos she had become smitten with one of their leaders—Melochofski, "a powerful giant of a man," who on the morning of November 11, 1918, had led his attackers in an assault on the undefended hospital village at Lower Toulgas.

Upon arrival at the cluster of log huts, Melochofski summarily ordered that every American and British patient be shot. And they most undoubtedly would have been, had not his lover, who would come to be known as Lady Olga, countermanded his orders.

Lady Olga was in love. But she was not a cold-blooded killer.

Olga had fallen in love with Melochofski as she traveled with him and his troops through the deep forests, and had shared all of the hardships that afflicted soldiers in the field—the damp, the cold, the endless marching, the lack of food.

She remained, however, "eternal feminine" and human, Moore et al. would write, and would not abide the slaughter of suffering invalids— even if they were the enemy. She demanded that Melochofski counter-mand his orders, and said she would shoot any Bolo who entered the hospital.

Earlier that morning, the Bolos spilled from the woods just west of Upper Toulgas, but it was a feint; the target of the Bolo assault was actually the hospital, the area around which the detachment of Americans and Scots had not bothered to fortify because the vast swamp and woods to the west were thought to be unpassable.

The hundreds of Bolos who stormed from those woods on the morning of November 11, 1918, proved otherwise. But their main objective was not the pitiful wounded and sick at the hospital; the target was the two Canadian batteries, manned by sixty men and a covering crew with a Lewis gun, both posted just to the west of Lower Toulgas.

As at Seltso one month before, the Bolos encircled the defenders and desperately tried to get to the Canadian guns. Isolated and with no reinforcements yet in sight, the pitifully small Allied force dug in its heels and once again cut down the attackers as they came in wave after wave toward them.

The artillery had been sited to cover Upper Toulgas to the south. But as the horde of Bolos attacked from the west, the Lewis gun leapt to action, spraying the oncoming horde and causing it to pause briefly. As well, some of the Bolos had been unable to resist the temptation of looting the buildings around the hospital and in Lower Toulgas.

That gave the Canadians time enough to laboriously swing their guns westward, and they began firing bursts of shrapnel at the Reds, who were just fifty yards away at their closest.

Swearing "fine, full chested, Canadian blasphemies," the artillerists worked furiously, and the Bolos quickly turned into "ghastly dismembered corpses," their flesh and blood thrown high into the sky "in sickening, splattering atoms," Cudahy would relate with some panache.

The Lewis gun—a light machine gun that could be operated by a single soldier and could fire between five hundred and six hundred rounds per minute—remained busy, too, while Canadians not needed to man the heavy guns went to work with their rifles, and a platoon of Royal Scots raced to the scene, losing heavily in the process. The dead and wounded Bolos also piled atop one another, as the cacophony of shot and shell and the screams of the wounded and swearing of Canadians, Scots, and Americans filled the air.

The Canadians, Robert Boyd would later write, "realized the artilleryman's dream, running their guns out of their emplacements and firing muzzle burst shrapnel against advancing infantry. The two gun section and one Lewis gun stopped 600 bolsheviks."

Meanwhile, a platoon of Company B that had been stationed in the homes and three blockhouses in Upper Toulgas was swarmed by Bolo attackers. Their commander, Henry Dennis, had orders to withdraw across the bridge to Lower Toulgas, and so they did, under heavy fire.

"Emerging from the woods came screaming Bolo Marines, so many were advancing on us, we all retreated very rapidly," Company B's Pvt. Bill Henkelman, stationed in one of the blockhouses, would say.

"We lost all issue and personal stuff. Those carrying packs dropped them."

Henkelman manned a Vickers gun—a machine gun bulkier than the Lewis gun that took at least several men to operate but could itself shoot up to 450 rounds per minute—at the blockhouse near the bridge. He watched as Sgt. Fred Marriott, in charge of the defense, rushed outside to direct his men and was cut down by a Bolo sniper. Pvt. Leo Gasper, meanwhile, was killed after crossing the bridge and attempting to find cover.

The Bolos made a mad dash toward the bridge, trying to join the force attacking Lower Toulgas. Henkelman, opening up his Vickers gun, "mowed these boys down." Not one survived. Henkelman estimated he had killed "between 30 and 70."

Just above Upper Toulgas, meanwhile, the Red artillery on land and gunboats were pouring shells into the blockhouses and other buildings—including the church—near the bridge, their fire directed by Bolo officers over phone wires strung through the woods.

The shells crept closer and closer to the blockhouses. "We could not run," Henkelman would say. "We knew death was imminent."

Clarence Scheu, manning blockhouse number six at the bridge, would remember the battle "raging all day, our front line defences [*sic*] still holding, but we are ignorant of conditions in our rear."

At about one P.M., a machine gunner was killed; a sniper shot Pvt. James Kooyers "as he was firing out a porthole," Scheu would write. "A while later, a bullet split my gun in two, rendering it useless."

At four P.M., a counterattack led by Lt. Henry Dennis went after a line of Bolo snipers at the fringe of the woods, driving them back. As evening fell, the Allies remained in control of much of Toulgas.

Estimates of enemy dead ranged to about four hundred; an exact count of the casualties would never be known, as untold numbers of the Bolos died later in the surrounding woods.

(Cudahy would write that the villagers in Nitzni Kitsa, twenty miles west of Toulgas, weeks later talked of three Bolos who appeared there "clad in rags, and half starved, babbling an incoherent story" of the battle and of its aftermath, when "hundreds" of their comrades perished in the cold swamps.)

Among the dead were three commissars—including Melochofski, who had ordered the deaths of the invalids at the hospital. He, in fact, would die there, in the arms of Lady Olga in the same room in which he had just hours previously ordered the deaths of the Allied sick and wounded. The Bolo commander, a former private in the old Imperial Army named Foukes, was also dead.

The battle of Toulgas, though, was far from over. Understanding this, three platoons from Company D, then at Chamova about ten miles down the Dvina, were put on a cross-country march toward Toulgas at one P.M. on November 11. After leaving one platoon en route to guard a telegraph station, the other two platoons arrived at two A.M. on the twelfth, as the battle continued to rage.

While they were en route, a force of Bolos at sunset attempted to rush the bridge separating the upper village from the lower. "We expected this and were ready," Scheu would write. "Many a Bolo, good or bad, fell in this attempt.

"Above the din of battle we could hear the Bolo officers shouting orders to cross, even when they knew it was plain suicide. My hat is off to some Bolo soldiers."

It would be rumored that Leon Trotsky, the Red minister of war, was directing the offensive from a Bolo gunboat just upriver. If so, it was he who on the next day, November 12, sent five of the armed watercraft toward Toulgas, where they lingered on the Dvina just out of reach of the Canadian batteries.

The firebrand Trotsky, born Lev Davidovich Bronstein in southern Ukraine in 1879, had long been a revolutionary but had joined the Bolshevik cause only in 1917, and he had been instrumental in the October Revolution that year, which brought the Reds to power.

Named minister of war following the signing of the Brest-Litovsk Treaty in March 1918, Trotsky by December would increase the size of the Red Army from a scant force to 600,000 men. Living aboard an armored train, he chugged from crisis to crisis along the vast Russian frontier, directing movements and inspiring his soldiers as they fought against the loyalist Whites.

If Trotsky was indeed in the vicinity of Toulgas, it was he who also decided to abandon the ruinous frontal assaults that had resulted in the deaths of hundreds of Reds. Instead, the Bolo land batteries kept out of reach and went to work on the blockhouses ringing Lower Toulgas, doing great damage.

At one blockhouse, a shell threw up straw from a nearby pile and blocked some of the loopholes; Sgt. Floyd Wallace bravely left the safety of the building and, under machine-gun and shell fire, removed the straw. He did the same thing once more that day, and was severely wounded, but would receive the British Distinguished Conduct Medal for his efforts.

Another of Company B's men, Pvt. Charles Bell, was later seriously wounded himself when a shell crashed into the same blockhouse and killed or badly injured all of the occupants. But Bell, dripping blood from a nasty gash to his face, gamely stuck by his machine until dark. He was awarded the Distinguished Service Cross.

Clarence Scheu, stationed in that blockhouse, would write that out of nine men, three were killed and five wounded—including himself when a piece of shell went through a hand and shoulder.

"We crawl out, bullets were thick outside, a shell buried its nose in the ground 10 feet away, but Luck was with me, it was a dud," he would write.

The church was smashed in, too, and was a "sad sight," Scheu would remember. Its occupants, the local priest and his family, were found in the rubble, all dead except a little girl.

The Bolo gunboats continued to pound the Allied positions through the twelfth and through the next day as well. Two more guns, six inchers, had been ferried downriver and were placed out of range of the Canadian gunners.

Hollow-eyed men manned their defenses while artillery rounds exploded around and on top of them. There could be no rest, no sleep, under the constant deluge of shrieking missives from the Bolos. And there would be no relief for months for the residents of the tiny Allied outpost that would continue to fight for their lives miles and miles away from the relative comforts of Archangel.

On November 13, the men found out an armistice had been signed with Germany. That night, Capt. Robert Boyd, who had in October been relieved of command of Company B and appointed commander of the Dvina column, and his officers appraised their "possibilities," just as Clarence Scheu and his mates had one evening not long before.

A siege was out of the question. And there was no thought of surrendering, as it was understood, Cudahy wrote, that the Bolos "would take no prisoners."

Their only salvation was a counterattack on a detachment of Bolos decamped around a cluster of small huts in the forest near Upper Toulgas.

It was decided that a surprise assault was needed on the Bolos there—
and the capture of the entire detachment if possible. If nothing else, a
"great demonstration" of force could lead the Bolos to believe the Allies
had received reinforcements. In fact, they had added but two platoons
from Company D, only one of which, the first, was thrown into the
assault.

Cudahy led the attack just before dawn on November 14, springing
from the woods and killing several Bolos before they knew what had
hit them. The rest fled in complete surprise, and reported that a large
force had attacked them.

Just for good measure, an observation post in the woods that contained numerous rounds of small-arms ammunition was set ablaze, and
"the explosions sounded like the musketry of a regiment," Cudahy wrote.

Company B advanced on Upper Toulgas, only to find no opposition.
The Bolos were indeed fleeing in the belief that a large Allied force was
advancing on them. The only Bolos there, some snipers, threw down
their weapons and came from their hiding places shouting *"Tovarish!
Tovarish!"*

Comrade.

Sgt. Gordon Smith of Company D would remember a Bolo officer
and his wife being taken prisoner that day. "Woman dressed in husband's uniform," Smith wrote. "A hell of a looking soldier she was."

The numerous Bolo dead scattered across the fields and woods were
pilfered. The Allies found "no end to rubles" in many of their pockets.
"Thousands of them," Smith wrote. "They are like so much newspaper
to us, but we take them anyway and use them for stakes in craps."

The Bolo prisoners taken during the four days of battle, Cudahy
would write, "expressed no martyr's devotion to the cause of the Soviets." Some had been pressed into the Red Army "at the point of a bayonet, and being kept in the ranks by the same argument." Others joined
so they could eat, as the Bolos had cleaned the countryside of food.

"They were a hardboiled looking lot, those Bolo prisoners," Moore
et al. would write. "They wore no regulation uniform, but were clad in
much the same attire as an ordinary moujik—knee leather boots and

high hats of gray and black curled fur. No one could distinguish them from a distance, and every peasant could be Bolshevik. Who knew?"

As for Lady Olga, she remained at Toulgas, and then went down-river to work at the hospital in Beresnik. Robert Boyd would remember seeing an open letter she had written to her former comrades, "telling them that they should not believe the lies which their commissars told them, and that the Allies were fighting for the good of Russia."

In the days following the fight, patrolling continued, and occasional skirmishes showed that the Bolos had not retreated far. On November 16, winter clothing sent from Beresnik finally arrived—a bit late, but still welcome to the men.

"It is November, and a raw Arctic cold 30 below zero has descended upon us with terrible ferocity," Smith would write.

Despite the numbing cold, and the advent of winter proper, a decision of savage military necessity was made. Upper Toulgas remained a threat to the outpost, as there weren't enough defenders available to man it in strength.

It was decided to turn the peasants—the *moujiks*—in Upper Toulgas from their homes, and then burn the village to the ground.

Some of the peasants were suspected of harboring pro-Bolshevik sentiments, and in any case some of the simple log homes had been used for snipers—"sniper's row," the men called it.

As well, men posted there through the cold, frosty nights were terrified, and saw in "every shadow a crouching Bolshevik," Moore et al. would write. "Often the order came through to the main village to 'stand to,' because some fidgety sentinel in Upper Toulgas had seen battalions, conjured by the black night."

In a scene that would repeat itself decades later in Vietnam, a cordon was thrown around the village, and the *moujiks* living on sniper's row were given three hours to gather what they could.

Then their homes were torched, as the first snow of winter drifted silently down and the women wailed and the children cried in deep despair, and the village men "looked on in silence, uncomprehending resignation on their faces, mute, pathetic figures," according to Cudahy.

Company B Sgt. Silver Parrish, in charge of the detail firing the homes, felt horrible about destroying the village. "My heart ached to have the women fall down at my feet and kiss my hand and beg me not to do it," he would write. "But orders is orders."

Orders is orders. But doubts were beginning to grow—about the exact aim of this strange war; about why the Americans were continuing to fight, despite the world war being over; about whether any of them would see home again, with thousands of Bolos out there and the port at Archangel about to freeze and leave them no way out should the worst happen.

"Sometimes I wonder, Why this expedition," Clarence Scheu had written on October 20, a full three weeks before the Armistice Day battle. "One man has to do the fighting of ten, and we can't replace men when they fall."

One Russian local at Toulgas had similar questions, asking, in effect, just what the Allies' aims in Russia were. Were they there to restore the czar? If so, why did they have to burn the simple homes of the *moujiks*—peasants—and requisition their meager possessions?

"It was small concern to Ivan whether the Allies or the Bolsheviks won this strange war," Cudahy would write. "He did not know what it was all about, and in that he was like the rest of us. But he asked only to be left alone, in peace to lead his simple life, gathering his scanty crops in the hot brief months of summer and dreaming away the long dreary winter on top of his great oven-like stove."

Even Robert Boyd was beginning to wonder what exactly was the point of his having lost nine men killed in action or dead from wounds received during those November days in Toulgas, with the armistice signed, and the world, supposedly, at peace.

"A mere statement from the United States and Great Britain that all aims and purposes of being in Russia had been terminated by the armistice, and that all troops would be evacuated when navigation resumed, would have been sufficient," he would write in 1939.

Col. George Stewart, though comfy in his steam-heated headquarters in Archangel, did appreciate his men's sufferings and situations across the wide northern Russia front, which by mid-November stretched from Archangel two hundred miles south to Ust Padenga, another two hundred miles from Ust Padenga to Onega, and one hundred miles east from Archangel to Pinega, or about as far from north to south as New York City is from Washington, DC, and about as far from east to west as New York City is from Pittsburgh, Pennsylvania.

Stewart, who had essentially abdicated his leadership of the Americans either out of a misunderstanding of President Wilson's wishes or an unwillingness to stand up to the British, coyly suggested in a November 14 cablegram to the British command in London that he felt it might be time to pull the plug on the expedition.

"Allies have not been received with the hospitality the object of this expedition warranted," he reported. "A certain amount of distrust of motive evidently permeated the Russian mind. The original object of this expedition no longer exists.

"The winter port of Archangel will be practicable for navigation twenty or thirty days longer and then closes until June. My inference is plain. Immediate consideration requested."

But there would be no leaving, and no relief. At Toulgas as all along the Allied front, "the long Arctic night was coming on," Harry Costello would write. "To our south and west the blackest cloud in social history was rising . . . It was spreading northward toward us—as the midnight sun receded."

By January, Cudahy wrote, Allied intelligence would report that the northern Sixth Bolshevik Army numbered 45,700 men, while the Americans, British, French, et al. would be able to muster 6,000, not counting the sometimes fickle Russian volunteers.

The Great War was over, but not this "strange war" in the Russian north.

It had, in fact, hardly begun.

CHAPTER SIXTEEN

THE PINEGA

He hadn't noticed the gore splattered over his neck and back until a few days later; only then did Pvt. John Toornman of Company G, 339th U.S. Infantry Regiment, realize that he was covered in the blood and brains of the late Jay Bournier Pitts, twenty-six years old, from Kalamazoo, Michigan, Toornman's own hometown.

It had been very cold, and between the bombardments and the shock of the December 1918 deaths of his pal Clarence Malm, known as a "prince" and "Our Clarence" back at the Pere Marquette Railway in Detroit, who had been kneeling next to him in the trench when a Bolo bullet sliced through the left side of his head, and Pitts, who had been just behind their sergeant loading ammo for the Lewis gun when a one-pound shell took off the top of his head, Toornman on the long, freezing slog back to Pinega hadn't been feeling much of anything.

By the time someone mentioned to Private Toornman of Company G, 339th U.S. Infantry Regiment, that he had frozen bits and pieces of people all over his coat, Malm and Pitts were stiff as boards and splayed on one of the sleds. By that time John Toornman, born in Austria, was numb, body and soul, and only wanted to eat for the first time in two days and then sleep, and forget, for a moment, Karpogora and what had happened there.

Company G had patrolled the city of Archangel and environs since arriving on September 4; six weeks later it was decided to open a new front, this one on the Pinega River, where the Bolos, having realized by then that this small force of Allies had no chance of defeating them, were gathering forces.

And so on October 20, 1918, two officers, a platoon from Company G, and some Russians were put aboard barges and towed east-southeast up the Dvina to where the Pinega branched off to the northeast, their destination a village of the same name some one hundred miles from Archangel.

They passed Leunova, and Ostrov, and Kuzomen before the river widened some. The journey took several days, in part because by then the tugs would freeze over at night, and the next morning the men would have to laboriously break the ice to free them. The men watched as the endless forests and tundra slipped past monotonously; it was monotonous, at least, until one of them found cases of rum packed aboard.

"Word got around and it didn't take long before everyone had a taste," John Toornman would remember. "Some had filled their canteens."

By the time the barge reached Pinega, a few of the men were too inebriated to carry their weapons. The officers, traveling on another barge, were oblivious to the state of their men.

Pinega was the largest town in the area, with about three thousand inhabitants. Some six to seven thousand people lived in the numerous smaller villages along the river. The locals had been elated and celebrated when the czar abdicated, but they had not taken warmly to the harsh Bolsheviks who replaced the old government.

"Some of their able men had had to accept tenure of authority under the nominal overlordship of the Red commissars," Company M's Joel Moore, who would himself become intimately familiar with the region, would write.

"When the Reds fled at the approach of the Allies, the people of Pinega had punished a few of the cruel Bolshevik rulers that they caught but [they] had not made any great effort to change all the officers of civil government even though they had been Red officials for a time."

The politics in the area would remain "a confused color scheme of Red and White civil government," Moore would add, with the local government being "half Red." Among the other half, the Allies would find three hundred volunteers.

Upon landing at Pinega, the Allied force moved through the town and dug in on both sides of its northern edge. The Bolos were in the next village to the north, but if they had any plans to confront Company G they would have had to do so by road, as the woods were too thick and deeply laden with snow.

The Allied force remained in place for several weeks, and was reinforced in late October by sixty-seven more members of Company G. Finally, responding to the locals' pleas for a column to be sent south along the river to flush the Bolos from the area, on November 15 thirty-five members of Company G and two hundred Russian volunteers headed toward the village of Karpogora, some sixty miles upriver.

The Bolos fled south before the column, "retreating from one village to the next, picking up Bolo sympathizers on the way," Toornman recalled. "I think the Bolos just wanted to draw us farther and farther from Pinega."

For ten days, the column moved with no opposition, and dug in on the southern end of each village they passed through. At each town, they scrambled for decent billets.

"When we got close, we run just like a bunch of kids let out of school," Toornman would remember. "Run to the first house, open the door, look, don't like it, close it, and run to the next one.

"You can imagine what those people felt like. They'd be scared to death when we come. Some of them started crying—the women. The men would still be in the army."

At one village, a patrol of Russian volunteers was captured by the Bolos; locals in a village up the valley said they had taken their prisoners into the woods and executed them. Indeed, their bodies were soon found, frozen in the snow and stiff as boards. "They had been brutally butchered," Toornman would recall. "I don't know how many, but I heard that it had been a large patrol."

While Americans celebrated Thanksgiving half a world away, the column arrived at the destination of Karpogora, and occupied the town "after a little engagement" with the enemy, Moore would write. Once again, the Allies dug in and built emplacements for their machine guns, and took over the last few homes on the south end of the village.

"We were there to stay a while," Toornman wrote.

For the next week, Bolo patrols came at night, fired at the Allies, and retired, using a schoolhouse just up the road for cover. The men urged their commander, a lieutenant, to let them burn the school down. "But nothing was done about it," Toornman would write.

On December 4, Toornman awoke to find most of his squad members in their nearby trench. Sgt. Michael Burke told him and Clarence Malm to go get their breakfast back in the center of the village, where a kitchen had been set up. But they never got their meal.

"We were halfway there when we heard the first shells coming over our heads," Toornman would write. "We ducked behind the log houses, not wanting to miss our breakfast." The shells, however, began to creep closer, so Toornman and Malm raced back to the trench.

After an hour of shelling, Bolos were spotted moving on their flanks through the deep woods. And before long, the Bolos attacked in rushes, racing forty feet and then dropping while their machine guns opened up, then moving forward again.

"The Reds certainly had plenty of courage," Toornman would recall. "They came deliberately up and fired at us . . . they attacked from every available point of shelter."

The Allies had three Lewis guns and one Vickers gun. The machine gun being worked in Toornman's trench soon malfunctioned, and Toornman saw that it had become clogged with dirt and sand blown up by the Bolo fire. While he attempted to clean it, Burke took a ring off of his finger and told Toornman, "They won't cut my finger off."

At about ten A.M., Clarence Malm, crouching to Toornman's right, was hit by fire from the schoolhouse. "His helmet flew off," Toornman recalled. "I knew he must have been hit in the head. A little blood came out his mouth and ear." A woolen cap, made by Malm's mother, Tillie, remained on his head.

Ten minutes later, Jay Bournier Pitts was hit. "He had been behind Burke handling the ammunition," Toornman would write. "We think he got hit with one of their 1 lb. shells. It took the whole top off his head which was inside his fur cap."

The battle lasted the rest of that day, and more men, all of them Russian volunteers, would also fall. The Bolos, meanwhile, were seen hauling as many as eighty of their dead away by sled.

That night, orders came to pull out. Toornman tried to lift his buddy Malm's body from the trench, but couldn't. After kneeling all day in the bitter cold, his legs were stiff. With help, he was finally able to slide Malm on his back through the snow to the center of the village. Others got Jay Pitts out as well.

In town, they found a large pile of military equipment that Allied soldiers were picking through. "No doubt they had intended to take all this along, but it was all left behind, as we were the last ones out."

Traveling on foot and by sled, "all day, all night, the next day and the next night," the column slogged the long way back through deep subzero temperatures to Pinega, where Toornman discovered to his disgust and sorrow that he had carried some of Jay Pitts back with him.

Jay Pitts and Clarence Malm were buried in Pinega, and remained in their graves there for almost eleven years before their bodies were recovered and sent home. John Toornman met Malm's mother, father, and younger brother in Detroit when Clarence's body arrived, and he returned to Tillie Malm the wool cap she had knitted for her Clarence, who had left home at the age of twenty-one so many years before to fight the Germans.

CHAPTER SEVENTEEN

THE LONELY DEATH OF FRANCIS CUFF

She never got a chance to speak to her father, and had no memory of him.

"We have been told that he was shot in the leg and then was finished off with an ax," Francis W. Cuff's daughter, Margaret, would tell a *Detroit Free Press* reporter on the occasion of Veterans Day in 1934, when she was seventeen years old.

"There's no use in being bitter now, but you can see from my background that I can't be very enthusiastic about wars. There's not much romance in it to me. All I can remember is that it cost me a father before he and I ever had a chance to say a word to each other."

Lt. Francis W. Cuff, of the tiny central Wisconsin town of Rio, enrolled in officers' training at Fort Sheridan when duty called in 1917, and was twenty-six when the Eighty-Fifth Division shipped out for overseas.

His father, Canadian-born William Cuff, had died at the age of thirty-nine in 1899, when Francis was just seven; a younger sister, Florence, died on her sixth birthday in 1901 from tonsillitis, and by 1905 Francis's mother, Maggie, was working as a laborer and doing what she could to support herself and her son.

When it came time to take a wife, Francis didn't have to look far;

he married a local girl, Erma Rausch, the daughter of Gust Rausch, a potato seller. Three weeks before the United States declared war on Germany, on March 17, 1917, Erma, just nineteen years old, gave birth to Margaret Florence Cuff.

On November 2, 1918, Francis Cuff and his unit, Company C, 339th U.S. Infantry Regiment, found themselves marching the road south from the Vaga River base at Shenkursk to Ust Padenga, to which Company A had retreated in late October. With them were thirty-five S.B.A.L.s, seventy-five Russian partisans, and Canadians with an eighteen-pound gun.

Since retiring from the far reaches at Rovdinskaya, Company A had had a relatively easy time of it in the area of Ust Padenga. The main work had been better preparing the defense of the vital area, which protected Shenkursk from invasion from the south.

The center of the position was the village of Visorka Gora, which sat on a high bluff above the west bank of the Vaga. Half a mile south sat the village of Ust Padenga; seven hundred yards farther south was the village of Nijni Gora. After forty days of continuous service, Company A on November 2 was finally relieved by Francis Cuff and Company C and headed north to Shenkursk.

Though there had been little action in the area, rumors were gaining steam that the Bolos were preparing to attack. Protecting the west flank of the Dvina column as well as Shenkursk, Company C had orders to hold at Ust Padenga "as long as possible." Any withdrawal would necessitate the evacuation of Toulgas above it, and even put the river base at Beresnik in peril.

The position on the upper Vaga River—isolated, virtually surrounded, increasingly hopeless—was not even remotely tenable, and embodied the worst aspect of Gen. Frederick Poole's grand plans of the early fall, when, as Moore et al. would write, the First Battalion had been sent upriver on its "fool's errand" to push through to Kotlas.

More rumors of a pending enemy attack reached Company C soon after it took over the post. On November 4, a Bolo patrol was seen and fired upon; the next day, a patrol sent to scout the village of Bresenik—not their base at Beresnik—nine miles to the south found twenty to thirty Bolos, "but the Russian in command pulled out," the company's Lt. Glen Weeks would write.

On November 11, as the force at Toulgas was fighting for its life, Francis Cuff took a patrol and traveled twelve miles through woods overflowing with deep snow and ran into a small Bolo force. "It was too dark for much action," Weeks wrote. "Got one prisoner."

On November 13, a patrol consisting of three Canadians and one Company C man went out on horses to patrol and "fell into a trap and one got away," Weeks would write. "The three were killed, then mutilated badly." Left dead and cut to pieces was Pvt. Adolph Schmann, of Milwaukee.

Four days later, two Bolo spies were caught "trying to find out our position, outpost strength, etc.," Weeks wrote. Francis Cuff, a Canadian artillery lieutenant, and Weeks "took one of them out in the woods and shot him." They let his body lie there for the next two days "so people could see it and tell the Bolos," Sgt. Robert Ray would write.

There were more incidents, most minor. A patrol of Bolos clad in white approached their post one night and left some propaganda, printed in English. On Thanksgiving Day, November 28, the company assembled and heard a proclamation from Woodrow Wilson. "Rum was given to the men," Weeks would note. "Everyone enjoyed the day."

The fun wouldn't last.

The next morning, Francis Cuff and Lt. Harry Steele left the post at 4:30 A.M. with sixty men and the intent of ousting a Bolo force from Trogimovskaya, five miles below Ust Padenga. The way led from the Vaga River over a forest trail, which had to be used because of the deep snow in the woods on either side.

At the deepest part of the woods, the patrol suddenly encountered a large force of Bolsheviks that had easily concealed itself amid drifts and thick spruce. Halting in the dim forest, and standing up to his knees in powdery fluff, Cuff ordered his men to fire, and after a sharp, quick fight he ordered a withdrawal.

Soon hearing the crackle of gunfire closer to the Vaga, Cuff—"one of the bravest and most fearless officers in the expedition," according to Moore et al.—and his party went to the rescue of the trailers of his patrol, who were being overwhelmed by Bolos. Cuff and his men sprang from the woods and opened fire on the attacking Bolos.

During the ensuing wild melee, Cuff and several others also became separated from the main force and were besieged by the Bolos. Cuff, though severely wounded, fought like a cornered animal, struggling to save his own life and extricate the sixty men under him. Some men were able to just barely escape into the thick woods, but were unable to bring Cuff and the other wounded with them. They had had no chance; the Bolos, a regimental report would note, had between six hundred and seven hundred men. It was, in fact, amazing that the entire patrol wasn't wiped out.

As it was, thirteen men—almost one-quarter of the patrol—were killed or had gone missing. The bodies of Francis Cuff, Cpls. John Cheeney and John Bosel, and Pvts. Raymond Clemens, Thurman Kissick, and Irvin Wenger were later recovered; all had been mutilated. The bodies of numerous Bolos slain during their last stand lay about them.

Of the others who went missing that day—Pvts. Elmer Hodge, Bolesaw Gutowski, Henry Weitzel, Johnnie Triplett, Nicholas Jonker, Walter Huston, and Mike Haurilik—only three would return home alive. The body of Gutowski was located and sent home in 1929; the bodies of Nicholas Jonker, Elmer Hodge, and Henry Weitzel followed in 1934. Johnnie Triplett, Walter Huston, and Mike Haurilik, all made captive, eventually made it home.

Two others were luckier. Pvt. Roy Clemens, whose brother Ray was among the dead, and Pvt. Oscar Greenlund became separated during the swirling fight and lost their way. They wandered for three days through the bitter cold and punishing snows, starving and hiding behind trees and in heavy brush "while bodies of enemy scouts passed by at almost arm's length," a newspaper would report the following July.

Finally hearing artillery firing, they made their way toward it and emerged at Ust Padenga. "Clemens was suffering from exposure and two frozen toes and his companion had parts of both feet frozen and he now walks with the aid of two canes," the Benton Harbor *News-Palladium* reported.

Francis Cuff and his men were buried in a solemn ceremony at Shenkursk on December 1, Cuff receiving military honors. Godfrey Anderson, serving there with the 337th Field Hospital Company, remembered his captain, Howard Kinyon, making a short speech.

"The enemy, he said, were castrating the wounded while they were still alive, when Lieut. Cuff pulled out his revolver and shot himself," Anderson wrote. "'That is the kind of enemy you are fighting,' he concluded."

Americans, British, Royal Scots, Cossacks, Canadians, and Russian volunteers, all in full dress, lined the street in Shenkursk as "the body of the brave Lieut. Cuff," encased in a simple pine casket, was borne to the cemetery down by the river.

"On top of the casket was his steel helmet," Anderson wrote. "The whole procession marched to the eastern outskirts of town where a grave had been dug amid a scattering of tall pines at the fringe of the dense forest."

Francis Cuff was then lowered into his grave "amid profound silence. There were tributes spoken and then the crash of a firing squad, which echoed and re-echoed through the boundless forest, and finally the melancholy notes of the bugler playing taps."

When the body of Francis Cuff—"whose name is known to every officer of the 339th," Harry Costello would write—was disinterred at Shenkursk for return home in 1929, it was noted in one record that he had indeed had his "skull shattered in left side & top," as his daughter Margaret Cuff had learned at a young age.

But that was just the half of it: "The bolsheviki [*sic*] had perpetrated one of their most common atrocities" on Francis, and had hacked him "almost beyond recognition. The legs and arms had been hacked from the torso," Harry Costello wrote.

It was better, perhaps, that Margaret Cuff had not known any of this, though what she did know was bad enough.

No, the Bolos had not been kind to Lt. Francis W. Cuff, nor to the daughter who never got the chance to know him.

CHAPTER EIGHTEEN

MEDICINE MEN

They were dying in droves, he would remember years later, dying in their simple village homes in which the women spent the winter spinning thread and weaving while the men lolled on the stove; dying and being buried by their black-bearded Orthodox priests who swung censers and chanted in deep basso voices as the miserable, endless processions made their way to the cemetery where graves had been laboriously chopped from the permafrost and in which they were laid, there on the banks of the Vaga River.

And young Pvt. Godfrey Anderson, late of Sparta and Grand Rapids, Michigan, and now of the 337th Field Hospital attached to the 339th U.S. Infantry Regiment, watched all of this in wonder, his part of the great adventure in north Russia being to somehow try to stem the tide of death enveloping not just the Americans but the local *moujiks* who struggled to eke a living out of the forests that surrounded their humble villages.

The flu had hit Shenkursk and its surrounding villages in November 1918, most likely brought to the area by one or two or more sick Americans who'd landed there that fall. It was an epidemic with "appalling virulence," Godfrey would write, and it afflicted the locals and Russian volunteers more than the other soldiers streaming back and forth from Beresnik in the north to Ust Padenga in the south.

"The Russians seemed to have no resistance whatsoever," Godfrey wrote. "By the 11th of November, both [of] our hospitals were filled; as was the Russian civilian hospital. The small stone hut at the rear of our barracks was full of corpses awaiting coffins, of which there was a shortage.

"It was the same in the outlands—people dying by the hundreds. Funeral processions were constantly wailing through the streets."

It was a daunting task that the men of the 337th faced. They were medics, but their few weeks of training at Camp Custer had been limited mostly to hiking and the kitchen patrol. On one occasion, a small class was held to teach the men the "names of all the bones in the body—occipital, clavicle, femur, etc.," Godfrey would recall. And just one other class was held on wrapping bandages.

In any event they had had little to no medicine to treat the dozens of their own flu cases upon landing at Archangel, and little to no medicine with which to treat the wounded at Seltso and Toulgas and Onega and Pinega and on the railroad front. The buildings selected to be used as hospitals were by and large covered in filth and vermin and stinking with the stench of indoor latrines.

And there were the undertakers. "Our first mortician, a fellow called 'Shep' lost his job because of purloining valuables from the pockets of the deceased," Godfrey would remember.

Another, Ethol "Pork" Nordman, had little sympathy for his Russian hosts. On nights when a Russian patient was expected to die, Pork could be found pacing impatiently in the hallway outside the door, in his hand a whittled "plugging stick" used to seal off the throat and anus of the dead. Pork Nordman would "profanely importune the unconscious patient to hurry it up and quit stalling."

On one occasion another man of the 337th working as an undertaker found one of his plugging sticks was too thick "and took out his army issued heavy duty jackknife and began shaving it down, smeared as it was by the raw sienna hued excrescence," Godfrey wrote. "After a cursory wipe off he stuck the knife back in his pocket."

That night, the undertaker went to the kitchen for a late snack, and "took out the same jackknife and began peeling an onion for his sandwich," Godfrey wrote. "He was later kidded plenty about it."

While treating their own men was difficult enough, it was the lack of sanitation among the populace that posed the greatest trial for the thin medical unit working in northern Russia that fall, winter, and spring. Arriving at Beresnik on September 25, the 337th's commander, Maj. J. Carl Hall, visited first a military hospital being run by the British, and then traveled two miles to a civilian hospital, which he had plans to convert into a new military hospital.

He encountered "vermin of all kinds, and cockroaches so thick that they had to be scraped from the wall and shoveled into a container," he wrote. "The latrines were built in the buildings, as is Russian custom, and were full to overflowing."

After inspecting facilities in other villages, Hall would conclude that sanitation was "almost an impossibility." Each rustic log home had a barn built at one end, with a hallway between it and the kitchen. A simple hole cut into the floor near the hayloft served as a toilet, and the excrement piled up beneath the home. On the Vaga, some of the wealthier villagers had a closed toilet between the barn and the kitchen. "These are the billets used by the Allied troops on the river front in North Russia," Hall wrote.

Wagoner Harold Weimeister of the 337th Ambulance Company would remember that in his quarters in Seletskoe on the Emtsa River the barn and house had been conjoined "for convenience in the extreme cold" of the Russian winter. The "toilet" was on the second floor, above the cattle stalls. "When used a turd would freeze before it hit the floor below with the consequences that in time it formed a tower about the diameter of a telephone pole."

When his Russian hosts asked him and the other men when they were going to leave, the men replied, "When we fill up the privy."

But the answer turned out to be less than funny. "We filled two up to the time we left Seletskoye in February. This tower of shit would grow steadily until it came abo[v]e the second floor too high to squat over—THEN WE MOVED."

The severe cold also led the Russians to seal their windows—and in some cases, their fates.

"In view of the Russian custom of keeping their doors and windows of their houses practically sealed during the winter and with their utter disregard for the most simple sanitary precautions, small wonder it was that in a short time an epidemic was raging in practically every village within our lines," Moore et al. would note.

At Shenkursk that November, Hall tried to convince a Russian doctor at the civilian hospital to open a window to air the place out. "No ventilation and practically all with Spanish influenza and, in addition, many with gangrenous wounds," Hall wrote of the situation. He tried to show the Russian doctor in charge that fresh air would be beneficial.

"But he seemed to think I was entirely out of my sphere and ignored what I said," Hall wrote. "I reported the situation to British headquarters and thereafter he reluctantly did as I suggested."

Hall also arranged for Russian medical officers to go out into the countryside with American medics, "instructing each to impress on the natives the necessity of fresh air and proper hygiene." In the villages, however, another problem was uncovered among the flu-ridden locals. "They found there was such a shortage of the proper kind of food that the people had no resistance against disease, and were dying by the hundreds."

In Ust Padenga at the southernmost front Lt. Ralph Powers, a 1915 graduate of the Eclectic Medical College of Cincinnati—a nontraditional medical school that promulgated noninvasive therapies and plant-based remedies—did what he could for the suffering villagers, but he was overwhelmed. Hall visited one peasant home there "where I found the father sick and in adjoining room the corpse of his wife and two children."

At another village, "I found twenty-four sick in four families; eight of which were pneumonia cases. In one peasant home, six in family, all sick with a child of eight years running a fever, but trying to care for others. All sleeping in the same room; three on the floor and balance together in a loft made by laying boards between the sills."

The room had double windows—"all sealed air-tight."

The peasants mostly suffered in silence, accepting, per custom, whatever Providence laid at their door. "The workers, however, devoted themselves to their errand of mercy night and day and gradually the epidemic was checked," Moore et al. would write.

Indeed, there was some slim silver lining among the doom and gloom. The work of the medicine men, and medicine women in the hospitals, "had a great effect upon the peasantry of the region and doubtless gave them a better and more kindly opinion of the strangers in their midst than all the efforts of our artillery and machine guns ever could have done," Moore et al. wrote.

While the fighting men would one day—if they were lucky—leave Russia still asking themselves, as Harry Costello would pose it, "Why did we go to Russia?" Godfrey Anderson and the medical corps could at least look back and feel they had done *something* of use through that long Russian night: they had saved lives, American and Russian, or at least alleviated some of the suffering of those doomed to perish in that disease-ridden backwater.

"It took strong qualities of heart and nerve to be a field hospital man, or an ambulance or medical man," Moore et al. would note.

CHAPTER NINETEEN

A THANKSGIVING OF SORTS

The major was drunk, stir-crazy, and looking for a fight that night, and so he grabbed some hand grenades, left his headquarters, and stomped through the subzero night air to the bridge where Company E men were watching the opposite bank for signs of attack. A Bolo commander had appeared at the bridge not long before, and assured the Americans—"comrades," he had called them—that the Reds had no interest in shooting at them unless they were shot at. Since then, a sense of quiet had reigned at that bridge over the Emtsa River.

The peace was shattered when Maj. Mike Donoghue, recently elevated from command of Company K and put in charge of the American force on the Kodish front, showed up out of that black night of November 27, 1918, intent on stirring things up, and blowing off some inebriated steam.

"Major Donohue [*sic*] came in drunk that night and began throwing grenades in the Bolo's line, this didn't go far before the Bolo's opened up machine guns on us, they kept firing until nearly morning," Company E's Cpl. Fred Kooyers, manning a Lewis gun that night, would report.

His work done and the rum wearing off, Donoghue returned to his headquarters "and the Bolo's quit firing. There wasn't anybody killed that day, but there were quite a few that were afraid."

"It was not a dignified tour of inspection in keeping with military tradition, but the disgraceful visit of a drunken ass," Company E's PFC Donald Carey would add of the major's buzzed, unilateral offensive. "Apparently not having secured sufficient excitement from the bottle or jug, he must necessarily attempt to supply it by opening fire upon the Bolos with a machine gun and by throwing a couple hand grenades into the river.

"Receiving no fire he even ventured part way across the bridge. Had an enemy bullet terminated such a fool-hardy stunt, little sympathy would have been forth coming from me."

It wasn't the first time the redheaded, hard-boiled major had turned into a drunken loose cannon. Days before, he had put on a show for Company E's Capt. Bernard Heil, and from his perch at the officers' quarters had tossed hand grenade after hand grenade down the road.

"He was far from being the gentleman that was to be found in the person of Maj. Nichols whom I never saw or heard of being intoxicated," Carey wrote.

But Major Mike was a warrior, and he wanted revenge.

Weeks earlier, the Bolos had blocked Donoghue and his men's way to Plesetskaya and very nearly annihilated them at Kodish. Donoghue had only just been able to get his command north and across the Emtsa River in a fighting retreat; almost miraculously, none of the men of Company K had been killed, but seven were wounded.

Since then, activity on the front had settled down and become a matter of watching and waiting on both sides of the Emtsa River, in accordance with the general cessation of offensive action ordained by Gen. Edmund Ironside.

Following its ordeal, Company K was relieved after six weeks of continuous service on the front by Company E, half of which had been living a fat, happy, and peaceful life back in the Smolny barracks at Bakharitza while the other half performed guard duty at Isakagorka to the south. Reunited for the first time since October 2, on November 8

Company E's four platoons headed south down the railway to Obozerskaya.

"The only signs of habitation were dinky jerkwater towns, mere sta-
tions, or peasant cabins, surrounded by small clearings," Carey would
remember. "Invariably at such points groups of natives in their quaint
costume were by the tracks to see us."

After arriving at Obozerskaya, two platoons of the company were
put under the charge of Lt. John Baker, who, despite express orders
from Major Nichols that were echoed by Captain Heil, insisted that
the men carry their heavy packs the thirty miles to Seletskoe instead of
having them ferried by the Russian droshkies.

"I heard Captain Heil tell Lt. Baker that the major ordered the packs
carried by droshkies," Carey wrote, "but the lieutenant replied that his
outfit was soldierly enough to carry their own packs."

They spent two days marching and two nights sleeping on the cold,
wet, muddy ground before reaching Seletskoe on the evening of November 11. Seventy-odd miles to the southeast, Company B and its allies were engaged in their Armistice Day death struggle with the Bolos
at Toulgas; at Seletskoe, the day passed almost like any other.

"That day so gladly hailed by millions of war weary people, we spent
hiking on the Emtsa front," Carey wrote. "Completely ignorant of what
was occurring on the Western Front."

After resting a day, the platoons were put on the march on November 13 for Mejovskayia, seven miles to the south. The next day,
they moved to the front's headquarters just to the south, on the north
bank of the Emtsa. There, about fifty men were selected to begin what
would become a numbing routine of one day on, one day off patrolling
the Allied side of the river.

"No trench or rifle line marked our line," Carey would write. "Only
the dark, deep, gurgling waters of the forest-fringed Emtsa River constituted the line of demarcation between the Bolsheviks and the Americans."

The line to be guarded, several miles long, was anchored on the right
by a position called "the church," after a log hut that sat on the south

bank on the Bolo side. On the left the line was anchored by what was called the "artillery position" just above the intersection of the Emtsa and the Plesetskaya-to-Kodish road.

At the center was a bridge built by the 310th Engineers near the charred remains of the bridge that had been burned by the Bolos in mid-September. "It was this that our force keenly guarded," Carey wrote.

The scene at the Emtsa was peaceful, bucolic, and yet disquieting. The Bolos were over there, somewhere, and could faintly be heard chopping wood or moving about, but could not be seen.

The days were growing ever shorter, as well, and the nights grew colder and colder, yet orders were given that no fires be made "lest the smoke attract artillery fire, or the blaze the bullet of some watchful rifleman," Carey remembered.

On his first night on duty at the Emtsa, a Bolo once more appeared near the bridge and began to calmly address the Americans across the river, employing workers-of-the-world-unite rhetoric and imploring the Americans to drop their arms and join the socialist struggle—or at least leave. As usual, the harangue went on for hours; Carey, who'd seen little of the world but the pleasures of Grand Rapids, was hit by the sudden incongruity of where his life had taken him.

"That I, a Michigan lad, reared amid the conveniences of an ordinary American home, should be standing in the shadows of a cluster of pines beside a large river flooded and sparkling with moonlight listening to Red nonsense in a most God forsaken country on such a hellish mission as war, far exceeded the wildest dreams of my childhood," he would write.

By then, winter clothing was being issued across the fronts, each man receiving two suits of woolen underwear and heavy knee-length socks and sweaters. Each also received a sleeveless leather jerkin, fur-lined headgear made of canvas that could be turned down to cover the neck and ears, and a long coat made from sheepskin that reached to the ankles.

The men also received wool mittens with a separate pocket for trigger fingers, plus a pair of oversized mittens that were worn on a strap around one's neck so a man could put his hands deep inside to warm them. To touch metal in temperatures that sometimes reached fifty below "was like grasping a piece of red-hot iron," General Ironside would note.

Shackleton boots were also issued but would be more often cursed than worn, the soldiers preferring hobnailed boots to the slippery soles of the mukluk-like winter footwear.

(Not all the men received their winter clothing on time. Fred Kooyers would write that when he and his crew returned to Mejovskayia for his issue of winter wear, they discovered that the company's supply sergeant, Fred Patton, "had sold about all that he could sell so we didn't get much warmer clothing to go back with to the front . . . It had now got so cold that some of the boys were freezing their fingers or feet nearly every night.")

A new problem also emerged as the temperature plunged: the machine guns. The Vickers guns, water-cooled, naturally froze and became useless in the frigid weather. But the Lewis guns, too, posed some trouble when it became so cold that the lubrication itself would freeze.

"If a machine gun jammed, the only way of getting it going again was by taking it apart and boiling it," Ironside noted. "This precluded their use in the open." As well, the range tables—a means of determining the distances of potential targets—had to be reconfigured, "owing to the loss of range in intense cold."

On one occasion when the temperature was thirty-five below, Major Mike, again wanting to take some potshots at the Bolos, set up a Vickers gun at the Emtsa—but as he prepared to fire he found that the gun had frozen solid, "as was to be expected," the Machine Gun Company's Harry Costello would write.

"Heating the water was out of the question. On this front one never struck a match even to light a cigarette, because a light would have drawn the Bolsheviki fire."

Donoghue returned to a shelter, "where crouched a Sergeant and Lieut. Johnny Commons" of Company K. Commons told Donoghue he'd heard of men on the Western Front sleeping with their machine guns to keep them from freezing, and Major Mike decided to give it a try.

After three nights, Donoghue called over to Commons: "Hey, Johnny, I've slept with this blankety-blank gun for three nights and it isn't even warm. I'll be frozen myself if I sleep with it any longer."

"And it was literally true," Costello wrote.

There was one more problem: as the gloom of General Winter descended, the men at all fronts began to lose heart. Many by late November had either heard rumors of the armistice or knew from various sources that the war was over in the west; meanwhile, here they sat in the vast Russian interior, freezing and waiting to attack or be attacked in a cause few understood.

"The black night and short, hazy days, the monotonous food, the great white, wolf-howling distances, and the endless succession of one [damned] hardship after another was quite enough," Moore et al. wrote.

Thanksgiving Day brought little respite from the ills. On that day Donald Carey and the Company E men not on watch were fed a dinner of "bread, butter, tea, and beans so scorched that it was almost impossible to eat them," he would remember. "It was a most thankless meal."

Added to that misery was an addendum to Woodrow Wilson's Thanksgiving message of November 16, 1918, which celebrated the ultimate "great triumph of right" in the just-concluded world war.

Wilson had made no direct reference to Russia in his message, but DeWitt Poole would. Poole, no relation to Gen. Frederick Poole, had replaced U.S. ambassador David Francis when he left Archangel on November 8 to have his prostate cancer treated in England. That Thanksgiving, Poole took it upon himself to issue his own proclamation to the troops, in which he blamed Germany's "intrigue" for putting much of Russia into "unfriendly and undemocratic hands."

He then offered some depressing news to the soldiers wondering why they were still fighting in Russia. "The president has given our pledge of friendship to Russia and will point the way to its fulfillment,"

The official "Polar Bear" insignia, designed and created while the 339th Infantry Regiment awaited transport out of Russia in late spring, 1919.
The Bentley Historical Library

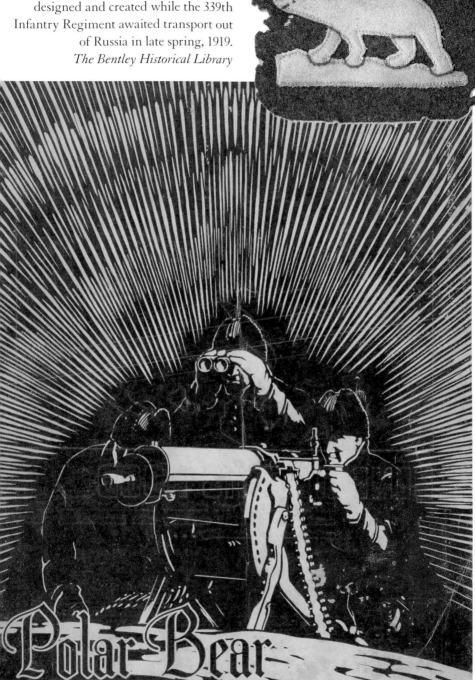

The cover of the program for the 1932 annual reunion of the Polar Bears.
The Bentley Historical Library, courtesy of the Frank E. Lauer family

Lt. Harry Costello of the 339th Regiment's Machine Gun Company, pictured in his glory days as a football sensation at Georgetown University, ca. 1913. *Courtesy of the Georgetown University Library, Booth Family Center for Special Collections, Washington, D.C.*

Medic Godfrey Anderson of the 337th Field Hospital Company shown wearing the Polar Bear patch on his left shoulder, ca. 1919. *The Godfrey J. Anderson Papers, Grand Rapids (MI) Public Library*

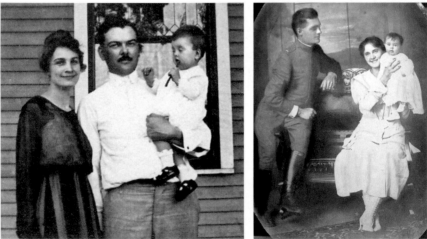

Left: Lt. Clifford Phillips of Company H, 339th Regiment, with his wife, Kathryn, and daughter, Ellen Jane, ca. 1917. Phillips was mortally wounded on April 2, 1919 while leading his men near Bolshie Ozerki, Russia, and died on May 10. *Courtesy of William Phillips Reich*

Right: Lt. Francis Cuff of Company C, 339th Regiment, with his wife, Erma, and daughter, Margaret, ca. 1918. Cuff was killed in action while on a patrol near Ust Padenga, Russia, on November 29, 1918. *Courtesy of the American Legion Francis Cuff Post #208, Rio, Wisconsin*

Lt. Charles Ryan of Company K, 339th Regiment. Ryan and his unit spent much of the fall of 1918 and winter of 1919 unsuccessfully trying to fight their way to the Bolshevik base at Plesetskaya, Russia. *Courtesy of the Charles Ryan family*

Pfc. Donald Carey of Company E, 339th Regiment, with an unidentified relative, ca. 1919. *Courtesy of Neil G. Carey*

The officers of Company A, 339th Regiment, and their Canadian counterparts at Ust Padenga, Russia, early in 1919. Lt. Douglas Winslow of the Canadian artillery is front row, right; to his right is Company A captain Otto Odjard. Lieutenant Harry Mead is to Odjard's right; Lt. Hugh McPhail of Company A is in the second row, far right. *U.S. Army Signal Corps, courtesy of the Bentley Historical Library*

Pvt. John Toornman of Company G, 339th Regiment. Toornman spent much of the winter of 1918-1919 on the Pinega River front. *Courtesy of Laurie Toornman Hare*

Sailors from the USS *Olympia,* the first American military men to arrive and the first to engage the Bolsheviks in northern Russia in late summer, 1918, pictured on September 6, 1918. *U.S. Army Signal Corps, courtesy of the Bentley Historical Library*

The three ships that transported the Americans from England, pictured at the docks in Bakharitza, Russia. Left to right are the *Somali,* the *Tydeus,* and the *Nagoya. U.S. Army Signal Corps, courtesy of the Bentley Historical Library*

Men of Company M, 339th Regiment, pushing south down the railroad front on September 29, 1918. An Allied armored car can be seen in the distance. *U.S. Army Signal Corps, courtesy of the Bentley Historical Library*

British general Frederick Poole, who commanded the Allied force in Russia in the fall of 1918. *U.S. Army Signal Corps*

British general Edmund Ironside awarding medals at Archangel in 1919. Ironside took over the war effort in mid-fall, 1918, and also oversaw the withdrawal of Allied troops in the spring of 1919. *The Imperial War Museum*

A look at the busy waterfront of Archangel. *The Bentley Historical Library, courtesy of the Frank E. Lauer family*

A soldier manning a Lewis gun.
The Harry Duink Papers, the Bentley Historical Library

Bolsheviks captured by French troops arrive at Bakharitza, Russia, on September 6, 1918. They were later sent to the prison at Archangel. *U.S. Army Signal Corps, courtesy of the Bentley Historical Library*

A cartoon imagining the Unites States' defeat of Bolshevism, drawn by Earl "Bug" Culver, bugler with Company A, 339th Regiment. *The Hugh D. McPhail Papers, the Bentley Historical Library*

The 339th's Michigan Barracks at Archangel, ca. 1919. *The Clay Grimshaw Schade Papers, the Bentley Historical Library*

ABOVE: American and Allied Russian troops in a snow trench at Cleshova on the Onega River front, ca. 1919. *The Edwin Flaherty Papers, the Bentley Historical Library*

A Christmas card created by the 310th Engineers in 1918. *The Earl V. Amos Papers, the Bentley Historical Library*

Men from Company B, 339th Regiment, on a snowshoe patrol on the Dvina River front on New Year's Eve, 1918. Lt. John Cudahy is farthest to the left, while Pvt. Clarence Scheu is farthest to the right. *U.S. Army Signal Corps, courtesy of the Bentley Historical Library*

Dog sleds were used to transport men and supplies along the widespread fronts. *The Harry Duink Papers, the Bentley Historical Library*

Outpost No. 4
Pinega —

4-8-19.

An outpost on the Pinega River front, ca. 1919. *The Clay Grimshaw Schade Papers, the Bentley Historical Library*

Barbed wire emplacements constructed by the 310th Engineers at Kleschuvo, Russia. *The Clay Grimshaw Schade Papers, the Bentley Historical Library*

A Bolshevik killed at the Company A, 339th Regiment's base at Visorka Gora on January 8, 1919. He was one of seven Bolos, all camouflaged in white smocks, that attempted to infiltrate the Allied line that morning. *U.S. Army Signal Corps, courtesy of the Bentley Historical Library*

The view toward the cathedral of Pagosta (on far horizon), looking south from Nijni Gora, Russia. Pagosta remained in Bolshevik hands through the war and was used for observation on the Allied outpost at Nijni Gora. *U.S. Army Signal Corps, courtesy of the Bentley Historical Library*

The railway front at Verst 454, looking north to the siding at Verst 455. A blockhouse guards the clearing at left. *U.S. Army Signal Corps, courtesy of the Bentley Historical Library*

The officers of Company M, 339th Regiment, soon after their return from the March 31–April 2, 1919, battle at Verst 18. *Left to right:* Lts. Clarence Primm, Milton Carpenter, Robert Wieczorek, Wesley Wright, James Donovan, George Stoner, and Captain Joel Moore. *U.S. Army Signal Corps, courtesy of the Bentley Historical Library*

A Bolshevik fighter killed during the March 31–April 2, 1919, attacks on the Allied position at Verst 18. *U.S. Army Signal Corps, courtesy of the Bentley Historical Library*

The graves of Lt. Frank Garrett and Sgt. Frederick Patterson of the 168th Transportation Corps, both of whom were killed by a sniper while attempting to clear the Murmansk-Petrograd railroad of Reds on May 2, 1919. *The Harry Duink Papers, the Bentley Historical Library*

A Red Cross caravan somewhere on the Archangel front. *Library of Congress*

Confirmer It or called mutiny of Co I 339 Inf. which proved to me a mutual interdaring of orders and not a mutiny.

1. Maj Genl Ironsides, British Army, Comdy N.R.EF.
2. Col Geo E Stewart, Comdy American Force N.R.EF.
3. Maj J F Rly. Chief Quartermaster Amer Force
4. Maj Charles Young - C.O. 3" Battl - 339 Inf.
5. Mr Francis, American Ambassador to Russia
6. Capt Jack Moore - P.O.C.M. 339 Inf.
7. Capt Horatio Winslow - C.O. Co I 339 Inf.

British general Edmund Ironside, right, and American colonel George Stewart, behind Ironside, address the members of Company I, 339th Regiment, following the unit's so-called mutiny of March 30, 1919. The company's captain, Horatio Winslow, is fourth from left while Company M's captain Joel Moore is second from the left. *The Chauncey C. Wade Papers, the Bentley Historical Library*

The Polar Bears' perilous situation in north Russia came under increasing scrutiny in the American newspapers, as this February 3, 1919 dispatch shows. *The Bentley Historical Library*

A newspaper notice of the death of Company E corporal James Mylon, who was wounded in the fighting at Kodish on December 30, 1918, and died the next day. *The Bentley Historical Library*

DETROIT BOY DIES OF WOUND IN RUSSIA

CORPORAL J. J. MYLON.

YOUNG DETROITER KILLED IN RUSSIA

Corp. Mylon Dies of Wound Received Near Archangel.

In the Arctic.

RUSSIA

—From the St. Louis Post-Dispatch. "O, Say, Can You See—Any Reason For it Being There?"

A political cartoon in the *St. Louis Post-Dispatch* displays Americans' growing impatience and concern over the Polar Bears' plight, ca. 1919. *The Bentley Historical Library*

Coming from Archangel Russ. June 19.19
A happy hour on the "Menominee"
6 X

A group of jubilant Polar Bears headed for France aboard the *Menominee* celebrate happ
hour, in June 1919. *The Bentley Historical Library, courtesy of the Frank E. Lauer family*

Co. G "339th In
BREST, FRANCE, JUNE,19
"BACK From Russia"

"Back from Russia": The members of Company G, 339th Regiment, were all smiles
after arriving in Brest, France, in June 1919. *The Walter C, Matuszewski Photograph
Collection, the Bentley Historical Library*

339th Infantry

"A" Co.
Carter, Wm. J.
Cwenk, Jos.
DeAmicis, Guisseppi
Hannon, John T.
Hutchinson, Alfred G.
Jenks, Stillman V.
Kowalski, Stanley
Kurowski, Max J.
Kussrath, Chas. A., Jr.
Lehmann, Wm. J.
McTavish, Stewart M.
Martin, Wm. J.
Peyton, Edgar W.
Peth, Russell A.
Rauschenberger, Albert
Retherford, Lindsey
Russell, Archie
Sajnaj, Leo
Williams, Edson A.

"B" Co.
Finnegan, Leo N.
Foley, Morris J.
Kuzba, Peter
Vandermeer, John

"C" Co.
Bosel, John J.
Casey, Marcus T.
Clemens, Roy C.
Cheeney, Roy D.
Cuff, Francis W.
Kiecz, Andrusci
Skocelas, Andrew
Speicher, Elmer E.
Szymanski, Louis A.
Wenger, Irvin

"D" Co.
Syska, Frank
Tamas, Stanley P.
VanHerwynen, John

"E" Co.
McDonald, Angus
Mueller, Frank J.
Zoltcha, Mike

"F" Co.
Bayer, Chas.
Berryhill, Chester W.
Conrad, Rex H.

"G" Co.
Malm, Clarence A.
Pitts, Jay B.

"H" Co.
Negako, Wm. W.
Richardson, Eugene E.
Silkaitis, Frank

"I" Co.
Hanley, John T.
Kalaska, Joseph
Kistler, Herbert
Wadsworth, Wm. L.

"K" Co.
Cronin, Louis
Fuller, Alfred W.
Gray, Alsea W.
Staley, Glenn P.

"L" Co.
Christian, Arthur
Dusablon, Wm. H.
Ozdarski, Jos. S.

"M" Co.
Hodgson, Fred L.
Niemi, Matti I.
Nunn, Arthur

"M.G." Co.
Meister, Emanoul A.

"H.Q." Co.
Jackson, Jesse C.
O'Brien, Raymond A.
Shaughnessy, John E.
Togges, Wm. G.

"SUPPLY" Co.
Berger, Carl O.

"337th AMB." Co.
Ida, Jas. T.
Paprzychi, Sylvester
Powers, Ralph E.

RECOVERED UNIDENTIFIED POLAR BEAR BODIES, MAY BE IDENTIFIED LATER

339th Infantry

"A" Co.
Cole, Elmer B.
Gottschalk, Milton E.
Lucioni, Sebastiene
Patrick, Ralph M.
Richey, August K.
Rodgers, Yates K.
Scruggs, Frank W.

"A" Co. (Cont'd)
Smith, Geo. J.
Stoir, Victor

"H" Co.
Avery, Harley
Bereson, John
Graham, Claus
Richter, Edward

And Three Unknowns Recovered from the River Front.

A list of the bodies of Polar Bears who were recovered in north Russia by the Michigan Commission in 1929. Eighty-six were located that year, and the bodies of twenty-one others were returned in subsequent years. The bodies of some two dozen Polar Bears were never found. *The Michael J. Macalla Papers, the Bentley Historical Library*

The scene at the May 30, 1930, dedication of the Polar Bear Monument and burial of remains at the White Chapel Memorial Cemetery in Troy, Michigan. *The Polar Bear Memorial Association*

Author's photograph of the Polar Bear Monument, sculpted by Leon Hermant, up close. Note the World War 1–era helmet and cross. *James Carl Nelson*

Poole would say. "Confident in his leadership, the American troops and officials in Northern Russia will hold to their task to the end."

With the world war over there were many among the troops who couldn't help but ask what, exactly, "the end" was to be. By then, most Americans holding the line south of Archangel knew the armistice had been signed, which meant their brethren in France would soon be going home. It also meant that the reasons for their being there—whether it was merely guarding stores or the grander idea of reestablishing the Eastern Front—no longer applied.

To Donald Carey, Poole's words meant that "we were in Russia for a definite, though unexplained, purpose and that there we would remain until the administration saw fit to withdraw us. To say the least such a statement was far from encouraging."

Meanwhile the Emtsa was freezing, taking with it as it did a natural barrier to a Bolo attack. On December 7, those fears were realized when the company was rousted at four A.M. and told to be ready for an assault.

It came at the bridge, but was quickly aborted. "We had good positions and four Lewis guns with us," Kooyers wrote. "So we held them off."

On December 12, Carey was assigned to Kooyers's Lewis gun squad on the extreme right. "That I had had no introduction in the operation of this deadly weapon appeared to be of no particular concern to the parties who assigned the guard detail," he wrote.

The next night, Carey patrolled through the woods near the church position alone, and came to fully appreciate "how easily a small group of the enemy could cut me off from my face."

Returning, he went to sleep, only to wake up violently ill. Corporal Kooyers "was very solicitous of my welfare and kindly supplied me with his overcoat when I laid down beside the fire to sleep as much as my condition would permit," Carey wrote.

On the night of the seventeenth, while Carey was recuperating from his illness in Mejovskayia, the Americans at the bridge received another visit from one of the Bolos, who approached under a white flag and tried to ingratiate himself with the Americans.

"He told [the] conditions we were fighting under also the condition they were fighting under," Kooyers would note. "They also told us a British officer died in their hospital, they found seven hundred rubles on the officer and he would be over in a day or two and turn it in."

True to his word, the Bolo returned three days later, and gave the officer's money to Lieutenant Baker. Baker also received an invitation to dine with the Bolsheviks, who, the Bolo at the bridge assured all, would not fire unless fired upon. Baker declined the invite.

Carey, though not at the scene, would report that as Baker and the Bolo talked via interpreters, an exchange of prisoners was discussed. By then, three men from Company C and George Albers of Company I were in enemy hands, and Captain Heil opened negotiations. Subsequent events would leave all four prisoners captives.

Carey spent Christmas Day at the front, happy to be nibbling on a package of candy that had arrived from home—but blue at the prospects before him.

"Contrary to the persistent rumors that we would be home for Dec. 25, that date found us all marooned in snowbound Russia and still at war with the Bolsheviks," he would write.

"No amount of dreaming or wishing could alter that fact."

CHAPTER TWENTY

BETTER THAN NO WAR AT ALL

Here we go again, he thinks, as word comes down that his company is to once more enter the woods and swamps around that goddamned village, the same one he and his company took in mid-October. Then, they had been very nearly surrounded and fled for their very lives, crossing the river in the black night with the Bolos on their tails.

He remembers lying flat on his stomach next to Sgt. Michael Kenney at one point during the advance as the Bolo bullets zinged above them, clipping the branches of trees and searching for flesh. That time, he laughs to himself, was no moment for levity, and yet as they lay there, they talked quietly about their present situation and the possibility that they might, one day, get out of there, escape this hell called Russia, and resume their more mundane previous lives.

What was it Kenney had said? "I only want to get back to the states to vote for Bryan, because Bryan was right." That would be William Jennings Bryan, who had initially opposed entering the war, and after feuding with Woodrow Wilson had resigned as his secretary of state in June 1915.

Lt. Charles Ryan, of Company K, 339th U.S. Infantry Regiment, could only laugh. By the time he'd made it out of Kodish by the skin of his teeth he'd also had it with wars—especially this one.

"Our dispatches all seem to point to an early settlement on the Western Front," he wrote in a letter to a friend on November 6. "Don't know how it will affect us up here. This is only a side show but it has all the thrills and all the sad scenes that go to make up a larger one."

Charles Ryan would soon be moving back toward his old haunts, to the dim village of Kodish, with the aim once again of pushing on to Plesetskaya farther down the line. He was not thrilled.

"The dope is out," he wrote on December 23. "We are to make another advance. The same old stuff. We made it once, got chased back, and now we are to try it again. This winter campaign is going to be hard on the men."

Although Edmund Ironside had called a halt to forward movement in October, others in the British command were able to convince him that another push on Emtsa and Plesetskaya farther south was needed, as they believed the villages afforded a more secure base in which to spend winter than would Kodish.

The push was planned for late December 1918. By then, however, the Bolsheviks had already reinforced the ground between Kodish and Plesetskaya, and at the direction of Leon Trotsky, veteran troops from the south of Russia had been shipped north to bolster the Sixth Bolshevik Army.

Now, two platoons of Company K and two from Company E would be advancing toward the heart of that army. The force would also include one Canadian artillery section, a platoon from the Machine Gun Company, a trench mortar section, and a detachment of engineers, all of whom knew how to handle a rifle if need be.

Two platoons of Company L, meanwhile, were brought forward to the north bank of the Emtsa to hold the front. The companies of the Third Battalion then holding the railway front to the west, meanwhile, were to advance at the same time along the railway.

In front of Maj. Mike Donoghue's force across the Emtsa River were 2,700 Bolos plus a reserve force of 700 men and four artillery pieces.

Once again, it was an insane idea; once again, an Allied force of a few hundred men would go up against the Bolos with the odds stacked against them, but then, *orders is orders.*

Donoghue, for one, seemed optimistic. "Each unit caught a gleam of fire from the old Irishman's eye as he looked them over," Moore et al. wrote. Despite Charles Ryan's misgivings, they would add, Company K was eager to "square the November account."

The advance was set for midnight on December 29–30, and though his platoon was not to be in the fight, Ryan was told to take Lt. Alexander Batsner's First Platoon. Lt. Lewis Jahns, commanding Company K since the elevation of Donoghue, and Gilbert Shilson would join Ryan.

"I am the poor goat," Ryan would complain. "I am supposed to know the country, being the only officer who made the trip before."

Still, Ryan approved of the plan, noting the presence of French mortarmen, the machine gunners, and the artillery. "We are going at it right this trip," he would write.

Ryan would lead on the left. With typical optimism the offensive's planners expected him to "hit at Kodish, Avda, and Kochmas" on the first day, Ryan wrote. He noted that the railway force "will also hit at the same time, so we will get Plesetskaya this time."

Meanwhile, the platoons from Company E would cross at and near the bridge, and also at the church position one mile to the right. Donald Carey went to bed early on December 29, but he was roused at 10:30 P.M. and told to fall in.

"We were given a few instructions and informed that the enemy was 'a bunch of damned cowards' that would run at the first shot," Carey would write. "I hoped the officer knew more about it than I."

Unknown to Ryan and the others in the attacking force, the railway push was canceled at the last minute, and so would not be able to pressure the Bolo rear. Donoghue's hopes of taking Kodish, Avda, and Kochmas in a single day, meanwhile, would prove to be overambitious to a ludicrous degree. As Moore et al. would write wryly, "Only a matter of twenty miles of deep snow and hard fighting."

Nevertheless, the force set out from Mejovskayia at midnight. Carey, assigned to a Lewis gun squad, carried a heavy load of machine-gun ammunition on a bandolier. Like all of the attackers, he was also burdened by his heavy winter clothing, his Shackleton boots, his leather jerkin, a pack containing rations, a canteen, and a cartridge belt for his rifle, which thankfully was carried by another.

Before long, he was unburdened to a small degree when his bayonet slipped free, an occurrence that went unnoticed at first. When it was discovered, "I was quite chagrined to think of going into battle handicapped in this manner."

Reaching the Emtsa, the column of winter soldiers passed down the northern bank and onto the river, which was now coated thickly with a deep crust of snow. It then moved along the south bank, which lay shadowed from the moonlight by the dark, brooding trees.

The ice cracked underfoot but did not yield as they made the other side; the advance through the bitterly frigid, subzero night was made almost in silence—that is, until the men reached the other side and began moving toward Kodish. Approaching a line cut into the woods to mark a future road, Company E's men were ordered to form abreast of it and fire their weapons into the dark recess.

"Heretofore our expedition had been conducted with remarkable quiet . . . I have never been able to perceive the object of this revealing to the Bolos our impending attack," Carey would write.

The Bolos remained in line at Kodish as the column moved on, now treading through the fluffy, thick snow in the forest. At a farther point, the order was once more given to fire into the woods. Carey, already less a bayonet, fired twice, and then found his rifle was jammed. After removing the fire plate and cartridge spring, he watched disconsolately as they slipped from his fingers into the deep snow.

"It was most disheartening," he wrote. "After firing about ten shots at nothing in particular, I ceased to be an active participant in the battle."

Finally, the Bolo picket line was struck. A sharp crackling of rifle and machine-gun fire erupted. In that first burst, Company E's Pvt. Frank Mueller, from Marshfield, Wisconsin, was hit and killed instantly.

Meanwhile, a force of Company E men under Lt. Carl Berger forced the bridge and joined the drive toward Kodish, and another squad, under Sgt. Edward Masterson, crossed the Emtsa and attacked the church position to the far right and easily routed the Bolo defenders.

First Lt. John Baker steadied the line, encouraging the squads under Lts. Verne McClung and Austin Jeffers.

"When the bullets ceased to zip and whine, one could distinctly hear at considerable distance Lt. Baker's, 'Ready Jeff, ready Mac? Alright, F-o-r-w-a-r-d,' the 'alright' and first syllable of the last word being long drawn out and delivered with a rising inflection," Carey would remember.

Baker, he added, "made a splendid officer in battle, daring almost to recklessness, heedless of danger and visiting all parts of the line."

On the left, the two platoons of Company K lost one man killed during the approach through the deep woods and snow and early-morning gloom. "We pushed on toward Kodish, had a little fighting on the way," Charles Ryan would write. "They had M.G. in the town and put up quite a defense."

"By this time it was quite light, and as we hurried along we obtained fleeting glimpses of the enemies' defenses which though far from pretentious were better than anything we had on our side of the river," Carey wrote.

The Bolos had erected shelters from pine boughs for their outposts, and work was under way as well on a blockhouse being hewn from logs. Behind a thick breastwork made from ice, a machine gun stood ready to make mincemeat of the advancing Allies.

"The noise of pounding and chopping, and other activities that we had heard nightly while on guard were readily explained—Old John Bolo was endeavoring to make his position impregnable," Carey remembered.

The outskirts of Kodish were reached at noon, and the attackers formed a semicircle in the woods on the north and east sides of the village. Both companies poured fire into the town and met serious resistance.

"It was no mere skirmish," Carey wrote, "but a veritable battle in which rifle, machine gun, trench mortar, and the two pieces of artillery at headquarters were actively employed.

"From every available door and window they returned our fire with rifle and machine gun, but most of it passed harmlessly over our heads. Bullets whizzed, whined, and sang in varying intonations; some closely resembling the long drawn out, high pitched, nasal twang of a tightly drawn wire, and dumdums—steel bullets with soft copper tips satanically devised to flatten upon striking and make a large jagged wound—cracked with the explosive report of a small calibre [sic] rifle."

Men fell, among them Company E's Cpl. James Mylon, who before the war had been a coproprietor of the Mylon-Galvin automobile company and, unlike a good proportion of his fellow soldiers, had believed in his new mission.

"The weather is cold, but healthy to live in during the winter months," he had written home as the days on the Kodish front had shortened. "We are all eager for the end to come soon, but I am sure most all of us would rather remain here until order is restored in Russia than to go back and leave these poor people in such destitute circumstances as they are in the present time.

"We have had many exciting moments . . . but we have stood it all and are now getting used to it." James Mylon would linger until the next day, his hopes of seeing order restored in Russia unfulfilled.

Farther down the line, Carey would witness only two of Company E's men being wounded during the fight, which lasted an hour before the Bolos began retreating from the village in small groups. The Allied force was ordered to hold back until the Canadians had quit shelling the town, which Carey would describe as "a dirty, unkempt place," adding "its drinking water was odorous and vile."

Situated on high ground at the northeast corner of a large clearing that sloped away to the south and west, Kodish was valuable only in that it blocked the sole route south to Avda, Kochmas, and the important Bolo base at Plesetskaya.

After taking the village, the Allied force quickly ran into Bolo dugouts guarding the road south. Nevertheless, it attacked.

The attackers were forced to go to ground. Digging furiously with their fingers, they made snow caves in an open field. There they would remain with "no overcoats, no eats, and a way below zero," Ryan wrote. The deep snow and a few isolated willow stands were their only protection.

The losses through the day and into the evening were heavy, with Company K alone losing about thirty-five men to wounds. Sgt. Michael Kenney, who'd wanted to live long enough to vote for William Jennings Bryan, was killed that night, along with Company K's Sgt. Bernard Grewe, both slain while moving among their men.

Lt. Lewis Jahns and Gilbert Shilson also made the rounds, ducking as flares from both sides illuminated the battlefield. They met "nothing but looks of resolution from them," Jahns would write, "for if this little force of less than a hundred men gave way the whole American force would be routed from Kodish."

Donald Carey remained with his Lewis gun crew and found some respite from the battle in a house in which he found a dead Bolo. "His upturned, pale yellowish face was a gruesome spectacle," he wrote. Just outside lay another dead Bolo, "mute testimony that at least some of our fire was effective."

There was little safety from flying bullets either out there in the snow or in the town. The Bolos began shelling Kodish as the afternoon wore on, and one man, Company E's Cpl. George Geyman, was wounded by a bullet to the hand even though he was in the house in which Carey sought refuge.

More Company E men arrived wounded from the firing line. "I was standing beside the house when 'Banker' Burnham, the first of the wounded to arrive in the village, appeared," Carey wrote. "He had scarcely left in a droshky for Mejovskayia just as Geyman and Seidenstricker had earlier in the evening, when one or perhaps two others appeared.

"I am sure that among those whose arrival I witnessed there was

Shaw, the Indian and finally Everett Roe who was badly wounded in the arm and shoulder."

For young Donald Carey, the battle was "most exhausting." But, he would write, "I had experienced a thrill—an unmistakable element of fascination. To flirt with death was novel, and to be under fire in battle exhilarating."

Wryly, he would add, "To have possessed a serviceable rifle with which to fire at human targets would have made it even more so."

Carey and a dozen others milling about in Kodish were soon commandeered by Sgt. Andrew Untener and ordered to deliver ammunition to the front. Carey carried a heavy box of shells across the field and into a willow thicket, where he found Sgt. Howard Reynolds, who told him to go to the relief of the wounded.

He soon ran across a Lewis gun and several of his company mates, one of whom, Pvt. Walter Franklin, lay severely wounded in the back, "groaning in a slight hollow . . . I concluded that Franklin's wounds were mortal and had no heart to talk to him." Walter Franklin, in terrible pain, was removed from the battlefield but died the next day.

Carey also discovered Fred Kooyers, with whom he had guarded the front through those many cold, cold nights. Kooyers and four other members of the crew were squatting in the snow around the unconscious body of Lt. Carl Berger, who "had been struck in the mouth by a bullet almost immediately after having lighted a cigarette on the line."

Berger, a twenty-seven-year-old from Mayville, Wisconsin, had only recently written to his mother, Elizabeth, and told her, "I have no worries." He died on December 31, leaving a wife, Adele, and a son, Carl Jr., who had been born just two weeks before the 339th left for England.

Fred Kooyers and his squad remained on the line until 8:30 P.M., and then took refuge in a building in town. When one of the men lit a candle to illuminate the new surroundings, a spate of Bolo machine-gun fire quickly found them. "Before we could put the light out we had six men wounded," Kooyers wrote.

Subsequently ordered back to the front to retrieve some of the wounded, Kooyers and his coterie located a building being used as a hospital, where "we found the British medical men and doctor which we had been looking for some time laying around the hospital drunk."

Later, the firing on the line intensified and all were ordered to man it. Kooyers, crawling on hands and knees under heavy fire, reached the forward line at about eleven P.M.

"All that could be heard was medicalmen, medicalmen, groans from the wounded and sounds of the guns," he wrote. "It was then about fifty below zero . . . our line was then covered with dead, dying and wounded men."

"The same old stuff," Charles Ryan had written upon learning of the new advance on Kodish. And it was indeed. The intent had been to reach Avda, then Kochmas, in a single day's advance. The reality was that this drive, too, had stalled.

The Bolos had not been ready to push back in September, but now they were massing, recruiting, conscripting, and stubbornly refusing to comply with the Allied notions and ambitions.

In the snow around Kodish, the bodies of Americans lay quickly freezing, both wounded and dead. The dead soon froze into grotesque shapes, their limbs splayed like the branches of a gnarly old oak tree. Perhaps they were the lucky ones; the survivors still on the line, still burrowed in their snow caves, began to suffer frostbite to fingers and toes, and there was to be no escape from the fierce Bolo fire.

"It was a sorry business that fine American lads far from home and the land they loved should die in such a desolate God-forsaken place," Carey would add.

Company K would lose two sergeants—Grewe and Kenney—and PFC Alfred Fuller. Company E lost its first dead—Pvt. Frank Mueller and PFCs Floyd Austin and Harold Wagner. The company's Lt. Carl Berger died the next day, as did Cpl. James Mylon and Pvt. Walter Franklin.

"Mournful Kodish," Moore et al. would call it. The Americans would remain in and near that hell while their luckier brethren floated past the Statue of Liberty and toward their new lives through the rest of winter and into the spring and summer.

Tomorrow would be New Year's Eve 1918, but the new year hardly held out much hope for the men freezing and dying at Mournful Kodish.

CHAPTER TWENTY-ONE

K MEANS KODISH

In another life, he'd been a metalworker at the Fisher Body Company, Building Number 14. But when the draft, and duty, had called, thirty-year-old Bernard Grewe had left his family's comfortable home at 415 Philadelphia Avenue in Detroit and gone to Camp Custer, where he was assigned to Company K.

On December 30, 1918, now-sergeant Bernard Grewe was killed as he moved among his men in that open field just south of Kodish, Russia; he lay out on the field as the battle between American and Bolo raged into the night. His death, and that of other "steady and courageous and loyal pals" who had been through so much together, made Kodish "a place horrible, detested, and unnerving to the small detachment that held it," Company K's Lt. Jack Commons would write.

It was the same back in Detroit, where Theresa Grewe had mourned ever since receiving word of her only son's death. "Everything in the Philadelphia Avenue house reminded her of her son, and added to the poignancy of her grief," the *Detroit Free Press* would report the following November. Unable to stand it any longer, Theresa induced her husband, Frank, to sell the haunted home, which he would, relocating his wife and four daughters to a new house, not far from the Detroit River.

Back at Kodish on that last day of 1918, with the rest of the world at peace for the previous seven weeks, there was to be little movement. Col. G. Lucas, commander of the railway front, had seen no point in holding on, and recommended withdrawal; but the British high command overrode him, and told Maj. Mike Donoghue: "Hold what you have got and advance no further south; prepare defenses of Kodish."

But holding the line there would prove difficult. Newly energized, the Bolos probed the lines held by the frozen, shivering men of Companies E and K, who lay low under the constant fire of Bolo machine guns and exploding bits of shrapnel. Holding Kodish, Moore et al. would write, meant the men "were to be penalized for their very desperately won success."

At eight A.M., the Bolos charged up and over a bank in front of a part of the line held by a combined platoon of Company K and Company E men. After pausing to reorganize, the piercing, harrowing sound of a whistle was heard, and the Red line "came dashing forward at us to make a bayonet charge," Company E's Fred Kooyers wrote.

The Bolos, Kooyers would claim, were 450 in number, the Americans' force just thirty-five. Company K's Lt. Alexander Batsner, in charge of the combined force, steadied the men, yelling to them: "Give us hell, boys, or they will get every one of us!"

Lewis guns and rifles scythed through the Bolo line, while Headquarters Company's Pvt. Vincent Barone, manning the sole mortar the Americans had, spent much of the rest of the day sending hundreds of shells at the throng of Bolos. Barone then turned his attention to the Bolo machine guns at the edge of the field, silencing many of them before he fell with a bullet in a leg.

The Reds spread their attacks and probes all along the American line, and were repulsed by the fire from snow trenches and men firing from dugouts hastily scratched from the frozen earth under the houses in Kodish. Meanwhile, an artillery duel between the Canadians and Bolos stretched through that day and into the night.

Even as the artillery traded shot for shot, Gen. Edmund Ironside arrived at the Kodish front. Unhappy with Colonel Haselden's command at the Kodish front, he relieved him and replaced him with another Brit, a Colonel Pitts, a "boy colonel who was a lieutenant a few weeks ago," Ryan would write derisively.

Ironside would admit as much, writing that he had had to turn the Kodish front over to "the newly arrived C.O. of a battalion of The Liverpools, whose substantive rank was that of lieutenant."

Ironside spent New Year's Eve with Company E's Captain Heil in a newly erected blockhouse on the Emtsa River, and was happy to have some action. In the faint gloom of late afternoon, "there was a sudden challenge, and looking out of the embrasure in the blockhouse I saw some faint figures, moving in front of us as if they were floating in the air above the snow."

The Americans' machine guns opened up, while a mortar sent over half a dozen shells. After five minutes, Heil and Ironside and some of the men went out to check the damage and found six bodies, clad in white and wearing short skis, in the snow at the position's wire. All were already dead, and had quickly frozen stiff, silent evidence that the intense cold of the Russian winter could do as much damage to a man as bullets and bombs.

"This little attack," Ironside wrote, "showed me once more the strength of the defensive in a Russian winter."

By the next day, January 1, all were on edge as a counterattack by the Bolos seemed certain. Within Company E, a chorus of discontented grumbling arose, as the two days of fighting "under conditions for an unexplained cause for which they entertained not the slightest enthusiasm" caused some of the men to consider other options, the unit's PFC Donald Carey would recall.

A party of Company E men gathered in the early hours with the intent of retreating to the river line, with the expectation that those in the forward snow trenches would follow. Their plot was discovered and reported to Captain Heil, and he told them such a move would endanger the men on the front line.

Lacking a courageous leader, the would-be mutineers returned to their quarters, "and the contemplated retreat resulted in a complete fiasco," Carey wrote.

Meanwhile, out on the forward line the heavy losses incurred by the Bolos during their attacks had made them hesitant to counterattack again. Instead, they continued to trade shots with the Canadian battery of artillery, which answered them round for round. And over the next few days the Bolos sniped from the low hills surrounding Kodish as well, to no good effect.

Having tasted the devastating, desperate fire of the Americans, the Bolos were now unwilling to approach close enough to do any damage. Still, they tried: shots rang from the hills all day, only to putter into the snow short of their intended Allied targets.

While the battle had raged, engineers arrived at the Emtsa to clear both sides of timber and build new blockhouses along its north bank. On January 4, Company E was pulled out of Kodish and sent north to the river to aid in the cutting and construction.

They also went to work burying the Bolos who had been killed six days before. PFC Sam Gordon, Carey wrote, "created no little hilarity" as he shouldered the stiff-as-boards bodies of the fallen Reds and carried them toward their newly dug graves while singing "Glory, glory, hallelujah."

The withdrawal of Company E left Lt. Alexander Batsner with a force of just seventy-six men from Company K and eighteen machine gunners to hold Kodish. Hundreds of Bolos remained to their front, and when on the pitch-black night of January 5 patrols brought word back that the strong Red forces had been located on the Americans' flanks, Batsner became convinced that a large-scale attack on Kodish was imminent.

Batsner, Lt. Charles Ryan would write, had been given orders "to pull out and burn the town in case of an enveloping attack." Fearing the village would soon become a mausoleum for him and his command, Batsner indeed ordered the buildings in Kodish to be fired, and then retreated with his men to the Emtsa River line.

"No doubt K. Co. was super-susceptible to such fears, for their experiences in this region in the fall were of such a nature as to unnerve veterans," Carey would write in sympathy.

But Maj. Mike Donoghue was not pleased with Batsner's action, and ordered the lieutenant to return with his men to the burning village. "The officers refused to go the men are all in," Ryan, back at headquarters on the river, wrote. Donoghue sternly rebuked them, and wound up leading them back to Kodish himself.

There, they settled once more into a defense of the smoldering town, suffering now with little shelter from the twenty-below-zero temperatures. Surrounded by the charred remains of the village, and surrounded once more by a Bolo force that sought to annihilate them, "no one but they can ever know how they suffered," Moore et al. would write.

Major Mike returned to headquarters the next day, seeking further reinforcements from Company E. Both Carey and Fred Kooyers would write that the major was drunk, as was Company E's Captain Heil. Heil told Donoghue to take as many Company E men as he wanted. "He got nearly all of our company," Kooyers would write.

Donald Carey was one of them. He and about forty Company E men followed "the doughty old Major" back to Kodish, where he and about ten men were sent forward to occupy a half-enclosed barn to the left of the road to Avda, where they kept watch on the Bolos.

"On the edge of the forest fully a half or three-quarters of a mile in front and slightly to the right of us we could see a Red guard walking his post," Carey would write. "We did nothing to disturb him; for no one desired to stir up that yellow jacket's nest in the forest west of us."

Companies K and E rotated men in and out of the destroyed village over the next few days. "We have two outposts and keep the patrols going," Ryan would write. But on January 9, Colonel Pitts ordered Company K to move up and take over Kodish—and stay there.

The order, and its reaction, revealed the strained relations between the Americans and their British overseers. "This is a farce," Ryan would write. "There is no more Kodish. We will have to build shelters for the men."

He would add: "I am afraid that there will be trouble with the company. This is spite work on the part of the British, who want to discipline 'K' after the mutiny of the other night. The major has nothing to say, an American major is like the 5th wheel to the wagon, the orders are made up in Seletskoe and he has no voice in them."

Company K's occupation of Kodish didn't last long, however. On January 13, it was finally relieved by a force of King's Liverpools and half a company from the so-called Dyer's battalion, which consisted of former Russian prisoners who had enlisted in the S.B.A.L. and had been led by Lt. Royce Dyer, a Canadian veteran, shortly after the landing at Archangel in August.

Some of the men were inmates from the prisons in Archangel who had been freed by the retreating Bolos the previous August. "No records of these men existed, and very naturally, when they were interrogated, they denied having committed any crime," Edmund Ironside wrote.

About three hundred of these men served under Dyer, who, Ironside would claim, had been very successful in "separating the goats from the sheep" and who had died while leading them in battle soon after the battalion's formation.

Moore et al. were not as admiring of Dyer's men, calling the battalion "an uncertain lot of change-of-heart Bolshevik prisoners and deserters and accused spies and so forth." Others were young street urchins who had enlisted for a uniform, tobacco, and three squares a day. The veteran regular Dyer, though, had done his best to make soldiers of them.

Major Mike remained to command this motley bunch of veterans, cynical Brits and questionable Russians, all of whom occupied Kodish until late January with little incident. In early February, however, orders once more came to retake the ground south of Kodish as a "defensive thrust" at the Bolos, who were causing trouble to the northeast at Shred Makharenga.

Major Mike had at his disposal the Liverpools and S.B.A.L.s, a section of trench mortars, the Canadian artillery, a new platoon of machine gunners, the company of Royal Marines who had fought at Kodish in the fall, and a detachment of coureurs de Bois, Russian Whites who had been trained by the French.

The main force attacked on February 7, and easily passed through the village while the company of Whites marched fourteen miles through the woods and captured the Bolo artillery in the rear, which they then turned on the enemy reserves in Avda. When those same reserves counter-attacked, the coureurs de Bois spiked the guns and took off to the north.

However, the Reds once again couldn't be budged from their position at Verst 12, where the late-December attack had also stalled south of Kodish. After a second attack on the Bolo position failed, the Liverpools abandoned the line and, unknown to either Major Mike or the machine gunners, headed for the river line.

"Brave, energetic, cheerful" Lt. Clifford Ballard of Cambridge, Massachusetts, shortly afterward took a squad of Russian gunners and a Lewis gun up to the line, thinking the Brits were still in action there. But he walked straight into the hole from which the Liverpools had retreated, and he and all but one of the Russians under him were killed.

The survivor "returned with his gun and dropped among the Amerikanski machine gunners, telling of the death of Ballard and the Russian soldiers at the point of the Bolshevik bayonets," Moore et al. wrote.

The body of Ballard, a thirty-year-old graduate of Amherst College and the eighth, and last, American to be killed during the winter offensive on Kodish, was never found. "Hope that he might have been taken as a wounded prisoner by the Reds still lived in the hearts of his comrades," Moore et al. would write in their 1920 book.

Later that year Miss Florence Snow, his fiancée, would travel to Detroit to meet the ships carrying the survivors of the Russian expedition. Those men, Moore et al. would write, "vainly wished to believe with the girl who piteously scanned every group that landed, that Ballard might yet be heard from as a prisoner in Russia."

Bowing to reason, however, they would add: "No doubt he was killed."

Red reserves coming from Avda finally tilted the day's battle against the Allied force, and Donoghue ordered a retreat at five P.M. Now, all manned the river line and waited for the expected Bolo counterattack, which arrived two days later.

The Reds attacked all along the front and managed to destroy one blockhouse manned by seven Liverpools, all of whom died after their ammunition was used up and they had to fight bayonet to bayonet. The trench mortar section and the machine gunners, hoping to avenge Ballard, did such deadly work on the Bolos that the Russians withdrew.

For all intents and purposes, the last-gasp Bolo attack marked the end of the action on the Kodish front. The Reds had Kodish, now just a burned-out shell. They also had Plesetskaya, long the object of the Allies' desires. Just a few months before, taking the village had been considered as just the first step in a race for Vologda; now it would remain but a dream, a mirage, an altar of sacrifice for many an American who died in the frozen, snow-choked woods around Kodish.

For the men of Company K, the K would forever stand for "Kodish," the unit's Lt. Jack Commons would write:

"There they had their first fight, there their dead were buried. There they had had their last battle. And there their memories will long return, mostly disagreeable to be sure, but still representing very definitely their part, performed with honesty, courage and distinction, in the big work that was given the Yankee doughboys to do 'on the other side.'"

CHAPTER TWENTY-TWO

THE SAD CASE OF
SERGEANT YOUNG

Ugh-chee-chy! Ugh-chee-chy!"

Powered by sturdy Russian ponies and the guttural chirp of their Russian handlers, the sleds flew over the snow and away from Smolny barracks and, finally, Archangel itself, following the wide, frozen Dvina River and headed for the new mysteries of the Pinega River Valley, one hundred miles to the east-northeast.

And aboard was Joel Roscoe Moore, late of Butte High School in Montana and the railroad front, now in command of two platoons of Company M as it pushed through the icy, almost crystallized air and short daylight of December, the sun barely hugging the southern horizon even at noon and then disappearing altogether by early afternoon, leaving the droshky drivers to navigate by the dim white of the deep, deep snow.

"A treat to our boys to see rolling, cleared country," Moore would write. "Fish towns and lumber town on the right. Hay stacks and fields on the left, backed by forests. Here the trail is bareswept by the wind from across the river . . .

"Tiny specks out on the ice below and distant are interpreted to be sledges bound for some river port. Nets are exposed to the air and wait now for June suns to move out the fetters of ice. Decent looking houses and people now face the strange cavalcade as it passes village after village. It is a new aspect of Russia to the Americans who for many weeks have been in the woods along the Vologda railroad."

The first night out, on December 18, 1918, the sixty-sled convoy, with one platoon marching ahead and one behind, stopped in one of those villages. "Halting," Moore wrote, "is a wonderful performance. The headman—*starosta*—must be hunted up to quarter officers and men. He is not sure about the drivers. Perhaps he fears for the neat haystacks in his yard.

"We cannot wait. In we go, and Buffalo Bill's men never had anything on these Russki drivers. But it all works out, *Slavo Bogga* [Thank God] for army sergeants. American soldiers are quick to pull things through anyway. Without friction we get all in order . . . Our lowly hosts treat us royally. Tea from the samovar steams us a welcome. It is clean homes, mostly, soldiers find themselves in—clean clothing, clean floors, oil lamps, pictures on the walls."

Joel Roscoe Moore had almost led Butte High to a state football championship in swirling snows; now he led soldiers as if they were players, *his* players, keeping the morale of all cheery through the travails of battle and cold monotony on the railroad front.

And he did the same hard work here, miles and miles to the north of Obozerskaya and Verst 445, as Company M raced to the aid of their brethren of Company G, who were being increasingly besieged by a Bolshevik force that had realized that the Allies had no intention of a large-scale invasion, but foolishly were parceling their men in dribs and drabs to far-flung outposts, most at least one hundred miles from the relative safety of Archangel, where each faced larger and larger numbers of the enemy.

The Bolshevik Northern Army had been busy recruiting, offering food, shiny new uniforms, and money, and stirring stories of how the Allies had been whipped across the Archangel District during the fall. They conscripted when necessary, as well, dragging men from their villages and into the Red Army and, in the Pinega area, sparking a refugee tide of anti-Bolsheviks who fled their remote homes and sought safety with the Americans and White Guards in Pinega.

In the Pinega River Valley, the local Bolo commander had also employed the now-frozen river and forest trails to haul bigger guns toward the main village of Pinega; five pieces of artillery, two 75 mm guns, and three "pom-pom" guns, all plundered from Archangel by the retreating Reds, had been retrieved from upriver at Kotlas and would soon "jolt" the men of Companies M and G in coming battles.

And the Bolos at Pinega were well led. One prominent commander who had fought Company M at the railroad front, Smelkoff, had gone north to assist a "rising young local commander" named Kulikoff. "These two ambitious soldiers of fortune had both been natives and bad actors of the Pinega Valley, one being a noted horse thief of the old Czar's days," Moore noted.

Since their battle at Karpogora in early December, Company G had remained in their refuge of Pinega. There, Pvt. John Toornman witnessed the execution of a loyal Russian officer who had been accused of cowardice after failing to show up at an assigned rendezvous for a pincers movement on a Bolo force.

Company G's commander, Capt. John Conway, had the man imprisoned, but then went to visit him. After talking for a time, Conway stood up to leave, and left his pistol on the table. The Russian either didn't or couldn't take the hint to shoot himself, so Conway took matters into his own hands and had him shot. On the day of execution, the officer was brought to the river, and lined up in front of a newly dug grave.

A row of Russian soldiers was placed in line, while Company G set up machine guns behind them. "More than one of them looked back, wondering what we were going to do behind them," Toornman recalled.

"Someone up front read Russian from a paper. The officer was blindfolded, but he pulled it off and threw it on the ground. Then he crossed himself." The Russians fired, and the condemned man went down "like his legs were putty," Toornman added.

Then, one of the soldiers removed the dead officer's boots, and he was roughly thrown into his grave.

To Toornman, Conway's cold actions were par for the course. All of his officers, Conway included, "forgot all about the Democracy we were fighting for," he would say. Even the sergeants, he added, "would sit and eat together, and have better food than the men."

In fact, Conway was nervous about his situation in Pinega, and had appealed to the high command in Archangel for reinforcements for his two platoons of Company G and the three hundred Whites he commanded. To that end, Company M, which had spent much of the fall rotating on and off duty at the railway front, was ordered to send two platoons to Pinega. With them would be a group of newly trained loyal Russian officers, whose mission would be to recruit and train conscripts in the Pinega area.

Their orders spelled out a twofold mission: to reinforce the men of Company G, and at the same time raise a regiment of loyal Russians from the valley, in which roughly half the residents were Bolo sympathizers. The Americans were told to walk tall and proud among the Russian populace, display a proud military bearing, and through those means relieve the anxieties of the loyalists.

It was a long, hard, cold slog from Archangel to Pinega. Company M's men slipped in their slick-soled and increasingly useless Shackleton boots, and at times only narrowly avoided being run down by ponies and the heavily laden sleds. And there was the biting, sapping, crippling cold unlike any felt even in northern Michigan or Wisconsin. Frostbite under such conditions was a common threat, especially to one's extremities, and the exertions of slogging through the deep, wind-driven snows that drifted over the trails caused men to sweat, and raised the specter of hypothermia when and if that sweat froze.

The men quartered with villagers as they traveled, and were alternately fascinated and repulsed by their experiences. "Five of us stayed all night with a Russian peasant family," twenty-one-year-old Pvt. Frank Sapp would write of his first night on the march. "The house was neat and clean. The people use fish oil soap and eat so many fish, they smell fishy."

The next night, Sapp stayed with another family in another town. "We bought fresh cow's milk at three roubles [*sic*] a pint," he wrote. "I went to a Russian dance that night the hours I was off guard. They dance the same as we do at home. Had accordian [*sic*] music. The girls refused flatly to dance with men who were drunk."

Christmas Day marked the eighth day of their journey, and still they continued. On the tenth day, Moore stopped at a telegraph station in the village of Yural and called ahead to Pinega. There, he learned that the Bolos had that day defeated a force of one hundred Whites at Viskagora, thirty-five miles south of Pinega.

The Whites had fought until their ammunition was depleted, then followed their leader, a Pole named Mozalevski, into the forests. Reaching the village of Peligorskaya, they reorganized and came under the command of a new leader, a Russian named Akutin, and each newly reorganized unit adopted the name of its native village.

The two platoons of Company M reached Pinega on December 27. It was then that Moore learned the situation. Downriver, at the villages of Leunova, Ostrov, and Kuzomen, the populace was "scowlingly pro-Bolshevik," he would write. One of the Red commanders, Kulikoff, hailed from Kuzomen and was constantly in communication with the Bolsheviks there.

His intent was to wait for the forest trails between Archangel and Pinega to freeze more solidly, and then cut the line behind the Allies, trapping them at Pinega. The Americans and their Russian allies would struggle through much of the winter to keep those lines of communication open even as they attempted to raise a new, loyal army.

"This as an intense little civil war," Moore would write. "No mercy and no quarter. The Reds inflamed their volunteers and conscripts against the invading Americans and the Whites. The White Guards gritted their teeth at the looting Reds and proudly accepted their new commander's motto: White Guards for the front; Americans for the city and the lines of communication."

Worried about those lines of communication, Moore sent a force under Lt. George Stoner forward to the area around Soyala, twelve miles southeast of Pinega, to guard and patrol. Then, on January 8, a White force, with the Americans in support, attacked the Bolo works at Ust Pocha, farther up the river. The villages of Priluka and Pochazero, just to the northwest of Ust Pocha, were taken, but the Whites suffered heavy losses before the Bolo works at the latter.

Shortly afterward, on January 14, the balance of Company M, two platoons under Lts. Clarence Primm and James Donovan, reached Pinega after a forced march of 135 miles in temperatures that reached forty below zero on three days, hastening to reach their comrades after being told "the other half of 'M' Company was in imminent danger of extermination," Moore wrote.

They were at least in danger. Counterattacking, the Reds nearly carried Stoner's contingent at Soyala on January 24, but were finally beaten off. On January 28, Moore, Stoner, and Primm led two platoons to the front at Ust Pocha to act as a rear guard for a preemptive attack of seven hundred Whites on the village.

The Reds fought them off, and in fact pushed the entire force north to Peligora, which had been fortified with wire, blockhouses, and trenches for an anticipated "last stand" before Pinega. The fighting went on for another six days until, unexpectedly, the Bolos retreated, burning the village of Priluka as they left.

"From Pinega we looked at the faint smoke column across the forest deep with snow and breathed easier than we had for many anxious weeks," Moore wrote. Allied pursuers found the Bolos holed up back at their base at Trufanagora, and on their return brought in forty sleds of supplies the Reds had left in scattered villages.

The retreat of the Bolos disappointed their Bolshevist sympathizers in Pinega and downriver, but for the anti-Bolshevists the weeks of drama had proven to be a boon to recruiting. Helped by a decree ordering conscription for all men aged eighteen to forty-five, the White force in the Pinega region would swell to more than two thousand men by March, and would include an eight-man machine-gun squad and artillery unit.

With the Bolo threat removed, the village square at Pinega "resounded daily to the Russki recruit sergeant's commands and American platoons drilling, too," Moore wrote.

Ever the enthusiastic instructor and coach, Moore was proud not only of his men's fighting ability but of their demeanor while dealing with the locals in the Pinega River Valley. Moore would credit the "faithful representation of American ideas of manhood and square deal and democratic courtesy" with helping them gain the support of the local peasantry—who in turn went from being a worried populace "to a confident, cheerful one."

During Company M's nine weeks at Pinega, not a single American had been killed, or even wounded. Meanwhile, after being dispirited by their rout at Viskagora on December 27, the White soldiers had gained their confidence back. Hard, resolute, and disciplined, the Americans had shown the Russians how to be soldiers, and instilled in them the desire to take command of their own fates.

"Those Russian soldiers made good," Moore wrote. "They wanted to be in the front and did not want the Americans to fight their battles for them."

Company M began pulling out of Pinega in early March, heading back to Archangel. But the balance of Company G remained. John Toornman's squad was sent eighteen miles downriver to Gbach to maintain a vital telephone line to Archangel, which the Bolos repeatedly cut.

The men occupied the top floor of a home in town, while the family of six lived on the first floor. His two months there were the best he spent in the army.

"There were no officers around, but we all had a certain job to do," he recalled. "One had to be at the telephone day and night. Two of us plus the Russian guide had to go out every day on patrol which took all day while it was daylight . . . We had a chance to see and to learn how those people, shut off from the world, really lived."

Toward the end of Toornman's duty at Gbach, he learned more of the local ways when two of Company G's sergeants—Edward Young and Michael Macalla—stopped over on the night of March 14 while on a reconnoitering mission.

Young—"my pal and bunkmate, a university man, a prince of a fellow," Macalla would say—had taken a bullet in his jaw in the December 4 fight at Karpogora, and the wound had never properly healed; now, traveling by snowshoe through the bitter Arctic cold had made him "morose and uncommunicative" by the time he and Macalla found shelter with Toornman's squad.

Despite Young's obvious discomfort, all seemed normal enough as the men headed for their beds. But as they lay sleeping, the calm was pierced by the sound of a pistol shot that rang out downstairs in the log home that served as the squad's quarters. Jumping from their beds, Toornman, Macalla, and the others quickly found the long-suffering Young dead from a self-inflicted bullet to his brain.

Toornman helped Macalla carry his dead friend's body to a sleigh, and a medical officer arrived the next day to hold an inquest. After ruling Young's death a suicide, he ordered Macalla to take Young's lifeless body back to Archangel—alone.

"[He] was my buddy," Macalla would say. "We had been together almost every day since I met him when they organized Company G in Camp Custer. The night before we left for the war we went down to Battle Creek and he blew his last dime buying a feed for the both of us.

"And now they were giving him to me dead, a bandage around his head, not even a coffin, but wrapped loosely in blankets."

Macalla drove off with his dead friend at his side, while the women of the house began furiously waving brooms and rags at the ceiling and blood-spattered walls. "The best I could make out is that they were getting the bad spirit or ghost out of the house," Toornman would say.

Macalla made about twenty miles the first day, and stopped in a small village where he was welcomed into a home. Before retiring for the night, the elderly grandmother brought the family's two little girls to Macalla, patted him on the head, and told them he was a "grand Americanski."

But the next morning another villager found Young's body in the sleigh, and in a moment "it was all different," Macalla said. "The whole village, including my host and his family, seemed in deadly fear of me."

Word of Macalla's macabre load spread down the Pinega, and terrified villagers mostly spurned him. On the second night, it was only with difficulty that he found a place to sleep, and on the third day he stumbled across a funeral.

"I thought that at last I would find a place where death was not so terrifying to the whole population," Macalla recalled. "But, when the word went through the town that an American was riding . . . in a sleigh, carrying another soldier who was dead, the same crazy fear seemed to run like wildfire through the village."

Macalla wound up sleeping in the building used for the funeral, and slept next to the "rough bier" that held the dead Russian. On the fourth day, he ran out of villages, and stopped on the river bank. He spent that long, dark night wrapped up in his blankets and those of the dead Sergeant Young, nearly freezing and all alone in the surreal and unfriendly dark wastes of northern Russia.

"I guess I was a little out of my head, too, for I talked to Young as if he were alive, and told him I was going to take his blankets because I had to have them and they couldn't do him any good anyway," Macalla said.

Finally, on the fifth day he reached the larger town of Kholmogory, just forty miles from Archangel. There, he found an American military policeman in a monastery that had been converted into a barracks, and he helped Macalla carry Young's body into a dining hall before directing Macalla to sleep there as well. Whether because of the cold or the presence of his dead friend's body, "there I slept one of the coldest sleeps of my life."

Given a fresh pony, Macalla and Young made it to Archangel the following day. Edward Young was then laid to rest in a section of a cemetery that had been devoted to American troops. By the following November, Sgt. Edward Young, Company G, 339th U.S. Infantry Regiment, was back home in Moosic, Pennsylvania; on November 17, 1919, he was once more laid to rest, this time at Langcliffe Cemetery in nearby Avoca.

"Full military honors, including a rifle salute and soldier escort, were given to the dead hero," the Wilkes-Barre paper would report, the writer unaware that the suffering Young had endured far, far away in the bitter wastes of northern Russia had led him to take his own life.

CHAPTER TWENTY-THREE

THE DEVIL COMES TO NIJNI GORA

Hugh McPhail would always be glad of at least one thing until his death at the age of seventy-three in 1968: fifty years before it had been Harry Mead, and not he, who had been ordered to bring his platoon to Nijni Gora on January 18, 1919.

"This I have always been thankful for," McPhail would say years later, long after the dawn had exploded early on the following day, shells plummeting from a dark, overcast sky that harbored a slim smudge of pink to the east.

The day brought grayish forms, hundreds of them, barely discernible through the gloom and coming on steadily down the wide, white, frozen highway of the Vaga River. It brought the shrieks of horses, men yelling, panic, temperatures of sixty below and the contrasting heat of villagers' smashed-in homes burning; it brought a disaster, months in the making and now descending, a disaster that would leave many Americans dead and dying, and turn Harry Mead's hair white almost overnight.

The day brought a disaster that was almost foreordained by their very circumstance, by the British high command's decision to push small bodies of troops hither and yon, miles from any safety or possible relief; it was the result of a question that would go unanswered, and which was perhaps best posed by Dorothea York, that question being "why it was necessary to maroon small detachments in precarious outposts which lay in the midst of hordes of the enemy about two hundred or more miles from the port of Archangel."

Since being relieved by Company C and leaving the upper Vaga River in early November, Company A had gone into quarters at Shenkursk and lived, for once, some semblance of a normal life. The men's barracks bags had arrived, and with them a store of tobacco. All assumed they would simply wait out the long Russian winter; all assumed the Bolos would as well.

Armistice Day passed unnoticed, but when word of the ending of hostilities on the Western Front reached them in mid-November, the men reacted with a cynicism born of their plight, men passing each other with a wink and a nod and sardonically exclaiming, "Congratulations on the end of the war!"

Thanksgiving brought a few fresh eggs and chickens and cranberry sauce for the enlisted men, and a party at the American hospital featuring vaudeville performances and a weak local beer known as *pevo*. By then the temperatures already stood at thirteen below zero, and an almost constant drizzle of snow had blanketed the town and surrounding forests in deep drifts. There was a coziness now to the place, which at moments resembled the serene interior of a shaken snow globe.

But Company A's strange, strange war beckoned once more, as in early December its four platoons were dispatched upriver to the area of Ust Padenga and the relief of Company C. The men once more took up the defenses: the farthest outposts at Nijni Gora and Ust Padenga on the west bank of the Vaga, and the main line of defense at Visorka Gora, seventeen hundred yards north of Nijni Gora and one thousand yards north of Ust Padenga.

Two blockhouses guarded the approach from the south at Nijni Gora. A trench line and a string of dugouts had also been chiseled into the permafrost on the southern edge of the village. Six blockhouses also lined the approach to Visorka Gora from the east and west, while a still-flowing stream on the southern edge of the village offered some protection from advancing infantry. It was here that two pieces of Canadian artillery, eighteen pounders, were also placed on a bluff above the creek. In addition to the Canadian guns, the defense offered one Russian one-pound gun and a pom-pom.

The Bolos held the ground directly south of Nijni Gora and were headquartered in the village of Pagosta, just several hundred yards from the Americans. The village was dominated by a three-domed cathedral used for observations as well as prayer, and its odd spires served as a reminder to the Americans standing lookout that while the wood-lined river might remind them of northern Michigan, they were in fact unwanted strangers in a strange land.

Within those Bolo lines the Red Northern Army had been gathering numbers, right under the noses of the Americans. By Christmas 1918 the northern Bolos had amassed 3,100 men, and were plotting a grand winter offensive on the area of Ust Padenga, where some 400 Allies—264 Americans, a company of Cossacks, and the Canadian gunners—stood and stamped their feet while on watch in the deepening cold, peering upriver for any sign of a Bolo threat.

And there were signs that something might be brewing out there in the far woods beyond the Vaga. The Bolos began staging brazen night patrols and advancing in their white smocks to within ten feet of the American outposts. As well, the Bolo artillery became more active, lobbing salvos toward Nijni Gora with greater and greater frequency.

Christmas came and went; on December 27, Col. George Stewart made his only visit to the area, and pronounced himself pleased with the troops and the defenses. Three weeks later—on January 18, 1919—Gen. Edmund Ironside made the same trip, arriving at Ust Padenga with the British lieutenant colonel C. A. L. Graham, who pinned a Military Cross on Company A's Capt. Otto Odjard.

Odjard subsequently took them on a tour of the outposts at Nijni Gora. Odjard told Ironside that he didn't think a Bolo attack was imminent, and in any case he was confident in the defenses.

Ironside then occupied a forward trench and looked south across the Vaga River, frozen white and stiff and windswept in the grayish, early-winter half-light, and tried his best to read the enemy's mind. He soon enough had a pretty good idea of what might ensue.

"I could see how easily they could launch a surprise attack against us, without giving much notice of their intention," Ironside wrote. He had faith that such an attack would fail if made upon the blockhouses and trenches that lined the southern front, but worried that enveloping attacks on the flanks could bring disaster.

His orders had been to hold the line across the various fronts while an army of Russians was being recruited, conscripted, and trained to eventually take over for the Allies. At Ust Padenga, he could only hope that the Bolos either would not attack before spring or, if they did, that their assault would fall on the fortified main line. But Ironside understood that the far-flung post would have to be immediately abandoned "should any kind of an enveloping movement show itself."

After visiting Odjard, Ironside and Graham left for Shenkursk; they would miss by mere hours the tragic, almost foretold climax of the strategy put in place by the British high command and zealously pursued by the long-departed general Frederick Poole.

Ironside and Graham, it would soon turn out, were lucky, very lucky indeed.

Not as lucky was twenty-nine-year-old Harry Mead, who relieved Hugh McPhail's Second Platoon that same January 18 with his Fourth and took up the defenses of Nijni Gora, as he and his men had done many times before. He had just forty-five men under him, and these he set to the routine of manning the posts and patrolling.

Nothing particular on the night of January 18–19 had pointed to an imminent assault on Company A's position. Still, the Cossacks had sensed something and had refused to man Nijni Gora, complaining that the position was too isolated and would be a death trap should the Bolos attack. The Cossacks instead occupied Ust Padenga, seven hundred yards to the north.

Harry Mead and his men would soon enough discover whether the Cossacks' concerns were valid. At 6:30 A.M. on January 19, 1919, Bolo shells began dropping, enveloping Nijni Gora, Ust Padenga, and Visorka Gora, killing or mortally wounding several men.

They were the opening salvos of an offensive aimed at rolling up the Allied southern defenses and then destroying the Shenkursk garrison; the Bolo commander, Alexander Samoilo, would commit 1,300 of his 3,100 troops, six big guns, and twenty-one machine guns specifically for the assault on the small garrisons.

Among the first to die was the weary Supply Company wagoner Carl Berger, who had just arrived from Shenkursk with an ambulance and gladly taken a seat that was offered to him in Lt. Ralph Powers's log billet in Visorka Gora. Berger had hardly sat down when a Bolo three-inch shell smashed through one of the walls and decapitated him.

His billet ruined, Powers raced through the continuing barrage to Hugh McPhail's headquarters across the road. That shelter also was soon battered into splinters, so McPhail moved on to the sergeants' quarters. When Powers followed him, McPhail worried the medical officer might be bad luck, and told himself, "This place is next." He took off for the dubious safety of a forward dugout.

Harry Mead was in bed when the first shell sailed right over his headquarters. He quickly dressed and ran to the forward position on the southern edge of Nijni Gora, which was manned by twenty men. He ordered one of the sergeants to take the balance—twenty-five men—and take up a position just north of the village to cover a retreat, should one become necessary.

The Bolo artillery shelled all three villages for the next half hour, then turned its attention solely to the dugouts at Nijni Gora. As the men lay low inside, they could discern a battle line of several hundred Bolos some eight hundred yards distant. They were coming on strong.

"They were too far to do much harm so we merely opened up on them in the intermittent bursts of machine gun fire," Mead would recall.

Suddenly, a sentry raced in from his outpost one hundred feet to the front and frantically reported that the ravine ahead of him was full of Bolos.

Just then, "there arose from the snow on three sides of the town swarm upon swarm of enemy troops clad in white," Mead recalled. "I at once realized that our position was hopeless." Mead telephoned Otto Odjard back at Visorka Gora and told him he and his men were going to have to withdraw, and would need artillery cover.

Odjard was already getting the balance of Company A ready for an impending attack, "but Lt. Mead's message made the impending crisis still clearer," York would write.

Odjard faced two major problems, however. The first was how he could cover the men who would soon be racing for their lives from Nijni Gora; the second was how he was going to defend his own position from an eventual, and certain, infantry assault.

Leaping to action, Odjard ordered one piece of Canadian artillery positioned to cover the road south to Nijni Gora, and had the other swung around and sited on the woods on the western flank. He also disposed skirmishers to the west, or right, and phoned the commander of the Cossack detachment in Ust Padenga and told him to send a platoon to the aid of Harry Mead and his men at Nijni Gora.

Odjard also made it imperative to the Russian captain that Ust Padenga, which had not yet been attacked by Bolo infantry, be held until he received orders to retreat. Meanwhile, the battle at Nijni Gora raged on.

"All this time of course we were sweeping the enemy line with machine gun and rifle fire," Mead would relate. "As soon as one wave of the enemy was halted on one flank another was pressing in on us from the other side. We held on as long as possible but the handful of men under me were being wounded right and left."

One of Mead's most trusted men, Pvt. Victor Stier, was shot in the jaw while manning a captured Bolo machine gun. "He did not leave his gun but coolly asked what he should do," Mead would say. "I shouted at him to dismantle his gun and get back to our rear position if possible."

Stier departed, but was still in the fight. He picked up a discarded rifle and joined the men from the platoon that had taken up the rear position at the north end of the village. Mead and his men were now nearly surrounded, and the Bolos were advancing on them with fixed bayonets. There was nothing those most forward—the survivors, anyway—could do but try to fight their way through the Bolos and reach Visorka Gora.

They withdrew in order, wading through hip-deep snow and fighting their way from house to house, "each new dash leaving more of our comrades lying in the cold and snow, never to be seen again," Mead recalled. "How the miserable few did succeed in eventually rejoining their comrades no one will ever know."

Mead himself only barely made it. Dashing behind a log home at one point to reload his pistol, he hesitated briefly before stepping out to the street. That slight tic saved his life—"because just then a Russian, who looked to be at least 10 feet tall, lunged with his bayonet and missed me by an inch," Mead would say. "I emptied my pistol into him and continued running."

Pursued by hundreds of Bolos, the survivors held on to the crest of the hill at the rear of Nijni Gora for as long as they could in the hope that the artillery could blast the village—and the screaming, yelling swarm of Bolos.

Mead would remember one man, Cpl. Giuseppe DeAmicus, racing to a point in the line that commanded a good view into the village, and moving right into the maw of the advancing Bolos. He put his Lewis gun to good use until being killed. Sgt. Thomas Kernan, thinking DeAmicus was only wounded, went to his aid.

"While he stooped over the fearless Italian veteran who was quite dead, Sgt. Kernan himself was badly wounded but still went on directing the fire of his men," Mead wrote.

The hoped-for shelling of Nijni Gora was delayed. The Canadian artillerists had been relieved just a few days before by Russians, and these deserted the guns—"something that no Canadian would ever have done in such a situation," Mead wrote. The Cossacks sent from

Ust Padenga to attack the Bolo flank had also done little good, as they fell into "wild disorder" as soon as their leader was killed.

Odjard collected the Russian gunners and drove them back to their pieces at the point of his pistol, but precious time had been lost. Pursued by Bolos, Mead and the remnant of his platoon had little choice but to retreat down the bare north side of the hill, and then cross an open plain of eight hundred yards that was covered with heavy snow.

All this, while under the direct observation and fire of the enemy.

The men, desperate, set out, floundering north. One by one, men fell wounded or stone dead into the drifts, which in the fifty-below-zero temperatures soon became icy, temporary coffins. The luckier ones waded on, and after a prolonged struggle Mead and the pitiful remnant of his platoon finally made it through to the headquarters at Visorka Gora. Of the forty-seven men who'd manned the defenses at Nijni Gora, just seven made it to the rear unscathed.

While they raced for their lives, Hugh McPhail was scanning the battlefield with his field glasses. Focusing on the site of the platoon's last stand on the brow of the hill north of Nijni Gora, he saw an arm waving feebly, and told Odjard about it. "Let me take your little black horse and a good tough sergeant and I will go out and rescue this lad," he told Odjard.

McPhail and Sgt. Tom Rapp left Visorka Gora with a sled and made it to the brow of the hill. There, he found two dead Americans, a wounded Russian gunner, and Victor Stier, who had been wounded again while defending the hill.

McPhail wrapped his overcoat around the Russian and then lifted Stier and got him moving to the sled, the effort forcing bubbles of air and blood from Stier's mouth. They made it back to Visorka Gora, but Stier died of his wounds later that day.

"Harry Mead always thought a lot of Victor's action in Nijni Gora," McPhail would say. "He said Victor tried to stop the 3,000 Bolos all by himself and his machine gun." Stier would be awarded a posthumous DSC for his brave actions on that terrible day.

The battle was far from over. Through that day, the Bolos hammered away at Visorka Gora, where men crowded into dugouts and watched anxiously for the Bolo attack that would surely come. That night, the Cossacks in Ust Padenga slipped out, and made it to headquarters with the Bolos none the wiser.

The tally of dead, wounded, and missing in the Fourth Platoon at the end of January 19 was staggering—and would come to be even more so as the days and years passed.

While only six men were known to have died by the end of that day, two more would succumb to their wounds in the coming days. Another seventeen of Company A's men who were caught in the death trap of Nijni Gora would be listed as missing until their remains were located in 1929. In all, twenty-five of the company's men died in action or from wounds suffered on January 19, 1919.

There was, however, one small silver lining.

Two men—Cpl. James Burbridge and Pvt. Peter Wierenga—had been left behind in Nijni Gora when the Fourth Platoon began its hasty withdrawal, and now faced the swarm of Bolo fighters by themselves. Quickly deciding it was time to get out, the two began moving, house by house, to the rear.

At one home, an elderly woman took pity on them and hid them in a closet, where they waited with their weapons in hand and their bayonets fixed. But they were quickly discovered as the Bolos themselves went house to house searching for Americans. When the closet door suddenly opened and revealed a Bolo soldier, Burbridge acted quickly and ran him through, and then shot a second Bolo.

Burbridge and Wierenga then kicked over a lantern, which left the room in darkness as they leapt from a window and hoofed it for a nearby marsh. They spent the rest of the day and into the night hiding in the deep subzero cold before locating and following the stream that flows before Visorka Gora. They were half frozen, but alive.

Meanwhile, the Bolos were in no mood to let up. "The following days were just a repetition of this day's action," Mead wrote. "The enemy shelled and shelled our position and then sent forward wave after wave of infantry."

The Canadian gunners, under the command of Lt. Douglas Winslow, finally returned to the scene and ran their guns out into the open. They then unleashed shots of shrapnel into the Bolo horde, "thus breaking up attack after attack," Mead recalled.

On January 22, the Bolos, thinking they had the Cossacks trapped, leveled Ust Padenga with artillery, and then advanced with infantry. Marching through the deep snow, they were quickly slaughtered by the Canadian guns, all the while ignorant of the fact that Ust Padenga was already a ghost town.

By the time the Bolos took Ust Padenga, hundreds of their number lay wounded and dying in the snow. "The carnage and slaughter this day in the enemy's ranks was terrific, resulting from a most stupid military blunder," Mead would remember. "The valley below us was dotted with pile after pile of enemy dead."

Having failed in the assault, the Bolsheviks in turn increased their shelling of Visorka Gora. "Shells were now raining into our position by the thousands," Mead would write, "but our artillery could not respond as it was completely outranged. By the process of attrition our little body of men was growing smaller day by day."

Toward the end of the day, a shell hit the log building in Visorka Gora that was being used as a hospital. Just prior to the blast the medic Ralph Powers, who had been heroically tending to the dead and dying for several days, was just preparing to operate on Pvt. Sebastiano Lencioni. A burst of shrapnel passed through the walls of the hospital and exploded outside, but the blast reentered the room and instantly killed Sgt. Yates "Curly" Rodgers, Cpl. Milton Gottschalk, and two others.

Powers also was wounded—mortally, it would turn out. Lencioni, who had already lost one leg, had the other torn off by the blast. Powers would be awarded a posthumous DSC for his work in saving the lives of many of the wounded from Nijni Gora and Visorka Gora.

The thirty-one-year-old Tennessean Curly Rodgers had been one of the most popular men in the company, and his death added to the already numb feelings of the men.

"His unquenchable spirit of laughter would never again relieve the tension and calm the raw nerves of an outgoing guard or patrol," Mead would write. "Curly was dead."

There was little time to mourn, however. Clearly, the far Vaga front had to be evacuated—and now. The desperate men of Company A would have to make a forced march through the bitter, sweeping Arctic cold for Shenkursk, which remained, at least in the short term, "the prize" for the Bolos, an American intelligence officer in Shenkursk would apprise the high command.

If Shenkursk fell next, Company B's position at Toulgas, to the northeast on the Dvina River, might also be imperiled, as would the Allies at Kodish and the railway—and eventually Archangel itself. The high command's folly was now in full collision with Leon Trotsky's ambitions to drive the foreigners into the White Sea.

CHAPTER TWENTY-FOUR

FLIGHT

O h, what a sight.

From the tower of the church, he could see for miles, see the long line of Bolo artillery plying the road to Shenkursk, see the Reds massing like angry ants in the villages that pocked the countryside, see the stiff, white Vaga stretching south for miles, and now covered with black-and-white forms coming on, advancing right toward him.

It was a horrifying sight for Harry Mead as he, Otto Odjard, and Hugh McPhail stood in the tower at Spasskoe and considered their options, of which there was just one. Orders were shouted, and the men of Company A, 339th Infantry Regiment, scrambled into position on the southern edge of the village, which sat twelve miles above Visorka Gora, now burned to the ground and smoldering,

And then the shells came fast and furious once again, one landing in the village center, even as Harry Mead descended the steps of the church and took a position with half of the men behind a stone wall. As he cleared the drifting snow from the wall he heard Cpl. Harold Danielson wryly remark how thoughtful it was for the United States government to have provided its soldiers with everything—"even tombstones for the men."

On the left, men raced to find what cover they could among the piles of wood and haystacks that sat here and there, while the lone Canadian gun was brought up. Here, Captain Odjard and the Canadian artillery captain just down from Shenkursk, Oliver Mowat, directed fire and positions, while McPhail and two Canadians blasted away at the Bolos with machine guns from the church tower.

"All that day the battle raged, the artillery was now shelling Shenkursk as well as our own position," Moore et al. would write. "The plains in front of us were swarming with artillery and cavalry, while overhead hummed a lone airplane which had travelled about a hundred and twenty-five miles to aid us in our hopeless encounter, but all in vain."

January 24, 1919, was the second full day of their flight, as the beleaguered garrison at lonely Visorka Gora had finally been ordered to retreat from the flaming village at 9:30 P.M. on January 22.

The entire surviving entourage was on the road north by two A.M., a Canadian gun in the lead and headed for Shenkursk so as not to be captured, while the second gun had been left behind because the horses were too tired to pull it.

The abandoned gun's breech had been removed, and would be carried back the fifteen miles to Shenkursk as evidence that it had not been captured intact, a point of pride with the artillerymen.

The column headed through deep, fresh-fallen snow and temperatures of forty-five below zero for the next village down the Vaga, Shalosha, eight miles away. "All that night, tired, exhausted and half-starved, we plodded the frozen trails of the pitch black forest," Mead would recall.

The despised Shackleton boots were no help on those frozen trails, and many of the men disgustedly unlaced them and continued on in just their socks. They reached Shalosha at daylight, "giddy from want of sleep and desperately hungry," Dorothea York would write.

They threw frozen tins of M&V—meat and vegetables—into stoves to thaw them, then greedily pried them open and devoured the contents as if they were the finest offerings from Detroit's swankest restaurants.

Paradoxically, the mail came into their frigid bivouac that afternoon, offering some cheer to their desperate march for life. Then orders came to continue on for Spasskoe, just four miles south of the presumed safety of Shenkursk.

There was one large problem: the Bolos had managed to get between the Allied force and Shenkursk, and had also occupied villages to the north on both sides of the Vaga River, the only escape route.

A conference of the officers was called to decide how to proceed, and the leaders settled on a plan of boldly marching straight down the Vaga in the hope that the Bolos lining both banks would mistake the desperate column for one of its own.

The plan worked perfectly, as the passing column drew only a single, wild shot. The Reds "could have surrounded and massacred the whole force that night," York would add, "but marvelously he did not, and some way wearied men and horses marched through the midst of them and escaped."

By two A.M. on January 24, the entire convoy had reached Spasskoe, and the men were greeted by the Canadian artillery captain Oliver Mowat and his crew, who had dragged a single gun out from Shenkursk.

The men fell out in billets about the town; McPhail when he arrived would find Harry Mead "in a chair sound asleep," a few feet from a brass featherbed. "Just three more steps and he could have fallen on the only bed I saw in Russia," McPhail would say years later.

At seven in the morning, a Cossack patrol sent south to ascertain the enemy's location and numbers raced back sounding the alarm. Hundreds of Bolos had been seen massing for a renewed attack; once again, the tiny Allied force was in danger of being annihilated.

That morning the temperature abated somewhat, but everyone in the Allied force was starving and suffering from exhaustion. Adding to their misery was a salvo of Bolo shells, which came roaring from the air at 10:30 A.M.

Oliver Mowat alternated between his only gun's position in the town and the church tower, from which he could direct fire to his sole battery and by telephone to a "Big Ben" piece in Shenkursk. The artillery duel continued for hours.

"There was scarcely any rifle fire although there were perhaps two thousand Bolos just out there," York wrote. "The enemy was not visible so there was nothing to do but conserve rifle shells, hang on to one's nerves, and wait."

Sgt. Evan Knox barked orders to the men on the right, while Sgt. Fred Nees imposed his will on the left. Before long, a large Bolo shell hit the road that divided the forces, and Nees went down, wounded.

"Clearly the Bolo was getting the range," York wrote. "Each shell dropped nearer with a deadly, devilish accuracy." Another shell suddenly landed nearly atop Mowat. Picking himself up, he said drolly, "One cigar." That broke up all within earshot, and for a moment the desperate misery of their plight was forgotten.

McPhail continued his machine-gun duel from the church tower, "absent-mindedly continuing the one-sided conversation with the enemy gunners," York would write. "Hit 'em again!" he yelled. "That's right. Get a cigar."

The laughter ended when a shell smashed almost into the Canadian gun and took off one of Mowat's legs at the knee. An hour later, a flying piece of shrapnel entered Odjard's neck, and also carried away an arm from Sgt. James Chesher; all three were rushed by sled to Shenkursk. Soon after, two more Canadians were killed at their now-useless gun.

With Odjard seriously wounded, perhaps fatally, the men felt more forlorn than ever. Morale all along the line wavered, as even more men fell wounded. Finally, Lt. Edward Saari, now Company A's senior officer, ordered a withdrawal to Shenkursk, even as the Bolos continued their pursuit, spilling from the snowy woods and the frozen river and threatening to envelop the command once and for all.

The men on the left lined up to begin another desperate flight. Harry Mead, in position in front of the church and unaware of Odjard's severe wounding, was summoned by a runner and, after learning the state of affairs, managed to find a Canadian sergeant to fix the phone wire to Shenkursk, which had been severed by the Bolo artillery.

Even as the sergeant went to work, Bolo shells continued to pour down. The wire fixed, Mead called headquarters in Shenkursk and asked what he should do. Before he got an answer, Mead decided everyone had had enough. "We're on our way," he said into the speaker.

At 2:30 P.M., the Allied force began its retreat to Shenkursk. Once more the men from Company A would have to cross open ground; once more they would flounder in the deep snow as they ran—waded—for their lives. "You may be sure no one dragged his feet or threw away his constant companion, the long Russian rifle," Hugh McPhail would say.

Halfway to Shenkursk, the ragged column was cheered by the sight of Capt. James Fitzsimmons and a platoon of Company C coming their way from Shenkursk to cover the retreat.

The company hastily raced forward and established a skirmish line, through which the freezing, desperate survivors of Company A passed. "We were shelled some while evacuating, but had no casualties," Company C's Lt. Glen Weeks would write.

Panting, sweating, and stumbling through the snow, still under fire from the Bolo artillery, the head of the column reached Shenkursk at four P.M., and all began thinking of hot food, steam baths, and a good night's sleep.

All also began to think they were safe.

The men fell out and found that their cooks had brought with them cans of hot M&V that they had been preparing for dinner before the order to retreat was given. The famished troops dug into the cans, grabbing globs of beef and vegetables with bare hands and stuffing them into their mouths in a frenzy of near starvation.

At least partly sated, the men fell out wherever they could, and most immediately fell into a deep sleep. While they snoozed, the hospital in Shenkursk was a scene of intense activity. "People were rushing about the corridors, clattering up and down the great central stairway, everyone busy and in a hurry," the medic Godfrey Anderson wrote.

More than ninety patients already lined the various wards, including the largest one, a room on the second floor that only a month before had been the scene of a Christmas party. Now, the sounds of labored breathing from the wounded and the dying replaced the gaiety of laughter and balalaika music, as did the heavy clomp of boots when orderlies carried the dead away to the morgue.

Among the dead was Lt. Ralph Powers, who had worked nonstop to patch up the Company A men and others wounded at Visorka Gora. Near him was the Canadian artillery captain, Oliver Mowat, his severed leg oozing blood. He would not last the week.

Hugh McPhail and Harry Mead had found a billet and hit the hay, and began dreaming of perhaps changing their socks, and maybe even their underwear, the following day. They had made it, they thought; they had seen and endured the worst and had made it to Shenkursk unharmed despite the long odds against them.

But their reveries were broken later that night when an American officer, Dan Steele, woke them and told them that Shenkursk was to be evacuated. McPhail and Mead couldn't believe the news.

"Here was a town well fortified, with many well-placed dugouts, much food, all kinds of ammunition, and we thought friendly people . . . and we are going to abandon the whole works," McPhail recalled years later. But the sound of the still-booming Bolo artillery, and the rounds plopping near and into Shenkursk, told the story.

The British high command had finally come to the conclusion that the position was untenable. The village had been shelled through the previous day from every direction, and the Canadian and Russian artillery was outranged. The Bolo had big guns that could pound Shenkursk to dust, with no chance of meaningful reply by the Allies.

Before long, the entire Allied force would be besieged and trapped within the walls of Shenkursk with little chance of much aid coming from Archangel or anywhere else. The Bolos had aimed on January 19 to roll up the small Allied force at Ust Padenga and continue on to take Shenkursk; now, they were here, and it was clear that their ambitions would be fulfilled.

Mead finally accepted the decision and made ready to leave after realizing that "every available approach and trail leading into Shenkursk was held by the enemy, who could move about at will inasmuch as they were protected by the trackless forests on all sides, and thus would soon render it impossible for our distant comrades in Archangel and elsewhere on the lines to bring through any relief or assistance."

As well, it would be months before the ice-smothered Vaga and Dvina Rivers would be clear enough to allow the British gunboats and supply ships access to the troops. And in any event, only two Allied-occupied positions existed between Shenkursk and the base at Beresnik, seventy miles down the Dvina.

In keeping in line with the ill-thought-out plan for the expedition, Shagovari, forty-four miles downriver, had a small force of Russians, while Kitsa, twenty miles beyond, had one American platoon and a small number of Russian troops.

Within days, or even hours, the Bolos now swarming the countryside could reduce those garrisons, and then attack Beresnik; with that base gone, Shenkursk on the Vaga and Toulgas on the Dvina would be cut off, and could be destroyed by the Reds at their leisure.

And so Shenkursk would be abandoned. The problem now facing the Allies, however, was how this garrison of perhaps one thousand soldiers, nurses, Cossacks, Russians, and residents of Shenkursk who feared Bolo reprisals could make their way north through a deeply frozen countryside teeming with an increasingly hostile enemy.

"All the principal roads or trails were already in the hands of the enemy," Mead would write. However, a Russian captain mentioned that a little-used winter trail through the forests existed that, if unoccupied by Bolos, could lead to the river trail to Shagovari. A Cossack patrol was dispatched to reconnoiter, and several hours later returned to report that the trail, heavily laden with snow, was open.

It was time to get the hell out of Shenkursk.

CHAPTER TWENTY-FIVE

VISTAFKA

The stables were burning, a single incendiary bomb having plopped onto the roof, and in the deep night of January 24–25, 1919, he could make out shadowy forms moving to and fro on Shenkursk's main street. Above, the sky was a dull gray, but to the north where it was clearer he could make out the dancing lights of the aurora borealis, billowing and green and incongruously silent compared to the "excitement and chaotic confusion" of the night.

Godfrey Anderson of the 337th Field Hospital Company had been given the task of preparing the hospital's patients for the coming hegira. "What it was all about we did not realize at the time, and no one bothered to tell us," he would recall. "Personally, I did not realize that we were leaving Shenkursk for good."

No one, apparently, had told Godfrey about the original orders from the British stipulating that all hospital patients were to be left behind as a matter of military expediency. The Canadians flatly refused to obey the order, and First Battalion commander James Corbly also told the Brits he would not leave any of his men behind.

Given what had happened to Francis Cuff and his men in November, "it was pretty certain that when the Bolo gained control of the town of Shenkursk, the wounded would be given the coup de grace," Hugh McPhail would note.

And so Godfrey Anderson and other medics and nurses tended to their charges late into the night, lifting and turning and bundling the almost one hundred sick and wounded into sleeping bags for their sled rides into the unknown in temperatures of sixty below zero.

"Some of these were so badly injured that the slightest touch would cause excruciating agony," Anderson recalled. The severely wounded screamed as they were tucked into sleeping bags, while those suffering from shell shock "raved and struggled and fought, and finally had to be overpowered by brute force."

The patients were carried out and placed in a bedding of straw atop a sleigh, covered with blankets, and "given a shot of medication or a swig of rum, as the case may be," Anderson wrote.

Along the main road in Shenkursk, a long convoy of ponies and sleds was being assembled. "We could but wonder where they had managed to commandeer all those sleighs and ponies," Anderson would write.

"They were filled up as soon as they moved into place, and then moved on to halt in a long line to await the order to move out. Those lying dead in the room upstairs were to be left behind."

All over the village, preparations for the nighttime flight were being made, with the orders maintaining that the men could bring with them only that which they could carry. A mountain of stores and ammunition would also be left behind.

"Each man chose hastily what could be carried in his pockets," Dorothea York wrote. "Souvenirs of heavy silver and other things of value had hardly a glance. Extra clothing, letters, diaries—all were thrown to one side."

Hugh McPhail and Harry Mead threw open their personal trunks and invited their men to take what they wanted from them. "All I took was a can of salmon," McPhail remembered.

Moving out into the crowded street, McPhail encountered a well-dressed Russian girl, and thought Lt. Edward Saari was trying to "snaffle" her for himself. McPhail found Saari and told him he didn't think it was a good idea to bring a civilian with him; Saari told McPhail he thought she was *his* girl.

"Give her a boot in the tail and get her out of here," Saari told him.

But other civilians, fearful of being left to the dubious mercies of the Bolos, poured into the street "in hordes," York wrote. "These citizens were supposed to follow the military from the city. The larger part did, but some sleighs mingled with ours all along the route."

"The dimly lighted streets of Shenkursk were crowded with confused and frightened people, milling about or scurrying hither and yon in all directions," Godfrey Anderson wrote. "Irascible staff officers were riding about, issuing instructions and trying to establish some sort of order."

At midnight, the convoy began to move, led by the Cossacks, who knew the way. They were followed in turn by the Canadians, Company A, the train of droshkies, and, finally, Company C, which guarded the rear and didn't leave Shenkursk until 2:30 A.M. Lts. Lloyd Fay and Glen Weeks were the last soldiers to leave. A gaggle of Russian civilians followed behind them.

The Shackleton boots continued to plague the Americans, who traveled by foot and slipped and skidded because of the boots' leather soles. As on the retreat from Visorka Gora, some of the soldiers removed the boots and tossed them away and continued slogging on wearing just one or more pairs of socks. As a result, "on the following day many were suffering from severely frostbitten feet," Mead wrote. McPhail eschewed the boots and wore eleven pairs of socks, a pair of moccasins, and overshoes. "I started out on skis but soon gave that idea up," he would say.

As the vanguard left Shenkursk, a local force of recruits—the Shenkursk Battalion—was ordered to take the trail to Kodima, thirty miles to the northeast, to protect the refugees' right flank—and to test their own suspect loyalty to the Allies. Not long after, the detachment ran into some Bolos. After a few shots, two companies of the battalion went over to the Reds, while the remainder had to flee for their lives.

The marching was agony, especially to the foot soldiers who had to struggle through the deep holes punched into the snow by the leading horsemen. "Time after time that night one could hear some poor unfortunate with his heavy pack on his back fall with a sickening thud upon the packed trail," Mead wrote.

They moved through the forest like an army of silent ghouls, the large spruce trees on either side of the trail snuffing out any trace of moonlight and impeding the leaders with snow-packed branches that leaned into and over the trail. The biting cold pierced lungs and slowly froze noses and extremities, even as the sheer effort of wading through the ponderous drifts caused sweat to flood from every covered pore.

By dawn, the vanguard was ten miles from Shenkursk. The booming of artillery could be heard once more pounding the town, as the Bolos remained unaware that it had been evacuated by the Allied force. The shelling only increased the pace of the column, which now plodded the hard-crusted snow of the Vaga River.

(The Bolos would eventually assault Shenkursk and, one intelligence report says, conduct "house-searches, arrests, requisition and registration of all goods." The Bolos also murdered the local priest and a merchant, and arrested, and later released, the Mother Superior of the convent.)

At nine A.M., the column halted at Yemska Gora, where locals served up hot tea, black bread, and strong fish cakes—"one of the most odiferous viands ever devised by human hands and which therefore few, if any, of us had summoned up courage enough to consume," Mead would remember.

"On this particular morning, however, it required no courage at all and we devoured the pasty mass as though it were one of the choicest of viands."

By five P.M., the weary party reached Shagovari, where a detachment of men from Companies C and D were awaiting. That village, too, had been attacked on January 21 by Bolos disguised as peasants, who struck an outpost and hacked Company D's Pvt. Frank Syska to death with axes and took his company mate, Pvt. Anton Vanis, prisoner.

As well, on January 23 a force of two hundred Bolos suddenly sprang from the surrounding forest and took the town before they could be detected; the defenders quickly organized and drove them out by hand grenade and machine gun.

Not long after the Shenkursk refugees arrived, a Cossack patrol stormed in and reported numerous Bolos were headed for Shagovari via the main road. "Soon the advance patrols of the enemy appeared and our artillery immediately opened on them," Mead wrote.

A detachment from Company D left town and fought off a Bolo attack, as the hundreds of weary civilians from Shenkursk plodded past, intent on reaching the safety of Archangel. The Bolos paused to wait for reinforcements, certain they had the pitiful Allied force in their grasp.

"All through the night we could see the flames of rockets and signal lights in surrounding villages showing them the enemy was losing no time in getting ready for an attack," Mead would remember.

Shagovari militarily was no better than Shenkursk, being easily approached from any direction under the cover of the surrounding woods. The convoy had little choice but to brave the trail once more and head for Vistafka, another sixteen miles downriver.

The column saddled up on the afternoon of January 26, waited for darkness, and then once more began its backbreaking flight north. This time the sleigh-ridden patients went first, having to be manhandled down a steep bluff to the Vaga, across which the trail north continued through forests. The long line of Americans, Canadians, and some lagging civilian refugees followed.

At about eleven P.M. Mead, looking back, saw a "brilliant flame . . . glowing against the sky, which rapidly increased in volume and intensity." The Cossacks covering the retreat were burning Shagovari, ensuring that the enemy would not partake of the stores and other supplies that had had to be abandoned.

Reaching Vistafka in the early hours of the morning, they found no safe harbor but another untenable position. "Of all the positions we had chosen . . . this was the most hopeless of all," Mead recalled.

The village sat atop a high bluff on the east bank of the Vaga, and was surrounded by forest there and across the river. Company C's

Edwin Arkins recalled that when the locals in the village were told they had to leave, some began crying; overwhelmed with either guilt or empathy, or both, Arkins gave one young mother a blanket to cover her shivering baby.

The men were soon at work stringing wires and, when the deeply frozen ground proved impossible to budge, constructing trenches out of snow. The sick and wounded, meanwhile, continued on, headed for the main base at Beresnik.

Godfrey Anderson traveled with that part of the convoy to Kitsa, four miles north, and was detailed to remain there. The next afternoon, he and another medic were ordered to unload a sleigh that had just come in from Vistafka. In it were two wounded soldiers lying on a bed of straw. Anderson and other medics managed to remove one of them and bring him into the aid station, but the second proved problematic.

As they moved the second soldier, Company C's Pvt. Isiador Dunaetz, he began mumbling incoherently, then managed to yell out, "Quit pulling my hair!"

Examining him, the medics found he had been creased by a bullet on the left side of his skull. They also found that some of his brains were oozing out and had frozen into the straw on the bottom of the sled—"and in moving him we were actually pulling out his brains," Anderson wrote.

The other patient had been hit twice by a dumdum bullet from a machine gun, and had two small holes on either side of his chest and two larger, "ragged" holes in the back where they had passed through. The unit's captain, Howard Kinyon, stuffed the holes with greased gauze, then turned his attention to Dunaetz.

Using scissors, Kinyon proceeded to cut the portion of Dunaetz's brain that was sticking out, then packed gauze into the resulting cavity. Dunaetz, Anderson recalled, remained conscious, but was in a "mental stupor" during the procedure.

Anderson was then detailed to join a sled convoy that would transport Dunaetz and the other wounded man plus some other wounded to Beresnik. By the time they reached Ust Vaga, at the confluence of the

Vaga and Dvina Rivers, Dunaetz was in a coma. After a short rest, they continued on, but at midnight Dunaetz—by now nicknamed "Doughnuts" by the medics—began to succumb to his injury.

"It seems that poor Doughnuts was going through a series of death struggles and his companion was upset and in need of moral support," Godfrey wrote. "The convoy was halted and we crowded around the sleigh and impotently watched the poor fellow breathe his last.

"His companion, tucked in beside him, pleaded with us to remain by the side of the sleigh, as he had no inclination to ride through the night alone with a dead man"—as would Company G's Michael Macalla in the coming months.

Anderson and his mates reached Beresnik later that night and handed over their "grim cargo" to the staff at the hospital. He was then assigned to duty at the aid station sixteen miles upriver at Ust Vaga, at which he would encounter many more wounded men coming from Vistafka.

There, Company A and elements of Companies C and D were holding on—barely. Within days of their arrival, the Bolos had brought up their light artillery, and began shelling the defenses intermittently. They also gave notice that they were prepared to lay siege to the village.

"Night after night we could hear the ring of axes in the surrounding woods informing us that the Bolo was establishing his defenses, but our numbers were so small that we could not send out patrols enough to prevent this," Mead would recall.

The Bolos also regularly probed the defenses. At three A.M. on January 30, Company C's Sgt. Wilbur Smith was killed and three others were wounded during a Bolo raid. That same day, the Bolos shelled Vistafka, tearing up several of the town's log homes, and then made a frontal attack at 8:30 A.M.

The defenders replied with machine-gun fire while an Allied plane came to the rescue, dropping bombs and scattering the attackers—and hitting one piece of Bolo artillery. The next day, January 31, a platoon of Royal Scots managed to make it through from Kitsa and relieved what remained of Company A.

For thirteen days the company and its allies had fought and re-treated, made stands and retreated, all while burning hunger ravaged their bellies and the unearthly cold Russian winter had attacked every uncovered piece of flesh. Numb now in flesh and spirit, the filthy, ex-hausted survivors exulted in their relief, clasping hands and slapping each other's backs before packing up their pitiful baggage and arms and heading for the trail to Kitsa, which was just four miles to the north but in their minds might as well have been Archangel itself.

Many of their friends had died in the smothering waves of Bolos at Nijni Gora and Visorka Gora, or on the trail between those tragic places and Vistafka, but they were alive. Somehow, by the grace of God or the Fates, they had cut their way through. With any luck their war was over.

"For eighty miles three hundred and fifty men had held off between five and six thousand," York would write. "The coming rest was well earned."

On February 1, 1919, Company A was reorganized. Edward Saari re-mained its commander, and Harry Mead took over the First Platoon; Hugh McPhail kept the Second Platoon and Arthur Collar the Third.

McPhail and his men were then sent to the nearby village of Ye-vievskaya, on the west bank of the Vaga and just between Kitsa and Vistafka. They would dub the tiny village "Potatoville" because of the stores of potatoes, turnips, and onions that were found buried in straw in one home.

Mead, meanwhile, took the First Platoon to Ignotovskaya, also across the Vaga, while Collar's company went to Maximofskaya, directly across the river from Kitsa. Edward Saari and the Fourth Platoon remained at Kitsa.

The population of Yevievskaya, McPhail would remember, had been forced to flee, leaving their livestock behind. Several of the company's farm boys quickly went to work, butchering a couple of cows and throw-ing steaks on the fire. For the first time in weeks, the men chowed down on fresh meat; the result was widespread cases of "the trots," McPhail recalled.

That was the worst of it, as for the balance of February, the men of battered Company A would live in relative peace until called upon again for duty at Vistafka, which was then slowly but surely being reduced by Bolo artillery and attacks.

The besieged Royal Scots huddled under constant artillery salvos that shook the roof timbers of their log refuges and splintered walls and floorboards; they constructed dugouts from snow on the forward perimeter and, with no way to cook, ate frozen, tinned corned beef and hardtack. Morale, such as there was, slowly ebbed—but with the Bolos on their front and flanks, there was no recourse but to grimly stick it out.

In early March, Mead's and McPhail's platoons were relieved by White Russians and reluctantly returned to Vistafka, the garrison of which had by then been reinforced by the relatively unscathed Company F. The balance of Company A remained at Maximofskaya with one platoon of Company D; it would be relieved by a platoon from Company F on March 6.

On the night of March 3, the platoon of Whites that had taken over McPhail's former position at Yevievskaya found a lode of English rum and soon began a whoop-and-holler celebration; it ended when the ever-watchful Bolo noticed the goings-on and quickly attacked and seized the town in just an hour. The men at Vistafka and Maximofskaya were now alone, virtually surrounded by the enemy and still 180 miles from Archangel.

On March 4, the Bolos, reinforced with heavier artillery, began shelling Vistafka. The bombardment destroyed the few homes and buildings that had been left untouched. The next day, the Bolo artillery lifted and began shelling the Allied artillery emplacements just to the north of the village—and then came the expected.

Wave upon wave of the Bolos swarmed from the south, gliding up the wide highway of the frozen Vaga and storming through the dark woods on either side. It "looked like the end had come," Mead recalled—but as at Nijni Gora, the men once more shouldered their rifles and loaded their machine guns and went to work, "pouring their hail of lead into the advancing wave."

The attackers were repulsed to the front and side, but managed this time to work into the Americans' rear, cutting the trail to Kitsa.

The defenders at Vistafka were, finally, surrounded.

Back at Kitsa, the garrison gave up all hope of cutting its way to the rescue, and instead began strengthening its own defenses. However, after a runner from Vistafka managed to slip through to Kitsa that night with a plea for help, a detachment of Royal Scots was sent south to try to bolster Vistafka's forlorn defenders. But the trails were too well covered by Bolo machine guns, and their effort was driven back.

The same afternoon, though, the command at Kitsa decided to make another daring attempt at rescue. A detachment of Cossacks and White Russians were issued a strong dose of rum, its commander "made a stirring address, calling upon them to do or die on behalf of their comrades," and the men set off through the forest for Vistafka, Moore et al. wrote.

In a lucky stroke, the men took a wrong trail, and wound up in the rear of the Bolo position. Before the full battalion of Bolos could ascertain whether the force was friend or foe, the mixed force of Russians pitched into them, the Cossacks mowing them down in long lines with their machine guns and quickly forcing a panicked retreat toward the Vaga.

Their stampede spooked the rest of the Bolos, who also took off for the river. Once on the wide, white expanse of the river, they became perfect targets for the American rifles and machine guns at Vistafka, as well as the Canadian artillery to the north, and they were slaughtered almost wholesale in the frenzied barrage.

Afterward, the friendly Russians entered the ruined village of Vistafka, where they were wildly cheered by the garrison. Almost by accident, the force of a few hundred Allies had put to flight four thousand Bolos, and afterward all "began to breathe more easily, thinking that perhaps the enemy at last had enough," Mead recalled.

A lull in the fighting ensued, but the reprieve could not last. On March 7, the Bolo artillery barked again, shelling Vistafka furiously and killing Company A's Sgt. Albert Moore. "He was one of four men in the company who always wore a tin hat," McPhail would say. "A bit of shrapnel had gone through the hat. I don't believe one could put his hand anywhere on Moore without covering at least three holes in his body."

Another of Company A's men, Sidney DeGraw, had also been hit, and with both legs "dangling" crawled from his machine-gun emplacement to a nearby dugout.

March 8 was ominously quiet. The defenders at Vistafka, no longer surrounded, were reinforced that evening by a platoon of Company F men. Finally, on March 9, "the storm broke," Dorothea York would write.

At three P.M. the Bolos attacked Vistafka and Maximofskaya, across the river, simultaneously. They were beaten off at the latter village, but tried once more at four thirty. "Their pom pom cost us two casualties before the Canadians found and silenced it with their faithful eighteen pounders," York wrote.

At eight P.M., the Bolos enveloped Maximofskaya, and came so near that the defenders could hear them talking. "The officers urged them to charge the slope and end the affair, but the men protested that they were cold and hungry and had no mind to brave that devastating small fire at close range," York wrote.

Vistafka, too, was once again under siege. "There were between two and three thousand of the enemy and we had two platoons and a few Cossacks," York wrote. The Bolos also had between ten and fourteen guns, while the Allied force had but three. The battle was "ridiculously, pitifully unequal," York would write.

A Cossack leader, Captain Kreetch, held dugouts on the left front of Vistafka while McPhail held the right with his platoon and Harry Mead, in command of the Company A men, occupied dugouts to the rear.

The Bolos shelled the village through the day, employing incendiary shells as well as high explosives. The men crouched and shifted positions through the day, trying simply to survive.

"We could see the hordes of the enemy everywhere," York wrote. "To pick off a possible fifty or one hundred [men] would draw their own small fire and not diminish their numbers appreciably."

Company A's Pvt. Earl Sweet was killed by a shell as he sat in a blockhouse near the Vaga; Pvt. Walter Welstead was also killed outright, while Cpl. Bernard Kenny was mortally wounded, as was Pvt. Benjamin Rose, whose legs were nearly severed but who, the frigid temperatures stanching the blood flow, was able to get to a hospital before dying on March 11.

Harry Mead was also severely wounded in his chest. "That was the end of Harry with the company until May," McPhail recalled. Mead was rushed back to Kitsa, taking with him all hope of communication with the forward posts. There, several of McPhail's men made a plea for a retreat.

"It appeared quite possible that the first platoon behind them had withdrawn and left them to fight their own battle as best they might," York wrote. McPhail tried to contact headquarters in Kitsa, but once again the wires had been severed. So he sent "three good tough men back to see what was brewing," he would remember.

One came back and told McPhail that they were to leave Vistafka "as quietly as possible. In the woods out front I could see the place was swarming with the Bolo."

As the Bolo machine gunners went to work each time an American or a Cossack showed himself, the evacuation would have to be made at night. Under cover of darkness, and crawling through the charred and smoldering timbers of what had not long before been a thriving village, the men assembled at the rear of Vistafka and then quickly moved north, where they bivouacked in the open a mile and a half to the south of Kitsa. There, they lay low and prayed that the Bolo artillery would not find them.

The Cossacks, though, had been left behind to the mercy of their mortal Bolo enemies. Their leader came back and, teary-eyed, begged for someone to order him and his men to leave Vistafka. The order was given, and he returned and brought his men out.

Company A was finally relieved later that day and went back first to Kitsa, then to the village of Malo Beresnik ten miles to the north. As they trudged over the snowy banks of the Vaga River the men could not know that their company had lost more men killed than any other American unit that was sent to Russia.

Since that awful morning of January 19, eighteen of its men had been killed in action or died of wounds, seventeen remained missing, and scores more were wounded. It was a hell of a price to pay for that long-forgotten, supposedly simple mission of guarding stores in Archangel.

CHAPTER TWENTY-SIX

TO WHAT END

By the time Cpl. Arthur Prince of Company B, 339th Infantry Regiment, came home, the girl he left behind had been dead for two years, and his mother, Jessie, who was already blind, had markedly aged from worry. By the time he came home, in October 1920, Cpl. Arthur Prince had been officially declared dead for months. He was crippled, suffering from kidney disease, and had wasted away on the scanty rations delivered to him at the various Russian hospitals where, at least, he had been treated.

A year and a half earlier, twenty-six-year-old Arthur Prince, of Onaway, Michigan, had been out on patrol around Toulgas on March 1, 1919, when he fell into the hands of the Bolos. He and his men had been ambushed, the enemy taking down the point man; when Prince went to assist him, he was shot in a knee, in a hip, and then, while he was trying to crawl away, in the side.

Hearing the firing, Capt. Robert Boyd sent out men from the fortifications at Toulgas in an effort to rescue the patrol, but they encountered a large force of Bolos. Before they could finally reach the men, three of them—Cpl. Joseph Pawlak and Pvts. Daniel Robbins and Frank Ruth—were killed; Sgt. William Bowman and Pvt. Frank Clish died of their wounds later the same day.

"Clish had been shot through the spine and died about noon," recalled Sgt. Simon Davis, who was sick in the hospital when Clish and Bowman were brought in. Bowman, he added, "had been shot through the bowels and struck at a glance on top of his head. He was conscious but had suffered terribly from the cold."

Cpl. Arthur Prince, meanwhile, was nowhere to be found. There was, however, a forty-yard, bloodied track in the deep snow indicating where the corporal, who had one leg broken by a Bolo bullet, had crawled in an attempt to reach safety. There were also shell casings showing that he had continued to try to fight off his Bolo attackers during his desperate, ultimately futile race for freedom.

The Bolos had finally managed to surround Prince and disarm him. He was placed on a sleigh, and his captors brought him 170 miles up the Dvina to Kotlas. There, he received his first bit of medical attention, and then was moved by train to Kostroma, about one hundred miles south of Vologda. There, he underwent three operations over the next seven months on his leg—"the tendons of which had become taut as a result of improper attention on the long journey from the front," the *Detroit Free Press* would report.

On September 28, 1919, Prince was sent on to a concentration camp 120 miles south of Moscow, where his wounds reopened. After a month, Prince was sent on to a prison in Moscow.

There, he experienced "the worst sufferings of his entire stay in Moscow," the newspaper would report. "The hospital was heated only two hours daily . . . there were untrained nurses and only a few doctors . . . and also a shortage of medicines. The food conditions were bad."

A fellow prisoner, an Englishman who had traveled to Russia to fight the Bolsheviks, told him of another hospital in the city that was run by Hungarians and was rumored to have better conditions, and Prince obtained permission to go there.

After three weeks, however, the crippled Arthur Prince still had not been taken to that hospital. His new friend, the Englishman, finally pressed the matter with the hospital's authority: he told the hospital's administrators that he had a pistol and five bullets, and would shoot four of them and then himself unless they moved Prince and himself to the other hospital.

Prince finally made it to the new hospital, where he found he had a new freedom and managed to recover enough that on one day he was able to get to the Bolsheviks' foreign office and "ask how to get home."

American diplomats were contacted, and they now cared for him and arranged for him to take a train to the Finnish border, where he was placed in a prison camp for Austrian prisoners who were being repatriated.

On August 4, 1920, Prince finally escaped Russia, but was placed in quarantine for two months. Eventually, Arthur Prince was sent on to the American consulate at Helsinki and thence to Coblenz, Germany, where he joined a contingent of American soldiers who had been detailed to remain within the Rhine bridgehead after the German signing of the peace agreement in 1919.

On October 18, he sailed with many of those men to the United States, and his odyssey finally ended with his arrival in Detroit on October 28, 1920. There, he found that his former comrades in Company B were planning a reunion in his honor for that night, but after his nineteen-month ordeal he didn't feel up to attending. "This has been a tough day for me and as much as I would like to see the boys of the old outfit, I must go to bed and get rest," he told the *Free Press*.

That "old outfit" had remained at Toulgas through the winter and into the spring following the terrifying Armistice Day fight the previous fall.

Robert Boyd would paint a portrait of his surroundings, and the nature of the locals, in a letter to friends:

"They have what is really a communal government," he wrote of the locals, "each string of villages chooses a 'Starasta,' or elder, who is the king bee. He decides who is to work for us and whose houses we are to use, and if we need men, hay, horses or anything like that we merely notify the Starasta and he supplies us.

"These people are really quite hospitable and very honest—no petty thieving is done but they would sell their soul for a drink of rum."

Boyd, who shared quarters with a local family, was not as admiring of the typical peasant's lifestyle.

"You cannot imagine how these native houses smell," Boyd wrote. "Below us in the combination living and dining room there are any number of kids—I've never been able to count them—some dozen chickens, and a lamb—all beautifully blended.

"We sprinkle the floor each day with creosote which kills some of the odors as they come up, and at that, this family is the cleanest one that I have seen."

His men, meanwhile, spent much of their time on patrol through the surrounding deep woods or simply trying to keep warm. And as patrol after patrol had been sent out, as probe after probe by the Bolos had continued through the long, bitter winter, the question of what, exactly, they were doing there began to dominate.

"Those long weeks of patrol and sentry duty were wearing on the men," Moore et al., with input from Boyd and John Cudahy, would write. Sentinels were continually seeing things at night that were not there.

And in fact the woods around them *were* alive, and not just with lurking Bolos. On one frozen, dark night a sentry on duty heard a number of mumbling voices coming toward him from the forest; certain he was about to be attacked by a gaggle of Bolos, he issued a challenge. The only reply was silence—but at daybreak, he discovered the fresh tracks of a large pack of timber wolves.

With the good work of the 310th Engineers, whose men sawed and hammered and constructed dugouts and blockhouses and strung wire around the position, isolated Toulgas had become a veritable fortress since November. But still the Bolos attempted with increasing frequency to penetrate those defenses.

One night, a band of Bolos crept up and began cutting the barbed wire between two blockhouses. Sensing something was brewing in the darkness, the sentry on duty sent a burst from his machine gun into the black.

An hours-long fight ensued, as this time, the threat was real. Piles of dead Bolos were found early the next morning, each lifeless body clad in a white smock to render himself almost invisible against the snowy background.

On another occasion, the enemy launched a large attack, sending men wading forward through thick snow and right into the maws of the Lewis and Vickers guns in the blockhouses. A vicious firefight raged for three hours before the Bolo line shuddered and then withdrew to the protection of the thick, surrounding woods.

The Bolos had yelled and screamed in terror as the Allied weapons fired on them, but their commanders urged and pushed them on at the point of their pistols and swords. In the end, Company B would capture seven Bolos, while killing nineteen and wounding another thirteen. The prisoners revealed that eight hundred Bolos were involved in the massed attack.

"So weeks passed and we held on, wondering what the end would be," Moore et al. would write of Company B. Some of the company's men had wondered that since at least Armistice Day—including their own captain, who on December 13 wrote and delivered through channels a tough list of concerns and questions meant for the American ambassador, David Francis, at Archangel (Francis had already left for England by then).

Conciliatory at first, Boyd went on to note the one question that was on the mind of almost every man under him: Why were they still there?

"While a state of war existed with Germany our mission, ostensibly at least, was to create an Eastern Front against Germany by developing a new Russian Army. The state of war is now over, and the fact of it being at present an armistice does not materially alter the situation.

"As one of the rank and file of the American Public I have always thought it one of our national policies that the settlement of internal dissensions in a foreign country, if not interfering directly with our international rights, was inherent with their power of self government [sic].

"If that is the case, what moral justification have the Allied forces, and particularly our own, in Russia since cessation of hostilities? If it is not the case, what is our national policy here?"

Aware he could be perceived as being out of line, Boyd assured his superiors: "I do not mean the above questions to convey an implication that I shall not continue to do my duty to the best of my ability in the future."

But, he would continue, "the morale of any force depends . . . a great deal on the rank and file knowing for what they are fighting. There has been no open dissatisfaction here, the men have gone thru hardships and fighting cheerfully, but will soon begin to say among themselves 'Why are we here.' It is my business to answer that question and I cannot."

By the time Arthur Prince was taken prisoner and Boyd had read the funeral service for the men who died on March 1—among them Sgt. William Bowman, "whom I loved like a brother," Boyd would write twenty years later—there was plenty of dissension to go around within Company B.

Clarence Scheu in a diary entry on February 26, 1919, would praise his comrades for their "wonderful spirit" under very trying conditions, considering that all were "operating in strange territory, have nothing but bare necessities, living practically like cattle, no immediate prospects of ever getting out of exile."

But after the massacre of Prince's patrol, Scheu would note in his diary that "it sure gets our blood boiling to see the chances we have to take on these damn patrols when we haven't men enough to man our fortifications properly."

In Sgt. Silver Parrish's platoon, meanwhile, a petition went around during the last days of February. The petition, according to a report by Capt. Hugh S. Martin of the American Military Mission, proclaimed that after March 15, the signers would refuse to stand on sentry, and would also refuse to go out on patrol.

"The principal grievance of the men at that time seemed to be that they were insufficiently protected by artillery; that they had been told that the ice on the river would begin to break about March 15 and they did not care to be caught like rats in a hole to be slaughtered by Bolshevik gunboats," Martin reported.

The petition was signed by about fifty men—an entire platoon. Martin would claim that when it reached Silver Parrish, he threw it into the stove and burned it. Parrish, he added, reported the petition to his higher-ups, who "apparently attempted to keep it quiet. I am not informed that any action was ever taken in the case."

Martin, however, did not have the whole story. Parrish himself took credit for the petition in his diary, saying the paper asked for "the reason why we are fighting Bolos, and why we haven't any big guns, and why the English run us, and why we haven't enough to eat, and why our men can't get proper medical attention."

Parrish made no mention of having burned the petition, but wrote that he, at least, did suffer a dressing-down by the British colonel, Graham, after someone "squealed" on him. Graham read him the Articles of War, "and showed me where my offense was punishable by death. But I knew it anyhow and should worry. I won't get my commission now (more luck)."

Perhaps not coincidentally, Parrish on March 11 was called out and handed the "English Military Medal," in recognition of his "gallant conduct . . . exceptional initiative and good judgment in action." The citation was signed by Gen. Edmund Ironside himself.

Still, his opinion of his and Company B's situation wasn't changed.

"The majority of the people here are in sympathy with the Bolo and I don't blame them," the firebrand sergeant would secretly write. "In fact I am 9/10 Bolo myself, and they all call me the Bolo, and my platoon the Bolo platoon, because every man in the platoon signed that petition against fighting the Bolo after the Germans had quit.

"But we have got the best fighting record of any platoon in the Battalion. So we should worry, and get home."

The constant shelling and patrolling continued until mid-March for the company, when it learned it would indeed be taking its first steps toward the United States after five long months in the wastes of northern Russia.

Rumors abounded that the Americans would be relieved by Royal Scots and new recruits from the Slavo-British Allied Legion, and head five miles northeast across the Dvina to the village of Kurgoman. The rumors turned true on March 16, when Company B was relieved and passed on downriver—"only across the river from Toulgas, yet the change will do us good," Clarence Scheu noted.

After several uneventful weeks at Kurgoman, the company would finally get its orders to withdraw. The long weeks and months of battle and privations would soon be behind them, and for all intents and purposes, Company B's strange, strange war was over.

When the company finally pulled out, it left behind the bodies of the three men who had been killed in action at Seltso the previous September. Two men—Cpls. Herbert Schroeder and Arthur Prince—remained missing. The men couldn't know it then, but they would meet Prince again.

Clarence Scheu would sum up the feelings of many as the company headed down the Dvina River toward Archangel. "Goodbye old Dwina [sic] river fronts, we never hope to see you again," Scheu wrote.

CHAPTER TWENTY-SEVEN

WHY DID WE GO TO RUSSIA

The long Russian winter had brought near-constant misery and hordes of Bolos screaming from the taiga and dark, scrub woods thick with suffocating snow. As the spring of 1919 approached, as the days grew a little longer and the air less bitter, a new menace was brewing in the ranks of the Americans and their exotic allies.

Dissension and mutiny had not been limited to Company B, but infiltrated the ranks across the still-frozen front as the soldiers obsessed over their predicaments and their fates—and received no good answers to just why they were still holding the line against an ever-emboldened foe.

Just weeks after the Company B petition had been circulated and signed by many, the corporals in Company E—some thirty men—held their own meeting while on the railroad front, and decided that they, too, had had enough.

They griped, they groused; with one voice they denounced their strange, strange war and their continuing parts in it. There was talk of a mass revolt, a refusal to leave for the battle lines when and if the time came. "The upshot of the affair bordered on mutiny," the company's PFC Donald Carey, who learned of the meeting secondhand, would recall.

Only one corporal, Earl Metcalf, came out against mutiny, and the virus of dissension spread to the ranks of the privates. But in the end, the decision of whether to disobey orders or not came down to the choice of one's fate.

As Carey would write, "Having no adequate idea of what punishment might be meted out to us as mutineers, I preferred to take my chances in battle with Bolo marksmen than at sunrise with an American firing squad."

The mutiny fizzled; Company E's war would go on.

The first mutinous grumblings had been voiced by the French on the railway front after word of the November 11 armistice reached their lines. News of the end of fighting in France had sapped their will, as had the "lack of definite policy in Russia," Capt. Hugh Martin of the American Military Mission would write in a July 6, 1919, report on the various uprisings.

Citing friction between the French troops and their British overseers as well, Martin would add that French morale had been lowered "to such an extent that open mutiny was momentarily expected."

The *poilus* returned to the front only after being promised relief by their officers. And in December the French ambassador, just before departing Russia himself, visited the French soldiers and made a personal appeal to them to stick to their posts.

"Although his speeches apparently had an immediate effect, it soon wore off and it seemed clear that the French troops in Russia could not be relied upon as a fighting force," Martin wrote.

As evidence, Martin pointed to an incident the following March 1, when a company of French soldiers mutinied and refused to perform their scheduled rotation to the railway front. Another French company was sent to Obozerskaya; it, too, refused to go beyond Verst 455.

"Only a few of the artillery personnel and machine gunners volunteered to go," Martin wrote. "The others remained behind." Hearing the whispers and seeing the cold, murderous stares of scores of their angry and disaffected men, many of whom had fought bravely on the

Western Front, French officers began to sincerely believe that they "were in great danger of being killed by their men."

Events would quickly prove that their fears were valid. The French troops spontaneously rioted on the night of March 1. They looted the Y.M.C.A. at Obozerskaya, and on the next day they stormed the "moving picture show" and hauled down a sign on the officers' box that read, "This box reserved for officers." The mutineers replaced that sign with a new one. It read: "The officers will be under the ground."

Their actions led to the arrests of 113 men, who were sent to Archangel and put under the guard of a detachment of French marines. Back at Obozerskaya, the lack of esprit among the remaining French was still such a problem that in the end the entire bunch was relieved and sent back to Archangel.

Mutinies had also occurred among the members of the Slavo-British Allied Legion as early as October 29. Ordered to turn out for inspection by General Ironside, a company of the S.B.A.L.s refused to leave its barracks. The men shouted, "We want more food!" "Our hours are too long!" "We do not want to be under the orders of foreigners!"

Their complaints having been at least acknowledged, the would-be mutineers after a few hours returned to their rooms, and the matter was not pursued further after Edmund Ironside discovered the reason for the outbreak.

"Someone in London," he would recall, had decided and decreed that the Russians were only worthy of half the rations the British soldiers were getting. "Nothing more disastrous to the formation of a new army could well have been received." Ironside ordered full rations for all, and all seemed well.

Then on December 11, another unit of Russians, the First Archangel Company, was ordered out of its barracks to parade before Ironside. But after being ordered to assemble, the S.B.A.L.s instead held a "soviet" and voted not to march, later citing grievances against their British officers.

The men locked themselves in their main barracks and hung red flags from every window, and several men climbed to the roof and fired their weapons. A Stokes mortar was brought up and fired a shell over the building and another one onto the roof. "Before a third could be fired the main door was burst open and the men came out with their hands in the air," General Ironside would write.

What happened next is unclear: Ironside said thirteen ringleaders were arrested, tried, found guilty of mutiny, and sentenced to death—after which, he said, he commuted their sentences and later allowed them to cross over to the Bolo lines.

Moore et al., however, said the leaders were killed by a Russian firing squad, an account echoed in Martin's report, which says the ringleaders were "immediately marched against a wall and a platoon of mutineers was forced to shoot them."

In any event, the rest of the Russians, terrified and pacified if still unhappy, dutifully packed off to the railway front later on December 11 and became, according to Martin, "a splendid fighting unit."

More Russian mutinies, however, were in the offing, including one in the Pinega River Valley in early March, where a company that hadn't been paid for months and had been ill equipped for the bitter cold refused to go to the front lines.

"There were a number of Bolshevik agitators among them and they took advantage of the situation to stir up mutiny," Martin wrote. In the end, twelve of the revolt leaders were shot; the mutineers ultimately were better supplied and agreed to go to the front, where they subsequently did "good work."

A decidedly more violent mutiny by supposedly loyal Russian troops would occur at Toulgas one month after the departure of Company B. Apprehensive as to what would become of them once the Dvina River was free of ice and the Bolo gunboats could freely ply its waters, a group of agitators and their sympathizers struck on the night of April 25–26.

That night, the Bolsheviks sent a delegation up to the forward line at Toulgas and told their White counterparts that they were surrounded. The Bolos gave the men two choices: they could either surrender, come over to the Reds, and be treated well, or they could resist. The latter choice, they were informed, "would mean death to all of them," Martin wrote.

In a panic, the S.B.A.L.s fell upon their officers, and were soon joined in their murderous spree by the Bolos. Seven of the White officers were killed, while the remainder managed to escape, as did some infantrymen. Meanwhile, about three hundred of the Whites went over to the Reds.

As for the British, there were various incidents of lesser mutinies and simple refusals to fight. Two companies of the Yorkshire Regiment flatly refused to enter the lines at the railway front in early February, and it took a good talking-to from Gen. Edmund Ironside and a grueling forced march before their "mutinous spirit" was broken, Martin wrote.

At about the same time, one company of the King's Liverpools balked while on their way to reinforce the garrison at Vistafka. These men, too, were given a "severe lecture" by their commanding officer, and agreed to enter the line at Vistafka only after being promised it would be their last action. And in March, a patrol of Royal Scots refused an order to burn a village on the Dvina River, seeing no point in destroying a village that was then occupied only by "a few families of defenseless peasants," Martin wrote.

The complaints of both Scots and Englishmen were similar, Martin wrote. As veterans of the Western Front and in many cases convalescents, they felt they were entitled to avoid front-line duty, and—there are echoes of the American complaints here—they said they also had been told they were to be garrison troops, not combat soldiers. In their opinion, Martin would write, fighting the Bolos should be the work of "men physically able to do the job."

The Americans obviously were not immune to mutiny, either. Martin, after interviewing enlisted men and officers both, summed up their feelings thusly:

"They wanted to know why they were called upon here after the fighting had ceased on the Western Front; they stated that they were

drafted to fight Germany, not the Bolsheviks; that we had never declared war on the Bolsheviks; that they had been sent here to guard
supplies and not to carry on an aggressive warfare; that after the signing of the Armistice with Germany their job was finished and if the
Government wanted them to stay on and fight Bolsheviks it should say
so and announce some definite policy regarding Russia."

Martin would note that even many American officers "unfortu-
nately" held the same views as their men; some, he would add, had
been "heard to express them within hearing of the soldiers."

The rank and file in northern Russia couldn't then know it, but their
concerns were being addressed back home. Vague expressions of their
feelings of discontentment had trickled home in letters, and in any case
the war wasn't being fought in a vacuum. The newspapers had brought
news of the collapse on the Vaga River front, and while many a worried loved one couldn't know exactly where their husband, brother, or
son was at any particular moment, the folks back home had not been
immune to the questions of just what Americans were doing in Russia,
and what might become of them.

President Woodrow Wilson was of course much more aware of the
rising cost his little war had been incurring in lives and misery. The
previous summer he had only reluctantly sent American troops to
guard Allied stores; by late November, he knew those same troops had
been hustled to the far frontiers of northern Russia; he knew as well
that Americans were dying.

In an echo of one of Felix Cole's arguments against intervention,
Wilson noted that the United States indeed was going to find it "harder
to get out than it was to get in."

As the months had passed since the armistice, he also had come under increasing political pressure to pull the men out, with politicians,
relatives of the men, and even civic institutions publicly questioning
why the 339th and its associated units were still in Russia.

Senator Hiram Johnson of California was particularly vocal. In a Senate speech on January 29, 1919—just one day before the front page of the *New York Times* reported on the running retreat from Shenkursk—Johnson blasted Wilson's government for being "weak, vacillating, stupid, and ignorant" in its attitude toward Russia.

"We have engaged in a miserable misadventure," added Johnson, who introduced a resolution calling for American troops to be withdrawn. Two weeks later, a vote on the resolution ended in a tie, forcing Wilson's vice president, Thomas Marshall, to cast the deciding vote against the measure.

Closer to the 339th's home, on February 5 a Michigan state senator, Herbert J. Baker, introduced a similar resolution asking Wilson's government to "immediately withdraw American troops from Northern Russia," the Lansing (MI) *State Journal* reported.

And according to an April 10, 1919, article in the *Detroit Free Press*, an organization called Detroit's Own Welfare Association was making similar pleas and trying to bring pressure on the government on the behalf of friends and family of the soldiers who were "in danger of massacre at the hands of the bolsheviki [*sic*] in northern Russia according to recent reports.

"Relatives of the boys are growing desperate and must have accurate information," the association said in its appeal to Wilson. "Thousands will volunteer if you need a relieving force. For God's sake say something and do something."

Even the Americans' own little-seen and often criticized regimental commander, Col. George Stewart, was sympathetic to their many sufferings and deprivations through the long fall and winter, and agreed that the men under his command should at the least be relieved—and soon.

In a February 13 cable to the War Department, Stewart wrote:

"Due to primitive conditions of life and continuous service in the field under almost Arctic conditions officers and men are beginning to feel the strain. Practically the whole Allied command has been on continuous duty in the field all winter with no reserves in Archangel.

"Limited Allied reserves are now being supplied from Murmansk a few coming on ice breaker and other by rail to Kem; and then by horses and sleds to destination. Recommend that present force be entirely replaced as early as practicable in Spring with an adequate force commensurable with its mission supplied equipped so that it can operate in an American way."

Where Wilson had the previous summer been torturously racked with misgivings about sending Americans into Russia, by mid-February the increasing clamor and his own growing doubts about the "miserable misadventure" caused him to quietly pull the plug on the expedition.

With little ado or fanfare, Wilson on February 16 notified Secretary of War Newton Baker that he wanted American troops out of northern Russia; Baker, who had opposed the intervention in the first place, quickly and quietly began making plans to begin withdrawing as soon as possible.

In a February 18, 1919, letter to the House and Senate military committees, Baker said he planned to have all Americans out of northern Russia by summer. He also announced that two companies of American engineers would be sent to Murmansk to repair the Murman Railroad—and "facilitate the prompt withdrawal of American and Allied troops . . . at the earliest possible moment that weather in the spring will permit."

The news was reported in newspapers across the United States, and soon enough it crossed the ocean to northern Russia. There it became a source of new frustration and tantalization for the men still waging war in the far outposts: when, they wanted to know, was "the earliest possible moment"?

Still, the cat was out of the bag: whether its allies—English, French, Russian Whites—liked it or not, the U.S. was pulling out. On March 4, the British war cabinet decided to follow suit, ignoring the arguments of the virulently anti-Bolshevik Winston Churchill, who as secretary of war had proposed *increasing* the Allied commitment in Russia to one million men. This after England had nearly been bled dry in the just-concluded four-year Great War.

After a winter of military disaster and unrest among the troops, it was also decided that George Stewart was not the man to lead any withdrawal. On March 10, Gen. Wilds Richardson, a veteran of service in Alaska who was then in France and commanding the Fifty-Fifth Brigade, Twenty-Eighth Division, was told by Gen. John Pershing that he was going to be sent to Russia to take over the 339th Infantry Regiment.

A week later, Richardson traveled to Paris and met with President Wilson, who was then attending the Paris Peace Conference. During that meeting, Wilson kvetched about how American troops had been mishandled by the British; he also told Richardson that his new mission would be to get American troops out of Russia "as early as practicable after the opening of navigation."

Richardson and his coterie didn't leave England until April 1, 1919, and arrived at Murmansk on April 8. There, he learned that one company of the 339th Infantry Regiment had mutinied on March 30—an incident that provided great fodder for the American press, and which was exaggerated and exacerbated by the gleeful reporting of the British press especially.

The unit cited for the alleged mutiny was Company I, which was stationed at Smolny barracks in Archangel. The men had put up some resistance when ordered to begin packing its sleighs for a return to the railway front, which was then being threatened by a large Bolo force that sought to take Obozerskaya and split the scattered Allied units.

"The sergeant in charge of the loading reported to one of the officers of the company that the men had stopped work and refused to load any further, stating that they would not go to the front," Hugh S. Martin would write.

The officer went to the scene and ordered his men to resume loading the sleighs. "He had to talk to them for some time before they would stir," Martin reported. Eventually, the work resumed, but one man continued to resist and was finally arrested and placed in the guardhouse.

In the meantime, Colonel Stewart was summoned, and he had the company assembled in the Y.M.C.A. cantonment, "where he gave them a long talk," Martin wrote.

Richardson, who arrived at Archangel on April 17, would write that Stewart read the Articles of War to the company, and then told the men he would be happy to answer any questions. The main question was simple: "What are we here for and what are the intentions of the U.S. Government?"

Martin would write: "The men finally agreed to go to the front on the condition that the man who had been placed in the guard house should be released. This was done and the company proceeded with their work and left for the front that afternoon."

However, the company's men would remain forever tarred with the accusation that they had mutinied. On April 10, a cablegram that had been sent from the American Military Mission on March 31 was released to the press.

The cable notified the War Department of the matter, and said that in fact the company's men had agreed to entrain only as far as Obozerskaya—and also let it be known that they warned of a "general mutiny" if American troops were not withdrawn "at the earliest possible date."

Two days later, the War Department confirmed to the press that the alleged mutineers belonged to Company I. Gen. Peyton March, Pershing's chief of staff, didn't help matters by claiming that the unit had been infected and affected by Bolshevist propaganda.

March announced that the men had asked questions of their officers that echoed those found in Bolshevik "propaganda leaflets," the *Washington Post* reported on April 13.

"I have not seen this leaflet, but I am very anxious to get it," March told the newspaper. "This is a very striking thing. I have had long experiences in the army and I do not recall ever having seen American soldiers who did not want to get into a fight. They always said, 'lead me to it,' and went into it."

George Stewart himself would later downplay the entire affair. "I did not have to take any disciplinary action against either an officer or soldier of the regiment in connection with the matter, so you may judge that the reports that have appeared have been very, very greatly exaggerated," he said.

"Every soldier connected with the incident performed his duty as a soldier. And as far as I am concerned, I think the matter should be closed."

Richardson, who ordered an investigation of the episode, agreed. "This incident was given wide circulation in the States, and I am satisfied from my investigation that an exaggerated impression was created as to its seriousness.

"It is regrettable that it should have happened at all, to mar in any degree the record of heroic and valiant service performed by this regiment under trying conditions."

As supposed mutinies go, Company I's was a tepid affair, more a brief outburst of pent-up frustration and homesickness than an actual rebellion. No one was imprisoned for long or executed as a result, and there was no good reason to reveal the damning cable to the press.

Because of that, Company I would remain forever and unfairly tarnished, and its men would face repeated questioning about the alleged mutiny upon their return home. In the meantime, there would be more "heroic and valiant service" to perform once more on the railway front.

CHAPTER TWENTY-EIGHT

THE BALLAD OF BOLSHIE OZERKI

A ll were certain that Clifford Fuller Phillips would live, that he would pull through. All thought he would return to Nebraska and the law firm of Phillips and Hebenstreit in Falls City, and to his wife, Kathryn, and daughter, Ellen Jane, who in a few months would turn three years old—old enough to wonder who her father was, and where her father was, but perhaps not yet old enough to understand any possible answers to those questions.

Lt. Clifford Fuller Phillips, Company H, 339th Infantry Regiment, and his Third Platoon had been sent east from Chekuevo on the Onega River on March 19, 1919, to reinforce a patrol led by Lt. Edmund Collins. Two days before, Collins had left with thirty men to see if he could confirm reports that the enemy was attacking the village of Bolshie Ozerki—twelve miles west of Obozerskaya—in force in an attempt to cut the lines of communication between the railway and Onega fronts.

One Company H patrol had already disappeared near Bolshie Ozerki on March 16 and was presumed to have been captured. Since, new reports claimed that the Bolos had attacked Bolshie Ozerki with between one thousand and fifteen hundred men. A small force of French defending the village had quickly melted away before the onslaught, offering a minimum of resistance before taking flight for the relative safety of Obozerskaya.

Across the fronts, the specter of annihilation loomed, even as rumors of a withdrawal gained strength. The Red Army had grown from almost nothing into a force of 600,000, and increasing activity by the Bolos had led to fears of a grand spring offensive.

With the rivers certain to be free of ice sooner than at Archangel farther north, there was the possibility that Bolo gunboats could reach and reduce the garrisons at Toulgas on the Dvina as well as Kitsa, on the Vaga River, with no fear of opposition by the British monitors—and with little possibility of reinforcements coming to the men.

The same was true in the Onega River Valley, held since December only by Company H and a force of Cossacks. And the railway front was also lightly held by a scant mix of Americans, Whites, and French. A concerted push by the Bolos at Bolshie Ozerki or Obozerskaya could leave that front unguarded, and the way to Archangel open.

And so Edmund Collins and his men had been sent east on a scouting mission to Chunova, which sat some ten miles northwest of Bolshie Ozerki and served as the headquarters for the railway front commander, Colonel Lucas. Upon Collins's arrival early on March 18, Lucas ordered Collins to accompany him on a move south to Bolshie Ozerki, and thence to Obozerskaya. But all were stepping off into the unknown, with no idea how many Reds were on their front.

As the small mixed force approached Bolshie Ozerki by sled, they came under intense fire from half a dozen machine guns. The barrage caused their Russian ponies to bolt, tossing Lucas and many others into the deep snow. While they floundered, the Allied force returned the Bolo fire, and before long they realized that the reports were true: Bolshie Ozerki was indeed heavily fortified, and an attack on it would be little more than suicide.

Luckily, the Reds were shooting high and only one man, Cpl. Nathan Redmond, was killed, and another wounded. Others, including Lucas—who became lost and wandered all night through the fifty-below temperatures—suffered severe frostbite as they sledded through the drifting snow to Chunova.

The next day, March 19, Clifford Phillips was ordered to take his men and reinforce Collins at Chunova. As well, a force of 320 men of the British Yorkshire Regiment were hustling south from Murmansk, and it arrived at Chunova on March 22. A new attack on Bolshie Ozerki was ordered by Lt. Col. N. A. Lawrie, who was in command at Onega and was fretting over an interruption of the flow of supplies down the Onega-Chekuevo-Obozerskaya supply line.

Despite fresh evidence to the contrary, Lawrie believed that the Bolo force at Bolshie Ozerki was only a large raiding party and could be easily attacked and swept aside, and the lines of communication with Onega reopened.

Lawrie would be proven wrong, but orders is orders. At two A.M. on March 23, the Allied force gathered, was put under the command of Lt. Edmund Collins, and shushed off toward Bolshie Ozerki, where not for the first time in this strange, strange war would a tiny Allied force confront, and be confronted by, a vastly superior number of Bolos.

The Allied force reached the northwestern outskirts of Bolshie Ozerki at nine A.M. As had happened five days earlier, they were quickly fired upon. Collins sent one company of Yorks through some woods on the right, and another company of Yorks was deployed to the left of the Americans.

This battle line, spread across 350 yards, advanced on the busy Bolo machine guns in Bolshie Ozerki, six hundred yards to the south. The Allies, easy pickings for the Bolo guns as they struggled forward through heavy, waist-deep snow, managed to cross five hundred yards of mostly open ground before Collins was mortally wounded by a sniper. Clifford Phillips took over, and though no further advance was possible, he directed the men to hold the perilous line; they kept up a furious fire for five hours before orders came from Lawrie to retire.

(Collins would not survive the trip back to Chekuevo; in the coming weeks and months, the fates of those in the patrol that had gone missing on March 16 would also be revealed. The patrol's Pvt. Earl Fulcher would write that a Bolo ambush that morning left two enlisted men— PFC Josef Ramotowske and Pvt. John Frucce—dead; Fulcher, who was wounded, and Pvts. August Peterson—also wounded, in his right leg—and William Scheulke and Cpl. Earl Collins were captured.)

Amazingly, among the Americans only Lt. Edmund Collins and Company H private Edward McConvill would die as a result of the March 23 battle. Two Yorkshire officers and two enlisted men also were killed in action, and ten more wounded. In addition, "many American and British soldiers were frostbitten," Company H's Lt. Harry Ketcham would write.

The survivors extricated themselves from the battle scene and once more headed for Chekuevo, while the Reds bolstered their numbers, their aim being to obliterate the railway force and then roll up the Onega force at their leisure.

While Company H and the Yorks were unsuccessfully trying to push the Bolos out of Bolshie Ozerki on March 23, another unit— Company E—attempted an attack from the east. The unit had been rotating in and out of the railway front over the past two months, replacing the worrisome French for a time and then being relieved by the same.

After the battle at Bolshie Ozerki on March 18, General Ironside had visited the front west of Obozerskaya and was alarmed to find it being guarded by just two hundred men and a handful of artillery. Returning to Archangel, he ordered reinforcements sent forward. To that end, Company E was rousted from Smolny barracks and sent down the railway with a force of Whites and a half company of Yorks.

And on the morning after the near mutiny by Company E's corporals at Obozerskaya, the men did indeed fall in and head once more for the front line, stumbling through the snow in their dreaded Shackleton boots with "depressed spirits and with the morale at an exceedingly low point," Donald Carey would write.

They were headed for Verst 18, which Carey would describe as a "poorly fortified position" between Obozerskaya and Bolshie Ozerki.

Stopping there, they built fires and warmed themselves while a number of Whites bound west for Bolshie Ozerki passed by, each man dressed in a "white sheet-like hood and cape which at once recalled to my mind accounts of the Ku Klux Klan of post-bellum days," Carey wrote.

At four A.M. on March 23, Company E was rousted and put on the road west as well, following, Carey would claim, "a couple of noble lieutenants stupefied with liquor, presumably rum."

After passing a battery of French artillery that was manned by Whites, Lt. Edwin Broer, "reeling and swearing," ordered the men to spread into attack formation. Then the company advanced, some following the road toward Bolshie Ozerki and others tramping through thick snow in the dense scrub forest.

At a turn in the road Carey noticed dark forms ahead in the early-morning gloom, and the red glow of a cigarette—White soldiers. Word was passed that the Russians would carry the attack on Bolshie Ozerki, while Company E would stand in support.

Soon enough, though, the Russians were discovered by their Red countrymen, and the air erupted with bullets and artillery shells. Carey, at a high point of the road, hugged the ground as shells burst about the company and the Russians manning the French artillery to the rear opened up.

As the men ate snow, Third Battalion commander J. Brooks Nichols arrived from the rear with Company E's Capt. Bernard Heil, already a pariah among his troops for leading from behind at Kodish.

Cpl. Fred Kooyers would derisively write, "Capitan [sic] Heil had stayed about two miles back of the men trying to dodge the battle until Major Nichols got there, when Major Nichols learned how badly we were outnumbered he told us to hold what we had for it was impossible for two hundred and fifty men to drive ten thousand."

At about eleven A.M., the company was ordered to move back, and it then swung north in an attempt to get around the Bolos' left flank. Dutifully following orders, Carey and the others began strenuously breaking trail through thick woods, their spirits sagging.

After an hour of struggle, a "miraculous transformation" in their moods occurred when word came over newly strung telephone wire that the attack had been called off. The Whites had been repulsed, and its survivors fell in behind Company E as it now turned and plodded east.

Company E was virtually unscratched, while the Russians had lost at least three killed and more wounded—some walking, some being borne on litters. The dead, "partly covered with a carpet-like material," Carey would write, were placed by the road in the rear of the artillery.

The company took up positions near the guns, which were protected by log barricades covered with pine boughs and snow. But there were few places to lie low at the lightly manned Verst 18 and few places to hide, considering that thousands of angry Bolos were just a few miles away and ready to pounce.

Over the next few days, men stood to in two-hour shifts in the fifty-below cold, peering into the enveloping darkness of night and the fuzzy air of day and expecting at any moment to see the Bolo horde coming straight for them. More artillery was brought from Obozerskaya and placed near the original pieces, and engineers cut wood and assembled blockhouses along the front with dizzying speed.

The Whites remained in the vanguard, camped in the woods to the west of the Americans, among whom a soldier's rumor surfaced on March 25 to the effect that Company E would be relieving the White Russians; the rumor turned out to be true. Once again, strains of defiance emerged among Company E's men—even in the very face of an overwhelming enemy. Some of the men had had enough.

Over their campfires, the men groused about their lot and their officers and once more broached the subject of refusing to move to the front lines. Once more, it was a corporal—Jim Sanders—who led the rabble-rousing.

When Lt. Edwin Broer subsequently ordered Sanders to lead a relief platoon toward the front line, he balked and said he and his men would not go unless a commissioned officer accompanied them.

"A heated argument" ensued, Carey would write, but Broer finally agreed to lead the party. "Thus we relieved our enemy's countrymen," Carey added.

Edwin Broer began leading the eighty-man detail, but turned back because he had forgotten to bring his overcoat. When the men began to turn back with him, Broer ordered them to continue on to the White lines. The men refused, complaining that they were being mistreated. Once more Broer backed down. He would spend his night coatless in the fifty-below temperatures.

Company E remained on the front and at Verst 18 for two more days, every member wary of an impending attack. Finally, after having camped in the snow for six days and nights, they were relieved by Joel Moore and Company M.

"No time was wasted in bidding the much cursed [sic] place a ceremonious farewell," Carey wrote.

Company M, veterans of the railway and Pinega fronts, had little time to get accustomed to their new surroundings. The Bolo force opposing the Allies had grown even as Company E manned the lines, and now numbered seven thousand men under command of Gen. Aleksei Kuropatkin, a former Czarist officer.

By March 31 this force had nearly surrounded Company M and the artillery; that day, the Bolos attacked the rear at Verst 18, where a pair of Russian 75s had been emplaced. The artillery was swung around, and bursts of shrapnel and fire from a Lewis gun were sent spewing toward the Reds, who were finally repulsed.

Four of the company's men—Sgt. Glenn Leitzell, Pvt. Freeman Hogan, and mechanics Charles Dial and Jens Laursen—were ambushed separately while making supply runs during the attack, and "brave, courteous, gentle Dial was shot through the head," Moore would write. The other three, plus a "Y.M.C.A. man," Bryant Ryal, were taken prisoner.

The Reds then attacked the company's front, but were also repulsed by rifle fire from the First Platoon's men and artillery. "Our communications were cut in the rear and it looked as if we would be in it when our ammunition gave out," Moore wrote.

On April 1, the Bolos charged from the woods at 3:30 A.M., the brunt landing on Company M's Fourth Platoon on the western flank. Fire from recently constructed blockhouses stymied three determined assaults that rolled as close as two hundred yards to a log barricade across the Obozerskaya–Chekuevo road.

Before long hundreds of Bolo dead and wounded littered the open taiga, as the Americans poured rifle and machine-gun fire and artillery into their oncoming, uneven ranks. On that day, "it was a glorious thing to be in the blockhouses and the log barriers and to witness those human multitudes surge on, then slacken, and falter and fail and shrivel as they came," John Cudahy would write.

There were losses within Company M. Pvts. Alva Crook and Frank Sapp were killed at their posts, and the Bolos repeated their assaults on the company's rear, but the effort was "as futile as it had been the first day's fight," Moore would write. "Scores of enemy wounded and dead lay in close range of our guns."

Among the Bolo dead was a commander who, thinking that a midday lull in the fighting signaled a Red victory, rode his large white horse nearly into the American lines before being shot down. The commander's sword was retrieved and presented to Joel Moore, a relic of an American success on this day.

At Verst 445 south of Obozerskaya, the maligned Company I, just two days removed from their alleged mutiny, also stood toe-to-toe with the Bolos attacking across the taiga and through the scrub brush and "never wavered during the ceaseless, storming battles that followed," Cudahy wrote.

The Machine Gun Company's Harry Costello, on the front with Company I, was also full of praise for its men. "The entire company went into the front lines, walked into a fight as they relieved the front, and withstood ten days of artillery and infantry attack without flinching, and defeated the enemy at every turn of the road," he would write.

As the second day's battle raged into the afternoon, two platoons of Company H, two companies of Yorks, and a detachment of Poles received orders to once more attack the Bolo force at Bolshie Ozerki to create a diversion and lessen the burden of those fighting at Obozerskaya and Verst 18.

By one A.M., the Allies were two miles from Bolshie Ozerki; at three A.M., they attacked along the road leading south into the village, their arrival heralded by the barking of dogs near the Bolo camp. One company of the Yorkshires subsequently stormed a ridge from which heavy machine-gun fire was coming, and its captain was killed.

Richard Ballensinger, captain of Company H, received orders to reinforce the Yorks, and he chose Clifford Phillips's First Platoon for the job. The other company of Yorks, meanwhile, was sent east to attack the northern edge of the Bolo position, but it also floundered in the dark and became lost. The detachment of Poles, sent to assault several small villages south of the Bolos, were easily repulsed by machine-gun fire.

That left Clifford Phillips, who led his men into the maw of the Bolo guns with a look of religious fervor in his eyes. "I have never seen a look like it before or since," Ballensinger would recall. "It was a look that made me watch him all the way out."

Phillips and his men joined the surviving Yorkshires, but heavy Bolo fire soon caused him to reconsider his position. As bullets, artillery shells, and the mechanical *put-put-put* of the machine guns filled the air, Phillips barked orders left and right, and urged the men manning the Lewis guns to pour it on as the Bolo hordes charged, retreated, and then charged again.

Pvt. Floyd Auslander was soon hit and killed instantly. Others, Yorks and Americans, fell as the deadly morning progressed. Phillips, Ballensinger would write, kept his cool even as Bolo bullets churned the snow around him, moving "without apparent thought of the bullets flying all around him" and giving ground "only very slowly, in spite of heavy casualties" until he, too, fell with a bullet in his chest.

Ballensinger, by then at the front and standing next to Phillips, said the shot knocked Phillips down "as if a ton of brick had fallen on him.

He said to me, 'My God, I got it. Captain, don't bother with me, I am done for, just look after the boys.'"

Lt. Howard Pellegrom, just returned from Archangel that morning, took command of Phillips's men and, together with the previously lost company of Yorks that had finally reached the scene, managed to beat off the continuous, massed Bolo attacks.

Company H and its allies held the rest of the day, and then escaped into the night. Company M, meanwhile, rebuffed the Bolo attacks of April 2, and held on at Verst 18 for two more days that featured little more than desultory back-and-forth firing.

All told, the Allies had fought off a force of some seven thousand men, two thousand of whom were killed in action, wounded, or died from frostbite after being incapacitated by their wounds and slowly expiring in the frigid temperatures of night. Other Bolo wounded, understanding they would be shot if they returned to their line, surrendered.

One American, though severely wounded, was still alive. Even while the desperate battle raged near Bolshie Ozerki, Clifford Phillips had been carefully carried to a sleigh and rushed toward Chunova, and thence Chekuevo. There, he rallied for a time despite a severe loss of blood, and was even "able to sit up in bed and talk to those who came to see him," Harry Ketcham would remember.

After a time, he was well enough to be carried on to Onega, "in the expectation that there he would be safer and have better care," Ketcham wrote.

On April 11, Ballensinger wired Kathryn Phillips at her parents' home in Neola, Iowa, and told her that her husband had been wounded but was "in hospital . . . no need to worry."

Clifford himself sent another wire to Kathryn three days later and told her he was "recovering rapidly. Don't worry." But doctors soon discovered that he had a hole in an artery, and was suffering massive internal bleeding. He needed surgery to repair the artery, but the primitive hospital at Onega had neither a surgeon nor the equipment for such a repair—and Phillips would never survive a grueling trip by sled to the better-equipped hospital at Archangel.

In Nebraska, winter was loosening its grip; the sandhill cranes were on the wing, headed north, the farmers were planting wheat, and the corn was sprouting. In a small hospital in godforsaken northern Russia, Clifford Phillips was breathing his last, his tortured body finally giving up its six-week fight for life on May 10, 1919.

On May 16, Kathryn Phillips would receive one last telegram, this one from the War Department. All hopes that Clifford Phillips would one day return were dashed as she read the first few words: "Deeply regret to inform you . . ."

The mourning for Clifford Phillips spread far beyond Neola, Iowa, and Company H. "The whole North Russian force is a loser by this gallant officer's death," wrote P. H. Edwards, a British officer Phillips had befriended on the Onega front.

Another officer, Glenn Birkett of Company G of the 339th, tried to console Kathryn in a May 18 letter. "One time when several officers had been talking about their wives he mentioned to me that he didn't care to speak about you ordinarily because you meant too much to him," Birkett wrote.

"You and his daughter were far dearer to him than the average family is to a man. His little girl, of whom he was so proud, can be proud of him as very very few children can be proud of their fathers."

Ellen Jane Phillips would grow up with no memory of her father. But she would carry some relics of his life, and his service, through her own long life, which ended at the age of eighty-nine in 2005. Among the relics were photos from happier times, and a shiny brass cross on which sat an eagle and the words "For Valor"—the DSC Clifford Fuller Phillips was awarded posthumously for encouraging and inspiring his men on that violent, windswept ridge in the middle of Russian nowhere.

CHAPTER TWENTY-NINE

GETTING OUT

The ice on the Vaga River was beginning to rot and heave and crack, and as the great winter thaw approached, the captain grew more and more concerned.

But Capt. Ralph Ramsay of Company F, 339th Infantry Regiment, had orders from the British commander on the Vaga front: he and his men were to remain at Kitsa until that commander, Colonel Poignant, deemed it the proper time to evacuate to the west bank.

But there was a great chance the ice could break, leaving Company F isolated and stranded on the east bank of the Vaga and at the mercy of the sure-to-come Bolo gunboats floating high on the swirling, churning spring waters.

And so Ralph Ramsay chafed and cursed and swore under his breath, and continued watching the river. As the ice grew weaker, he decided he'd had enough, and declared to the colonel he was getting out, and damn the consequences.

The colonel in turn ordered the Canadian artillery, already on the west bank, to fire on Ramsay and his men should they attempt to cross. The Canadians refused, telling Poignant "they would not fire on the Americans under any circumstances," Capt. Hugh Martin of the American Military Mission would write in a report.

And so two days before the evacuation date chosen somewhat arbitrarily by Colonel Poignant, Capt. Ralph Ramsay led his men down the steep east bank of the Vaga and across its jostling, melting floes. He did so, in the end, with no repercussions, even though Martin would note that Ramsay's refusal to stay at Kitsa could have been seen as "an outstanding act of insubordination."

But Martin would also write in Ramsay's defense: "Everybody acquainted with the situation knew that had Captain Ramsay not disregarded the order of Colonel Poignant he would have jeopardized the lives of all his men and apparently for no good purpose."

Similar drama, and similar activity, was taking place across all of the various fronts of northern Russia. On the Dvina, the Vaga, the Onega, the Pinega, and the railway, soldiers were going to find out whether what Woodrow Wilson had said five months earlier—that it was going to be "harder to get out than it was to get in"—would prove true.

Gen. Edmund Ironside had been thinking and worrying over the subject of withdrawal—both American and British—for some time. The "ideal solution" he found was to "hand over our defensive positions to the local Russians and to withdraw as a peace-operation," he would write.

But he worried over the fragile morale of those same Russians, and knew that handing the overall defense to them would constitute a "critical moment." "There was always the chance of a sudden collapse on one side or the other. If the Whites collapsed, we should have to fight hard to save our own skins and those of the friendly Russians."

Gen. Wilds Richardson arrived in Archangel on April 17, 1919, with a similar plan for withdrawing his American units. As in the "Vietnamization" in Southeast Asia fifty-odd years later, in which South Vietnamese soldiers slowly took the place of American troops, the Americans would be withdrawn and replaced with Cossacks and units of the Slavo-British Allied Legion.

Looming over the situation was the strong possibility of a spring drive by the Bolsheviks, especially on the river fronts. Timing would be everything, where with the spring thaw the Bolo gunboats would have the upper hand for at least a few days. Looming as well was the fealty of the White troops; at Toulgas, an S.B.A.L. mutiny on April 25 that had left seven Russian officers dead had brought new worries.

The incident caused great concern among the Allies, and Ironside would call it "a sad beginning to bringing a Russian Army into the field." Luckily, "it proved to be an isolated incident with no collusion with sister units in the area."

And so the men of the 339th Infantry Regiment began withdrawing, slowly and cautiously, in places leaving behind examples of their American ingenuity.

Booby traps and incendiaries were being prepared along the Vaga River front in anticipation of the Reds' arrival, engineers rigging machine guns that could be fired independently by stringing buckets of water to triggers.

As well, wires attached to the pins of hand grenades were strung through the woods, and explosives and flammable material were crammed into each building at Kitsa and Maximofskaya across the river.

As the last man stepped onto the western shore of the Vaga on the night of April 19, he sent a rocket up to alert the engineers. "The following moment the entire surrounding country shook to a series of terrific explosions both at Kitsa and Maximofskaya and then a great red glare emblazoned the sky as the two oil soaked [sic] villages burst into flame," Moore et al. wrote.

At its new positions at Malo Beresnik and Nitzni Kitsa above Kitsa, the recently evacuated Kitsa force awaited the arrival of the Bolo flotilla of gunboats, still aiming to drive the invaders into the White Sea. Come it did, but it turned out to be no match for the prepared fortifications and the entrenched Canadian artillery, which mauled the Red boats.

On the lower Dvina, meanwhile, engineers were also working, there using dynamite in an attempt to effect an early ice-out. British gunboats were soon on the move south toward Toulgas, where they battered the former Company B outpost that had fallen to the traitorous S.B.A.L.s and their new Bolo friends.

On May 17, the famed commander Frank Worsley, who had survived Ernest Shackleton's doomed Antarctic expedition aboard the *Endurance* and had more recently been appointed director of Arctic equipment and transport by Ironside, headed up the Dvina on H.M.S. *Cricket*, a heavily armed British gunboat.

Worsley's gunners shelled the Bolos' gunboats, occupied villages, took land batteries, and recaptured ten miles of the Dvina. The flotilla reached Toulgas on May 18, and by two P.M. the village—what was left of it—was back in Allied hands.

"My knowledge of ice stood me in great stead," Worsley said. "I had two happy months of fighting: that is, we'd have two hours fighting every other day . . . we shelled 'bolo' gunboats, land batteries, villages and troops and assist[ed] in the recapture of some ten miles of ground lost in the autumn and winter."

Meanwhile on the Pinega River front, a force of British, White Russian, and Chinese troops were attacking east through deep woods from Leunova toward Karpogora in an attempt to trap a Bolo force that threatened the village of Pinega. The attack, though, ended in disaster.

Within the woods, Red machine gunners had a field day slicing up the assault columns, and the Allied colonels, one Russian and the other British, "threw their men into death traps as they had done previously on other fronts," Moore et al. would write.

Emboldened, the Bolos attacked Pinega with greater determination, while Company K's men, positioned at Kholmogory near the confluence of the Pinega and the Dvina, anxiously watched and waited. Though their position was well fortified with blockhouses and emplacements, if the Reds took Pinega they could easily steam downriver and reduce the village at their leisure.

Fortunately for the Americans, the Whites held Pinega, and with the breakup of the river, Allied gunboats headed northeast once more, and the threat to Kholmogory and even Archangel was removed.

On the Onega River front, all had been quiet since the Bolos withdrew from Bolshie Ozerki on April 19. Company H continued to send out patrols, but once the ice on the Dvina below Archangel was out, the supply route from Onega to Obozerskaya, so vital during the winter, lost its importance.

On the Vaga River front, there would be one more piece of work for the column to perform before they were pulled out. Late on May 19, the Allied force, now grown with the addition of fresh White recruits, moved south to retake Ignotovskaya, directly across from Kitsa.

British gunboats and Canadian batteries bombarded the village for twenty minutes, splintering homes and setting fires. Then the infantry went in under a creeping barrage and recaptured the town, which had been lost to the Bolos more than a month earlier.

They found numerous dead and wounded Bolos, and in the coming days brought in more than two hundred other wounded and surrendering Reds. Then they sat and waited; reinforcements were finally on their way.

British authorities had promised Gen. Edmund Ironside relief through the winter, and during that time they had raised two brigades, one consisting of conscripted men who had been too young to join the fighting in France, and the other made up of veterans. Some of these "longed again for the thrill of the war," while others were simply "out of work and could get no other employment," John Cudahy would write.

The leading brigade reached the mouth of the Dvina on May 26, and the second a few days later. As Frederick Poole had done in early September, Ironside sent the new arrivals straight up the Dvina River, where on June 6 Frank Douma and Company D were relieved at Kurgoman.

Reaching Archangel on June 8, the Americans—few of whom had spent any time in the city since the previous September—gawked at the amenities as if they were cavemen suddenly transported into the twentieth century.

"We saw autos, street-cars and trains today, the first time in nine months," Douma wrote. "We also saw civilized girls for the first time, regular dresses and silk stockings. I am going to try to date up some of them as soon as possible.

"We must surely be on our way home by now."

Indeed, Americans were now withdrawing across the front. Russians relieved the Third Battalion on the railway front on May 7, and before the month was out Companies E and G were also on their way to Archangel.

Company K, too, left Kholmogory for Archangel, while Company F, which became the last American unit to get into the fight when it relieved the Allied force at Kitsa in early April, performed its final patrol on May 20. It would be the last American unit to leave this strange, strange war behind.

Company E's PFC Donald Carey would recall his company commander, Lt. John Baker, and other officers putting some ballistic oomph into their celebration of withdrawal while at Obozerskaya on May 21.

"In the evening I heard a number of revolver shots," he would remember. "Our officers were celebrating. One was our tall, red-faced company commander, Lieutenant Baker, who, as he said, 'had been for six months as sober as a Philadelphia judge and now I'm going to enjoy myself.' He staggered about, firing his .45 revolver into the forest."

As the Americans headed north for Archangel and their British and Russian counterparts went south for the river and railway fronts, a large question loomed in the minds of those who looked beyond their own desires of simply getting out of Russia. It seemed to some that the Bolsheviks had held back through the early spring, as the feared large-scale offensive the Allies had been sure would come had not materialized.

The Bolos, it appeared, were "content to merely harry the Americans, but not to take any more losses going against them," Moore et al. wrote. Instead, the Reds seemed to be biding their time and waiting for the Americans to pull out.

In fact, Leon Trotsky and Vladimir Lenin were more concerned at that moment with the White forces that threatened the country's breadbasket below the northern reaches of frozen Archangel, and they had turned their attention toward the south and east. As well, there were political considerations.

The fate and future of Russia were at that moment part of the conversations at the Paris Peace Conference, and Lenin was hoping for wide recognition of the Red government. Because of the delicate politics involved, the Reds did not want to agitate and alienate the Allies with a final, crushing, bloody defeat, but had decided to wait them out in the hope that they would soon enough simply leave.

Cudahy offered a further reason for the Red pause, citing Bolo prisoners' tales of low morale among the Bolos' rank and file. Some had been holding protest meetings, while in at least one instance more drastic action had been taken: Bolo soldiers had executed their commander, retribution for driving his men into the Allied guns at the point of his sword.

In late May and early June of 1919, the Americans slowly assembled in a canvas-tent city at Economie, north of Archangel on the White Sea. The trip wasn't always easy: the barge on which Companies A and B traveled became stuck on a sandbar in the middle of the Dvina shortly after leaving their base at Plesso, and the men spent the rest of that day and all of the next stranded and chafing at the rotten turn of events.

"Still fast on sandbar, we are taken off by tugs to lighten load and landed on island, four tugs busy with no success," Company B's Clarence Scheu would write. "We reboard barge, taken off again at 9 p.m., and reland on island, build fires to keep warm, expected aid does not arrive.

"We reboard barge after midnight, should have been in Archangel today, fine stuff, more swearing going on." It would be several days before the men reached Archangel, and then Economie.

There, the 339th Infantry Regiment's men fought off a new enemy— hordes of mosquitoes—and drilled, went company against company in baseball games, and paraded through Archangel on Memorial Day.

Considering their ordeal over the past winter, they also put their heads together and reached a consensus that they should have some distinctive collective name, and an insignia to go with it.

They decided to call themselves "the Polar Bears" and submitted their idea for a moniker and a corresponding patch that featured a polar bear against a blue background to Gen. Wilds Richardson. Richardson gave his approval and instructed the regiment's quartermaster to produce the patch.

And so it was that as Polar Bears, the 339th and its associated units continued to wait for deliverance.

"'At the earliest possible moment' was the date set by the War Department for the withdrawal of troops from Russia," Moore et al. would write. "This was the promise made the American people during the ice-bound winter . . .

"To us wearied veterans of that strange war, the nine months of guerilla war, always strenuous and at times taking on large proportions—to us the 'earliest possible moment' could not arrive a minute too soon."

Their transports arrived carrying the new British volunteers. They in turn brought with them chips on their shoulders as to which Allied country, exactly, had won the Great War; they weren't about to give much credit to the Americans, who had entered the war almost three years after its outbreak.

British-American relations, never good in northern Russia, turned even worse as Limey encountered Yank in Archangel.

"Certain replacement troops—British—arrived at the end of May and in early June, inoculated, apparently, with the virus of the wordy conflict then beginning to rage in England as to 'who won the war,'" Wilds Richardson would write.

"Previous differences had by this time been fairly well smoothed out or adjusted, but they broke out anew upon this issue and several incipient melees arose in the streets of Archangel which required prompt repressive measures to quell."

On June 2, Moore and his men, Donald Carey's Company E, Harry Costello's Machine Gun Company, Harry Mead and Company A, John

Toornman and Company G, and Companies I and L boarded the *Czar* and began their journey to a better reality.

The *Czar* left port at 7:45 the next morning. "Balance of boys on the dock including the band and *some* noise," one anonymous member of Company A would write in his diary. "At the entrance to the White Sea the American cruiser sent us on our way by blowing a screeching salute on her sirens. She blew and blew. The sailors were cheering in every part of the ship."

Moore et al. were more circumspect about leaving. While they were happy to finally be on their way, they remained haunted by those friends and company mates who would not see their homes again.

"Come vividly back into the scene the winter funerals . . . of our buddies, brave men who, loving life, had been laid away there, having died soldier-like for a cause they had only dimly understood," they wrote. "And the crosses now rise up, mute, eloquent testimony to the cost of this strange, inexplicable war of North Russia."

The balance of the regiment and its associated detachments followed in other ships, the last being the *Menominee* on June 15. Several days later those hard feelings between Brits and Yanks surfaced once more when the ship moored near an English vessel at Murmansk.

The Brits and Americans began "catcalling and exchanging insults, and presently they began throwing various missiles at each other— whatever was at hand," Godfrey Anderson recalled. A few Americans unscrewed the nuts from on-deck machinery and took aim at the cocky Brits; one resorted to throwing an orange. "Before it was over the Limeys were forced to retreat out of range."

On board the *Menominee*, too, was John Cudahy, who felt a wave of melancholy tinged with some anger wash over him while he watched the coastline of Russia fade into the distance as the ship plowed through the drifting ice of the White Sea.

He would sum up the feelings of many an American who took part in that strange, strange war:

"When the last battalion set sail from Archangel, not a soldier knew, no, not even vaguely, why he had fought or why he was going now, and why his comrades were left behind—so many of them beneath the wooden crosses. The little churchyards and the white churches and the whiter snow!

"Life will always be a crazy thing to the soldier of North Russia; the color and the taste of living have gone from the soldier of North Russia; and the glory of youth has forever gone from him."

The always outspoken Harry Costello would agree. Also looking back in anger, the machine gunner and former football star would detail the odds stacked against the Americans—among them "inferior fighting equipment" and the fact that "units holding the front line were outnumbered as much as 30 and 40 to 1"—and conclude:

"Officers and men returning to the United States from their campaign in Russia against bolsheviki [sic] have been forced to the conclusion . . . that they did not receive a square deal."

The Murman coast slipped away, and as the ships carrying the 339th Infantry Regiment churned through the icy, gray water and headed west, then south, for France, each man carried his own memories of the strange past year.

There was the propaganda-spewing Bolo at the Emtsa River bridge; Harry Mead's brown hair turning white during those desperate weeks of fight and flight from Ust Padenga and Shenkursk; feverish, dying men coughing their lifeblood away in Archangel and upriver; the crimson-stained snow from the slaughter of Bolos at Bolshie Ozerki; the kindness of Lady Olga; and the horrible visage of hacked-to-death Francis Cuff in those bloodstained woods near the Vaga River.

And there was of course the cold, the bone-stinging cold and the monotonous, monochromatic vista of the Russian winter; the deep, ponderous drifts and the Russian ponies straining to pull the droshkies; the filthy peasant huts and an engineer performing a field amputation to save a wounded man's life; the suffering, the heroism, the near mutinies.

And the waste—the utter waste of men's bodies and souls—and, in the end, for what?

No, the men sent on a fool's errand to northern Russia had not received a "square deal"; in the end, though, they could console themselves with the knowledge that though they had suffered and sacrificed terribly, they had also endured and persevered and performed heroic acts, many of them, and stood to for the man to the right and the man to the left.

At least there was that.

CHAPTER THIRTY

THE GULAG AMERIKANSKI

In July 1919, Freeman Hogan was showered with flowers, a returning hero. Private Hogan, Company M, 339th Infantry Regiment, the prodigal son, captured by the Reds somewhere in northern Russia and now miraculously returned.

"Everybody said I was a hero and the girls all sympathized about my wound and how the Russians treated me," Hogan would tell a reporter for the *Detroit Free Press* in 1929. "A fellow pretends he doesn't like that stuff, but it was great.

"They wouldn't believe I didn't know how I got that scar on my temple. I told them over and over I must have been nicked by a piece of shrapnel because I woke up a prisoner, but I finally had to invent a story about a hand to hand bayonet duel."

In a quirk of fate, Freeman Hogan and a handful of other Americans who were taken prisoner would, like Herbert Schroeder, penetrate deeper into Russia than any of their still-free comrades; in a quirk of fate, Hogan and the other captured men would, in their own small way, fulfill the grand designs of the British architects of the Allied invasion of northern Russia and, though hardly traveling first-class, visit Moscow, Petrograd, and Vologda, which had seemed so near, so attainable, in the late summer of 1918.

On March 31, 1919, Freeman Hogan and Sgt. Glenn Leitzell, both thirty-one, had just left the rear of the position at Verst 18, on their way to Obozerskaya by sleigh on a supply run, when the Bolos enveloped much of Company M's position. They were jumped by a band of Bolos about five hundred yards from their lines, and hustled into a nearby wood.

There, they were joined by Bryant Ryal of the Y.M.C.A., who had been in a sled just ahead of them. Leitzell, Hogan, and Ryal were then quickly turned west and hustled off toward Bolshie Ozerki, "with one guard in front, three in the rear and three on snow skis on each side of the freshly cut trail in the deep snow," Leitzell would say.

Their arrival among the large force of Bolos, who were at that moment assaulting Joel Moore's Company M, was unceremonious. "Some tried to beat us with sticks and cursed and spat on us as we were shoved along to the Bolshevik commander," Leitzell recalled.

One "scowling" Bolo soldier tried to cut the gold filling out of one of Leitzell's teeth, but was violently shoved aside by his guard. Hustled now to the Bolo headquarters, they saw a former loyal Russian they knew who had gone over to the Reds. "They demanded our blouses and fur caps, also our watches and rings," Leitzell said of his captors.

Other Allied prisoners soon appeared, among them Father Roach, chaplain of the Seventeenth King's Liverpools, and the mechanic Jens Laursen, whose sled had been ambushed on March 31. A British flier with a shattered arm was also brought in.

They were interrogated by a Bolo intelligence officer, but Leitzell, Hogan, and Laursen pled ignorance of the Allies' "scheme of defense." Taken away to a filthy hut, they encountered other prisoners—loyal Russians, a few locals, and suspected Bolo deserters. All were fed half a fish and a lump of frozen black bread.

The next day, even as the renewed Bolo attack was raging, the Americans were brought to see the Bolo commander, Aleksei Kuropatkin. He passed out smokes, and pointed with his pistol to a large wall map.

He promised his prisoners that the Reds would soon crush the Allies and roll right on into Archangel. "Then he informed us that we were to be sent as prisoners to Moscow," Leitzell said.

They would be traveling in the footsteps of the first American prisoner, George Albers of Company I, who had been taken five months earlier on the railway front, and not long after brought to the bridge over the Emtsa for propaganda purposes.

"A guy crawled up on me in the snow while I was on sentry duty," Albers would say of his capture. The Bolo knocked him senseless with the butt of his rifle, then took Albers's fur coat, his shoes, and even his uniform.

"When I came to I was being carried away on a stretcher," Albers said. "We hiked 200 miles toward Vologda with the temperature 40 below. It was pure hell. We got black bread and fish soup—once in a while. We slept in peasant huts alive with vermin." Albers's only revenge was to curse and swear at his captors, who obviously had no idea what he was saying.

Albers would claim to be the first American brought to Moscow, further deepening the mystery of the whereabouts of Company B's Cpl. Herbert Schroeder. Eventually, other Americans would drift in, among them Company D's Pvt. Anton Vanis, captured at Shagovari on January 21, and Mike Haurilik, Johnnie Triplett, and Walter Huston of Company C, grabbed in the November 29 ambush that left Lt. Francis Cuff dead.

Those captured while on the ill-fated Company H patrol on March 16—Pvts. Earl Fulcher, William Scheulke, and August Peterson—were sent to Vologda. Cpl. Earl Collins, who led the patrol, was severely wounded and was last seen in a Bolshevik dressing station near Bolshie Ozerki, newspapers in the United States reported later in April. "His fate is still unknown but doubtless he is under the mossy tundra," Moore et al. would write in 1920.

The survivors would see much more of Russia than they bargained for, but interestingly most, if not all, would report having received decent treatment by their Bolshevik counterparts, at least once they reached Moscow.

There were difficult moments, however. Leitzell and Hogan were put on the trail south to Emtsa, and then locked into a boxcar on the railway siding for the night. The next morning, the door opened, and they found themselves confronted by an angry mob of Bolos that was "kept out only by our guards' bayonets," Leitzell would write.

"I paid a British two-shilling piece which I had concealed in my shoe to a guard to get me a tin to put our food in, and we made wooden spoons. That night we were lined up against the car and asked if we knew that we were going to be shot. But this event, I am happy to say, never took place."

Whereas Father Roach managed to convince his captors that he was a Red sympathizer and was ultimately released with Bolshevik propaganda bulging from his pockets, the others were sent down the line to Plesetskaya and then Vologda, which ironically had been the original, dreamy destination in Gen. Frederick Poole's long-forgotten plan of campaign.

Earl Fulcher, wounded in both thighs, and August Peterson, wounded in his right calf, were sent to a hospital. There, their injuries were dressed, Fulcher would later report.

"There were four female nurses. At this hospital we had soup twice a day and hash once a day. Very bad cases received milk once a day and sometimes twice a day," Fulcher wrote.

One day, a young female interpreter visited Fulcher and Peterson, and gave them soap, forty rubles, and tobacco and rolling papers and matches. She also asked a number of questions—among them how many machine guns their company had, the name of their commander, and the number of officers.

Two soldiers also interrogated them, and tried to reassure them that "they did not blame the soldiers in the Allied Armies for being up here," Fulcher said.

"They also asked us if we were drafted. The woman did most of the talking to us . . . The woman told us not to worry and that we would be sent home as soon as we were well."

Soon after, Fulcher was moved to another hospital, where he found among the patients five Englishmen and four Frenchmen. Peterson remained behind, fading in and out of consciousness while obsessing over his predicament, no matter the reassuring words from the Red interpreter.

Earl Fulcher endured, and was rewarded. On May 3 he was sent by train north to Plesetskaya, and on May 5 he was sent to the front line in the company of Capt. J. A. Harzfeld of the American Military Mission and turned over.

Leitzell, Hogan, and Laursen, meanwhile, joined George Albers in Moscow on April 10. The city was in the midst of a severe food shortage, as most provisions went to the Red Army. Half of the populace— one million people—had left the city in search of food, while those remaining, one official would say, were demanding "not that we agitate about bread but that we provide it."

"On our arrival we found the streets sloppy and muddy, with heaps of ice and snow and dead horses among the rubbish," Leitzell remembered. "Few business places were open, all stores having been looted." The men were placed with other prisoners—French, English, Scottish, and also Americans who had preceded them in Moscow.

(Laursen would in an affidavit claim that Cpl. Herbert Schroeder, who went missing on September 20, 1918, while on patrol at Seltso, was also in Moscow, and that Laursen visited him "at his quarters where he was confined with a British prisoner," a consular cable reported in 1923. No further news was ever heard of Schroeder.)

The next day, they were fed cabbage soup, horse meat, salt fish, black bread, and water. "We learned that the people of the city fared scarcely better," Leitzell would say. "All were rationed."

While Red soldiers received a pound of bread per day, workmen received just half a pound—and others one-quarter. Residents, Leitzell would write, had three choices: "Fight, work for the Red government or starve."

He would add disdainfully: "Some argument. Liberty is unknown under the Soviet rule. Their motto as I saw it is: 'What is yours is mine.'"

By luck, the prisoners encountered an American Y.M.C.A. worker who, like Bryant Ryal, had been captured in late March. Merle Arnold took them under his wing for a short while until he was freed; upon his release he contacted Red Cross officials in England and Denmark— and he also managed to have two hundred rubles a week placed into the hands of the interned.

They managed by hook and by crook to find food, and ultimately were given almost free rein in the city, even being allowed access to a club used by government officials; the Bolsheviks, finagling vainly to be recognized during the ongoing treaty negotiations in Paris, were wary of angering the United States and its allies with any reports of maltreatment of prisoners.

At the club, the men found books, and for a few rubles they could purchase a bowl of soup or a piece of horse flesh. While the city's population starved, they made do.

They were also put to work, in return for payment. "When we worked we got our 25 roubles [sic] a day," Albers added. "Sometimes it was carrying out furniture seized by the government in the homes of the wealthy, sometimes it was digging graves for the people who had died of starvation . . . the frozen bodies laid out in a row while we blasted through four feet of frozen earth."

However, they pushed their luck and almost had their privileges taken away when to a man they refused to march in the May Day parade. Hoping not to make any further waves, the Americans pretended to sympathize with the Bolshevik cause, Leitzell wrote.

"The Red fanatics really thought we were converted to the silly stuff called bolshevism [sic]," Leitzell would write. "It was plain to us also that they were playing for recognition of their government by the United States."

With the help of Frank Taylor, a correspondent for the United Press who convinced the Reds that the Americans were soon going to pull out of Russia, and another Y.M.C.A. worker, Louis Philip Penningroth, an Iowan who had been involved in relief work for war prisoners in eastern Europe, some of the Americans gained their release in the third week of April.

Penningroth, the famed correspondent Frazier Hunt would write, "dropped into soviet Russia from the blue sky" and suggested to Georgi Chicherin, the commissar of foreign affairs, that the Americans should be released. Chicherin, then dealing with more important matters, blithely agreed.

But as it turned out it wasn't quite that simple; Chicherin would only allow wounded Americans to leave. In addition, he agreed to the release of six British prisoners.

In a dispatch on May 14, Hunt painted the scene when the Americans were notified of their pending release.

"Six Americans were swapping yarns with British Tommies, with an admiring row of French poilus as audience," Hunt wrote. "It was a motley crew. All were attired in strange combinations of Russian, American, French and British garb, but we did not have any trouble picking out the Americans.

"There was a certain little lilt of confidence about them; then, too, each had held to something of his old uniform—regimental button shirt, overseas cap, or something from home."

After some small talk, Y.M.C.A. man Penningroth asked the Americans: "Well, how'd you fellows like to go home, anyway."

"There was silence for about three seconds," Hunt wrote. Then Albers spoke. "Say whatya kidding us this way for? This going home ain't no joke to us."

Penningroth managed to prove they were being freed, after which "there were yells, dancing, prancing, and tearing the roof down," Hunt wrote. The French prisoners remained ignorant as to what was going on, but when one of the forty British soldiers explained it in "limping French, with a word or two of Russian thrown in," the *poilus* joined in "the mad dance around the room."

Company D's Pvt. Anton Vanis soon appeared with one of his Red guards; informed of the pending release of some of the prisoners, the guard left and returned with several of his comrades. Congratulations—in English, in French, in Russian—swelled the room.

Incredibly, it was at that moment that two men from the Company C patrol that had been ambushed on November 29—Mike Haurilik and Walter Huston—arrived at the prison, with the Y.M.C.A.'s Bryant Ryal, taken March 16, in tow.

Haurilik "would soon be sticking his feet under pa's table at 446 Hastings Street, Detroit, and Walt Huston would soon be telling the girls around Muskegon, how they had it over all the Moscow dames he had met when he was a guest of soviet Russia," Hunt wrote.

The first to be released were Albers, Vanis, Haurilik, Huston, and William Scheulke. By May 15, 1919, they were on their way to the United States aboard the S.S. *Harrisburg*. Leitzell, Hogan, Laursen, Company C's Johnnie Triplett, and Ryal were released soon after the first five, but were sent to Finland, where they were quarantined.

The correspondent Frank Taylor caught up with them at their internment camp in Terijoki.

"The Bolsheviks did their best to convert the Yankees, who kept their peace, and expressed no opinions until they had crossed the border into Finland," Taylor wrote in a July dispatch. Now freed, the doughboys told Taylor just what they thought of their captors.

"They're not making any Bolsheviks of American prisoners," Leitzell informed him. "They try to preach bolshevism [*sic*] to us, but it doesn't go. They'd take men who've got brains, who've accomplished something by ability and work, and reduce them to the lowest level. Who's going to stand for that?"

Turning passionate, Leitzell would add: "They're a bunch of thieves and robbers. The leaders are preaching that everyone ought to have the same amount of money, but every leader has a pile of rubles stuck away that would knock your eye out."

"I figure they're crooked and deceitful and are a bunch of cut-throats," Jens Laursen chimed in. "All the honest ones want to get out of Russia as soon as possible. They all want to go to America. Like hell we'll let them in—if I see any I'm going to shoot 'em!"

Freeman Hogan, too, had not exactly been swayed by his Bolshevik teach-ins. "If America ever went bolshevik [*sic*] like Moscow, I'd make myself a lone hand to stand out against them. If you want to be a good bolshevik [*sic*], you've got to be crumby and dirty."

After finally being released from the internment camp, Leitzell, Laursen, and Triplett rejoined the 339th Infantry Regiment in France. They sailed from Brest aboard the S.S. *Troy* on June 20, and reached the docks at Hoboken ten days later, their strange war concluded.

Freeman Hogan would soon enough be showered with flowers; it would be, he would say years later, "a great day."

CHAPTER THIRTY-ONE

A RETURN TO RUSSIA

They came for his body, and she told them no; she would not tell them where he was buried. For more than ten years she had watched over his grave, covered it with flowers and wax blossoms, tended it with a love and care that perhaps went beyond human understanding.

"She refused to give up the body of the man she had loved in life," one newspaper would report in 1929, long after the surviving Polar Bears had returned home, and longer still since Lt. Ralph Edgar Powers of the 337th Ambulance Company had died from his wounds in Shenkursk on January 24, 1919.

"They threatened, they offered rewards, but she would tell them nothing. Then she gave them false directions. At last, weeping, she begged them not to take his body away, but the Americans told her they could not disobey orders.

"So she took them to a grave marked with an ikon and covered with flowers. And the body of Lieutenant Powers came home with those of his comrades in arms."

Powers had worked furiously to save the wounded men of Company A during those awful days at Ust Padenga, and had gone to death "a victim of the shells, because he would not have his wounds bound up while a single, private soldier was not relieved," John Cudahy would write.

He was remembered by his comrades, Cudahy added, as a "symbol of moral grandeur and noblest self-abnegation, that will ever inspire faith in the immortal, spiritual entity of man."

The body of Lt. Ralph Powers, awarded a posthumous elevation to captain, had been left behind at Shenkursk when the Allied force fled north. His body had been left behind as well when the 339th Infantry Regiment boarded its transports and began quitting Russia and their silly and strange little war, bringing with them just 108 bodies out of the 235 men who died in Russia.

But he was not forgotten; nor were the others, those 127 as-yet-unclaimed American soldiers who had headed Over There and wound up instead dying Up There by a strange quirk of regimental, political, and personal fate.

When the regiment left Russia, the ships steamed for Brest, France, where the 339th remained until the third week of June 1919, when it was dispersed to several ocean-going transports.

The ships carried more than just happy American soldiers: aboard, too, were eight new brides, Russian women who had fallen in love—or at least pretended to have fallen in love—with handsome doughboys.

One woman, Nena Alexandra Rosov, had through the long winter become enamored with Company E's Pvt. George Cleveland Geren while he was stationed in Morjagorskaya, where she taught school.

When his unit pulled out, Nena pined for a time, then headed out on foot for Archangel, seventy miles distant. She intended simply to say good-bye; when she arrived, she found that Geren had been hopeful she would see him off, and with the help of the American consulate had arranged for them to be married.

They were wed on May 28, 1919, at Archangel's large cathedral, repeating their "I dos" in front of Priest Papoff. George was thirty-two and already divorced, and Nena was just eighteen, but the age difference hadn't mattered as love blossomed between the two.

Aboard the transports headed blissfully for the United States were other blushing brides, and at one point a beauty contest was held. The prettiest, it was decided, was Alexandra Kadrina, who had become Alexandra Karouch just days before after marrying Russian-born John Karouch, of Company G.

By early July, the happy brides, their ecstatic husbands, and the homesick and jubilant men of the 339th Infantry Regiment arrived at ports on the east coast and then entrained for Detroit; they were back, "back to receive the hospitable welcome of a gracious city, a happy state and a grateful nation," Company E's Donald Carey would write with some exaggeration.

On July 3, Companies A and L were the first to arrive at the Michigan Central train station at 7:20 P.M. They were greeted by thousands of family members, friends, and well-wishers. "'Polar Bears,' Arctic Heroes Loudly Hailed," the *Detroit Free Press* would headline the main story on their arrival.

"Like magic the throng around the depot grew" as three separate trains arrived one by one, the paper reported. The story would add, "It was a hardy, happy fit-as-a-fiddle army of tough young fighting men which poured out of the station, whooping like Sioux Indians and so deliriously joyful that the spirit spread through the crowd like a spark to tinder."

The mayor, the Honorable James Couzens, issued a proclamation. In praising the 339th's men, he displayed a familiarity with their battle zones that might have surprised many of the soldiers; the folks back home, it seemed, had indeed been following them in the newspapers.

"We at home may have only a vague conception of the Dvina, the fight at Shenkursk or the Archangel-Vologda front, but for us you have made the numerals the 339th the title of a long-to-be-remembered Michigan epic," Couzens proclaimed.

"They are no longer the mere badge of an infantry regiment of the

United States army. They symbolize in our minds a story of magnificent endurance, sacrifice, and obedience."

After billeting in local homes overnight, the men took their places in a July 4 parade, and then were feted at a celebration on Belle Isle, a large park in the middle of the Detroit River. That evening, the 339th's tireless champion—California senator Hiram Johnson, who had pushed and issued resolution after resolution to have the Polar Bears pulled out of Russia—spoke to the crowd.

"Thank God the boys are home from Russia," Johnson said. "Thank God their trials and tribulations are at an end. They served under conditions that were the most confusing and perplexing that an American army was ever asked to contend with, but they did their duty, and I contend that duty was more truly done than that of any other soldiers in the great war. To have done their duty as they did it marks every one of these boys a hero, for all time to come."

(Though the crowd cheered the exhortations of Senator Johnson and other speakers, their words rang a bit hollow to some of the Polar Bears. "When the speakers said the people would be eternally grateful to us for our great accomplishment," the former prisoner of war Freeman Hogan would later say, "we wondered what that accomplishment was, but were proud anyway.")

The celebrations would go on as the rest of the survivors of that bleak, strange, confusing Russian expedition trickled home. Company D's Frank Douma arrived at Boston aboard the *President Grant* on July 12, and finally made it to Detroit on July 16.

"Detroit is giving us a special welcome because this is her special regiment," he would write in one of his last diary entries. "We have free entertainment and free eats wherever we go. The people seem to be very anxious to do everything they can for us."

After that, it was back to Camp Custer and mustering out. The regiment was deactivated, its war finally over.

That, however, was not the case back in Russia. Even as the Americans were cruising home, plans were being laid for an all-out, new offensive up the Dvina River—and another pie-in-the-sky scheme to reach Kotlas emerged, this one with the further ambition of connecting with the large army under Adm. Alexander Kolchak, supreme commander of the Whites.

Gen. Edmund Ironside had orders to get his men out of Russia by September 30, 1919, but he wanted to first create a buffer zone to safely allow their removal without an attack by the Bolos. He also wanted to ensure that the recently recruited Archangel army of Whites was capable of taking up the defense of the port from the Bolos.

Ironside aimed to push a combined force of British and Whites up the Dvina River, scattering whatever Red forces might be there and then leaving White Guards in place above the old haunts at Toulgas and Seltso. The bulk of the Russian force would then move farther upriver and, hopefully, reach Kolchak's White Army then attempting to take Viatka—now called Kirov—three hundred miles southeast of Kotlas.

If Kolchak's army could capture Viatka, the British War Office optimistically concluded, the Reds would have to abandon the railway that ran to Kotlas; a farther advance to Kotlas by Kolchak to the north and a White force to the southeast would clear the Dvina River all the way to Archangel, and create a buffer for the departing British troops and the remaining White force in the Archangel District.

On June 20, a combined English-Russian force launched an attack on both sides of the Dvina, and met some success. The advance, General Ironside wrote, found the Bolsheviks "in hopeless confusion." Their flotilla of gunboats had dispersed upriver, and they were reduced to floating mines downriver toward the British gunboats.

The way to Kotlas appeared open; then the roof caved in.

Lt. Royce Dyer's battalion of the Slavo-British Allied Legion reached the Dvina front on July 4 but mutinied three days later. "They had all seemed quite contented," Ironside wrote. Contented, that is, until 2:30 A.M. on July 7, when Lewis gun and rifle fire was heard coming from the village where Companies B and C of the S.B.A.L.s were quartered.

Eight mutineers had entered their officers' quarters and, after shooting three orderlies guarding the billets, killed three British officers, and mortally wounded two others. Four Russian officers were also murdered.

The mutineers then called on Company C of the S.B.A.L.s to follow them toward the Bolo lines, and about twenty of them did so. They had greater success with Company B, from which about eighty men went over—or at least tried to go over—to the Reds.

Ironside was shaken to his core by the incident, and had an almost instant change of heart about continuing the offensive. "I now felt a distinct urge to extricate myself and my troops as quickly as I could," he would write. "The danger of further mutinies amongst the Russians had been greatly increased."

Indeed, Ironside on July 20 learned that another Russian mutiny had occurred, this one on the Onega front. There, the mutineers handed the front to the Bolos, and Ironside realized that his right flank was in enemy hands. Then came news on July 24 that Kolchak's force had failed to take Viatka, and was in fact in full retreat.

As always, reaching Kotlas would remain a dream.

Ironside saw clearly now that it was time to get the British out of Russia—and soon. He decided to perform one last operation that would clear the Dvina front and buy some time and space, and then begin pulling out. This the Russian-English force did on August 10 and August 11, attacking once more on both sides of the river, killing hundreds of Bolos and capturing several thousand more. Allied casualties were 145 men killed or wounded.

The move, said Gen. Wilds Richardson, who had remained in Archangel until August 23 while sorting things out, "practically destroyed the advance Bolshevik forces on the Dvina, steadied public sentiment and permitted the British to withdraw several weeks later without material interference."

The British began leaving the various fronts on August 20, and were safe within the lines at Archangel by August 23. By September 27 the war was over for them, too, as the last of the English soldiers departed, taking with them—over a disgusted Ironside's initial refusal—more than five thousand "friendlies," anti-Bolshevik Russians who feared for their lives under Bolshevik rule.

The war was left to the sixteen thousand White soldiers whom the British had trained through the year. They were put under the command of the anomalously named Gen. Eugene Miller, a Russian who had essentially taken over as governor-general of the Archangel District when Nicholas Chaikovsky had left earlier in the year to attend the Paris Peace Conference.

He had a hopeless task: stopping the inexorable tide of history.

Miller enjoyed some breathing room as the Bolsheviks deployed their forces to fight White armies in Siberia and the south. However, once Kolchak's army had been defeated, and he executed, the Reds turned their attention once more to the north.

New offensives in early 1920 brought the Bolos back to the railway front and the Dvina, and Miller could only watch as his own army disintegrated and his men deserted in droves.

He would flee as well as the inevitable loss of Archangel approached. On February 19, 1920, Miller and his deputies boarded an icebreaker and steamed for England; on February 21, Archangel fell peacefully to the Reds, who went on to plunder northern Russia. In an orgy of retribution, they executed as many as thirty thousand people.

By then, the postmortems of the American intervention had been written. Capt. Hugh Martin, in a report to the American Military Mission, would blame the ultimate abject failure of the Allied intervention on three key points: a lack of enough manpower to do the job right, a lack of clear aims for the intervention from the start, and friction between the Americans and French and their British overseers.

In fact, there *were* clear aims for the intervention; the problem was that the British had one aim and the Americans another. Woodrow Wilson had sent in troops with instructions to guard stores and stay the hell out of Russia's internal affairs.

The British, on the other hand, were intent on fomenting a full-blown counterrevolution against the Bolsheviks. When the Brits were put in charge of the entire affair, the die was cast; 235 Americans would die in Russia because the British used the 339th Infantry Regiment as it saw fit, while the American leaders sat on their hands.

The American ambassador, David Francis, was a vocal proponent of the British vision and had not protested when the men of the 339th were hustled from their transports and packed off south on the railway and up the Dvina River. The 339th's commander, George Stewart, meanwhile, lost whatever nerve and backbone he may have once had and, feeling he had been ordered to, acquiesced in the theft of his regiment, and basically abdicated his command—and in his own way caused more than 150 of his own men to die in battle during the grueling winter of 1918–1919.

The British plan as put in motion was beyond a fool's errand—it was based on a hallucination, a belief that the local Russians would spontaneously rise up and join the Allies and wipe Bolshevism from the face of the earth. It was hubris of the highest order, hubris promulgated on fantasy, to think that a handful of Allied soldiers could be spread thinly across thousands of square miles of northern Russia and defeat a Red Army that would number 600,000 by the end of 1918. Right. *Cheerio and all that . . .*

Yes, we can blame George Stewart and David Francis for the invasion-turned-debacle, but the buck has to stop with Woodrow Wilson. His tortured aide-mémoire, over which he had vacillated and sweated and come up with excuses and contradictions, in the end wound up making no sense at all; perhaps ironically, it instead remains a classic example of presidential vacuity and short-sightedness.

It was, in the end, the reason that Clifford Phillips lingered for six weeks with a bullet in his chest before dying; it was by Wilson's hand that Harry Surran and Clyde Clark and scores of other flu-ridden men perished in their virulent fogs; it was because of a poorly thought-out and self-contradicting screed that Francis Cuff would never return alive to his wife and small daughter and Herbert Schroeder would fall forever off the face of the earth.

Men die in wars, and the 235 men killed in the 339th Infantry Regiment and its associated units can seem insignificant when placed in the context of the Great War, during which millions of men were lost on the battlefields of the Somme, at Loos, at Verdun, and in the Meuse-Argonne, where some twenty-six thousand Americans perished during the last six weeks of the war.

But all died fighting for a cause they understood; the dead in the 339th Infantry Regiment had no such luxury, and died, in the end, for no good reason the survivors could ever figure out. One hates to say that anyone ever dies in vain, but the sad reality remains that militarily, the ill-begotten, ill-conceived Polar Bear Expedition did little more than cause the deaths of more than two hundred good, brave American soldiers.

Politically, some would claim the Allied invasion of northern Russia actually helped the Bolsheviks consolidate their power through the crucial early days of the Revolution, and led to their ultimate victory over the Whites in 1922. The weak Allied effort, and the Reds' quick victory, gave the Bolsheviks "new confidence" and helped create public support for the Revolution, Robert Lockhart, a British attaché in Moscow in late 1918, would write.

The expedition also sowed the seeds for recriminations and distrust that would plague U.S.-Russian relations throughout the twentieth century—and beyond. The United States would recognize the Soviet government in 1933, and it became an uneasy ally with Russia in the fight against Germany and the Axis during World War 2. But that alliance descended into the chilly and even dangerous relationship that marked the Cold War, as the two superpowers sought dominance on the world stage in the last half of the century.

Most Americans—excepting those who fought in Russia and their families—quickly forgot about the Polar Bears and their bizarre war with the Bolsheviks. (Two American presidents, Richard Nixon and Ronald Reagan, would assert in speeches that American and Russian troops had never fought each other.) But the Soviets knew better and remembered that the United States and the British had landed on their shores and attempted to overthrow the young Soviet regime in 1918 and 1919.

"For the American people, the cosmic tragedy of the intervention in Russia does not exist, or it was an unimportant incident, long forgotten. But for the Soviet people and their leaders the period was," according to historians Jeremy Kuzmarov and John Marciano, writing in 2018, "an experience burned into the very soul of the nation, not to be forgotten for generations, if ever."

In 1959 Russian premier Nikita Khrushchev would remind the world—and the U.S.—of America's part in the affair. "We remember the grim days when American soldiers went to our soil headed by their generals," he said. "Never have any of our soldiers been on American soil, but your soldiers were on Russian soil. These are the facts."

He might have mentioned one other fact: the bodies of two dozen American soldiers remain on Russian soil even now. But there would have been many more left behind in frozen graves had not their living comrades never forgotten their sacrifice.

The veterans of the expedition formed the Polar Bear Association in 1922. "From its inception one of its most important objectives was the return of the bodies of those who died and were buried in Russia," Company G's Michael Macalla, he who had devotedly brought the body of his fellow sergeant Edward Young to Archangel, would write.

To that end, Macalla, Company M's Walter Dundon, Joel Moore, Harry Mead, and others pressured politicians in Washington, DC, and Michigan for funds to cover the costs of another expedition, this one with the aim of returning to Russia to locate as many of the 127 bodies that remained there as they could.

Federal funds in the amount of $200,000 were allocated for "the expense of negotiating, locating, exhuming," and the return and reburial of the soldiers. The state of Michigan kicked in $15,000 as well. On July 18, 1929, Macalla, Dundon, and the three other members of what they called the Michigan Commission—Gilbert Shilson, manager of the Associated Press bureau in Lansing; Roy Derham, formerly of Company D of the 339th; and John Evans, formerly of the 337th Ambulance Company—sailed for Germany.

Upon their eventual arrival in Berlin, they were met by a representative of the Veterans of Foreign Wars, "under whose sponsorship we were forced to travel due to non-recognition and diplomatic relations prevailing at the time," Macalla wrote.

Despite the delicate relations, within ten days they were issued visas, and were also met by Americans with the Graves Registration Service. Macalla and Dundon then flew to Moscow, while the others came by train and plane in ensuing days. After "3 days in Moscow where there was more red tape," Macalla wrote, the entourage spent five days traveling by train to Archangel.

The party split, Macalla and Dundon appropriately heading to Kodish and the railway front, the other three heading up the Dvina River. Once more Americans plied the rickety railway through the vast scrub forests and swampland of northern Russia, and coursed up the sluggish, wide Dvina, passing the simple hamlets and villages that were almost totally obscured by the black woods lining the banks.

Searching for the wooden crosses in the "little churchyards," as referenced by John Cudahy, the commission located the remains of eighty-six soldiers, eighty-four of whom were identified by tags, tooth charts, personal belongings, and other means. As they dug, locals came out of hiding, and passed on information on the locations of American graves they had found in the various locales.

They spent two months at their backbreaking work, sleeping once again in the peasants' homes and awaking once more deprived of food and smokes. It was all too familiar. Eerily familiar.

Among the bodies ultimately located were those of the seventeen Company A men who went missing during the fight and subsequent flight from Nijni Gora. Thus did Stillman Jenks return home, and Max Kurowski and Joseph Cwenk, too. At the cemetery at Shenkursk, they also located Francis Cuff and some of those others from Company C who were killed in the November 29, 1918, ambush.

Ralph Powers was found at Shenkursk and removed as well, despite the best efforts of his female grave tender—had she been a lover? a friend? a patient?—to keep him in Mother Russia forever. In any event, "the woman was left kneeling, crying, beside an empty hole," the *Detroit Free Press* reported upon Powers's return to the States.

After processing and identification, the bodies, now placed in large wooden caskets, sailed from France in November 1929. Upon arrival in New York, forty-one of them were claimed by relatives or friends for private burials. The remaining forty-five bodies, Ralph Powers among them, were sent in nine train cars to Detroit, where they arrived at 8:30 A.M. on December 1, 1929, their long and strange odyssey over.

The next day, a memorial was held downtown, and thousands of people—including many former soldiers of the 339th—attended. Crowds fittingly lined Fort Street in a cold and swirling snowstorm as speeches were made and the sacrifice of the dead honored.

A long line of hearses then made its way to White Chapel Memorial Cemetery in nearby Troy, Michigan, where the bodies were put into storage until the following Memorial Day. Then, they were again laid to rest—this time for good—on May 30, 1930, with full military honors in plots surrounding or near a newly chiseled marble bear standing over a helmet and cross, a monument to the Polar Bears.

Four years later, more bodies returned. The Soviet government allowed the U.S. Graves Registration Service entry into Russia to search for American bodies in the summer of 1933, and nine were located. These arrived in Detroit in September 1934 and lay in state until November 11, when they, too, were reburied in the Polar Bear site within White Chapel's grounds.

That same year, the Soviets notified the United States that they had located and would release twelve more bodies. Among those were Cpl. Earl Collins of Company H, who had been captured on March 16, 1919, and had last been seen being tended to in a Bolo field hospital near Bolshie Ozerki. For reasons unknown, his family had him buried in England.

The bodies of about two dozen more Americans remain in Russia, interred in battlefield graves obscured by wood and brush and by time—mute evidence of an ill-conceived invasion that pitted bewildered American youth against determined Bolshevik revolutionaries.

On a warm and bright summer's day, the Polar Bear Memorial and its quiet, well-kept grounds seem incongruous with the circumstances of the deaths of many of the soldiers who died in the icy winter wastes of northern Russia so long ago, and who now lie in the shadow of that great, snarling marble polar bear.

They will lie quiet forever, but the bear will continue to tell their story, symbolizing the Arctic cold and icy snow in which they suffered, and symbolizing Russia itself; the bear stands guard over Francis Cuff and Ralph Powers and Victor Stier and the other heroes, and represents all the Polar Bears, now gone, who fought and died and sacrificed themselves in the hostile wilds of north Russia with little understanding of why they were there.

But all had done their duty; all could at least be proud of that. As one anonymous Polar Bear would write in an echo of the Canadian John McCrae's famous Great War poem "In Flanders Fields":

Comrades, as you gather far away
In God's own land on some bright day
And think of us who died and rest,
Just tell our folks we did our best
In the far off fields of Russia.

EPILOGUE

In the summer of 1919, the survivors of the Polar Bear Expedition came home, were celebrated, and then melted back into civilian life. But not all of them did so quietly: John Cudahy and Harry Costello wrote and had published damning accounts of their misadventure, Cudahy in his book *Archangel: The American War with Russia* (he used as his nom de plume "A Chronicler"), and Costello in *Why Did We Go to Russia?*

Cudahy would go on to become ambassador to Poland from 1933 to 1937, and then he was reposted to Belgium, which he was forced to flee at the beginning of World War 2. He later published another book, *The Armies March*, about the lead-up to the Second World War. He died on September 6, 1943, after being thrown by his horse while riding on his family's Wisconsin estate.

Costello went on to a career of sports writing and coaching football. He also became the director of publicity for the Louisiana State Athletics Department in 1935, and his eternal gift for storytelling made him a favorite on the sports rubber-chicken circuit. He died at the age of seventy-six on August 24, 1968.

Joel Moore, Harry Mead, and Lewis Jahns of Company K, meanwhile, formed a publishing company—fittingly, the Polar Bear Publishing Company—and produced the 1920 book *The History of the American Expedition Fighting the Bolsheviki*. Moore later became the warden of the Michigan State Prison and died in 1953. Mead went into politics, managing campaigns for the mayor of Detroit and the Michigan governor's office. He died at the age of seventy-nine in June 1969. Jahns, who mainly handled the business side of the book, "dropped out of sight" after its publication, one author notes.

For Col. George Stewart, the Polar Bear Expedition was his last. He closed out his army career in 1931, when he retired on disability, and died at the age of seventy-three in 1946.

The medic Godfrey Anderson, meanwhile, married his girlfriend, Ruth Anderson, shortly after returning home and spent forty-five years working for the Johnson-Handley-Johnson Furniture Company in Grand Rapids, Michigan. Through the years he worked on his memoirs of his service with the Polar Bears, and died at the age of eighty-five on April 23, 1981. The memoirs were published as *A Michigan Polar Bear Confronts the Bolsheviks* in 2010.

Donald Carey became a school superintendent and later in life returned to farming in Vermontville, Michigan. He married and had a son, Neil, and spent years of his off time putting the memoirs of his service with the Polar Bears to paper. He died of a massive heart attack at the age of fifty-three in April 1945; his son edited his memoirs and published them in 1997 in the book *Fighting the Bolsheviks: The Russian War Memoir of Private First Class Donald E. Carey, U.S. Army, 1918–1919.*

ACKNOWLEDGMENTS

I would like to thank the staff at the Bentley Historical Library at the University of Michigan in Ann Arbor for its help in researching this book. The library is the first stop for anyone researching the Polar Bear Expedition, as it holds an extensive collection of diaries, photos, memoirs, and the like from the expedition's veterans.

Thanks also for the help of author Dennis Gordon, who besides being an expert on the Lafayette Escadrille is an authority on the expedition to north Russia, and spent years collecting the reminiscences of various Polar Bears before publishing them in 1982 in *Quartered in Hell*, which has become the go-to book for anyone wanting to research the Polar Bears.

I'd also like to thank Michael Bracey for his help at the U.S. National Archives in College Park, Maryland, and Mike Grobbel, president of the Polar Bear Memorial Association, which helps keep the memories of the expedition alive. Thanks also go to Jerry Traut; Cathleen Ruth; the family of Lt. Charles Ryan of Company K; Donald Carey's son, Neil G. Carey; author Gordon L. Olson; Janet Chobanian; the photo-sales staff at the Grand Rapids (Michigan) Public Library; and Gene Toornman and his daughter Laurie Toornman Hare.

I would also like to thank my editor at HarperCollins, Peter Hubbard, whose enthusiasm for and interest in the story of the Polar Bears resulted in this book. Thanks go as well, and as always, to my literary agent, James D. Hornfischer, for being my advocate, mentor, and friend.

NOTES

Albers, George. Albers's account of his capture and imprisonment from the article "Michigan Soldiers Taken by Reds Help Bury Starved" in the Lansing (MI) *State Journal*, June 6, 1919.

Anderson, Godfrey. Anderson's memoir "The 337th Field Hospital in North Russia, 1918–1919" found in the Michigan Historical Collections, Bentley Historical Library at the University of Michigan, Ann Arbor, MI (hereafter BHL). Used with permission.

Arkins, Edwin. Arkins's quotes from the "Edwin L. Arkins Diary and Scrapbook 1918–1922," BHL. Used with permission.

Birkett, Glenn. His letter to Kathryn Phillips provided by William Phillips Reich, Clifford Phillips's grandson.

Boyd, Robert. Boyd's account of Col. George Stewart's visit to the front from *The History of the American Expedition Fighting the Bolsheviki*. His criticism of the campaign from the article "Americans at Archangel" in the March 12, 1939, *Chicago Tribune*. His description of the conditions at Toulgas from the February 26, 1919, *Eau Claire Leader-Telegram*. His letter to the American ambassador from the records of the expedition in the National Archives, College Park, MD.

Carey, Donald. Carey's memoir of the expedition found in "Overview of the Donald E. Carey Papers" in the Hoover Institution Archives, Collection Number 98014, Stanford University, Stanford, CA. Used with the permission of Carey's son, Neil G. Carey.

Clark, Clyde. Account of Clark's death from the Lansing (MI) *State Journal*, November 26, 1918. Account of his funeral from the *State Journal* of November 20, 1919. Biographical information from the *State Journal*, November 13, 1919. The double funeral for his ex-wife Bessie and her brother, William from the *State Journal*, January 25, 1919.

Cole, Felix. His cable opposing intervention from "Papers Relating to the Foreign Relations of the United States, 1918, Russia, Volume II," Office of the Historian, U.S. Department of State (hereafter OHDS). Accessed online at https://history.state.gov/historicaldocuments/frus 1918Russiav02/d589.

Commons, Jack. Commons's quotes from *The History of the American Expedition Fighting the Bolsheviki*.

Costello, Harry. Costello's account of the expedition from *Why Did We Go to Russia?* His description of Archangel from the article "Harry Costello Scores Russians" in the February 16, 1919, *Detroit Free Press*. Accounts of Costello's college football career from the articles "Harry Costello Is Worst Enemy of Old Dominion" in the *Washington Times*, November 17, 1912; "Costello's Long Run Brings Victory to G.U." in the November 25, 1910, *Washington Post*; "Meriden Is Proud of Young Costello" in the *Bridgeport (CT) Times and Evening Farmer*, December 5, 1911; and a short article about his professional career in the same paper on January 6, 1917. Also see the story "Nine Point Harry and the Kingfish" from the Booth Family Center for Special Collections, Georgetown University Library. Accessed online at https://www.library .georgetown.edu/special-collections/archives/nine-point-harry-and -kingfish.

Cudahy, John. See *Archangel: The American War with Russia.*

Cuff, Margaret. Margaret Cuff's quotes about her father, Francis Cuff, come from the article "Death, Bad Debts and Depression Is All We Got, Says Son of a Soldier" in the November 11, 1934, *Detroit Free Press.*

Davis, Simon. Davis's quotes from *Quartered in Hell.* Used with permission.

Doe, Charles. The story of his field amputation was told by Mike Grobbel in "Amputation by Pocketknife: The Story of Pvt. Charles R. Doe, Co. A, 310th Engineers, 85th Division, U.S. Army." Accessed at http://pbma.grobbel.org/doe/index.htm. Used with permission.

Douma, Frank. The "Frank W. Douma Diary" found in BHL. Used with permission.

Edwards, P. H. His letter about Clifford Phillips's death provided by Phillips's grandson William Phillips Reich.

Francis, David. See *Russia from the American Embassy.* His June 22, 1918, cable to the secretary of state from OHDS. Accessed online at https://history.state.gov/historicaldocuments/frus1918Russiav02/pg_220.

Fulcher, Earl. Fulcher's account of his capture and imprisonment from the "Earl Fulcher Papers," BHL. Used with permission.

Geren, George. Account of his marriage to Nena Rosov from *The History of the American Expedition Fighting the Bolsheviki.* Account of beauty pageant among Russian brides from the *Detroit Free Press,* July 15, 1919.

Grewe, Bernard. Account of mother's grief and relocation found in the *Detroit Free Press,* November 17, 1919.

Henkelman, Bill. Henkelman's quotes from *Quartered in Hell*. Used with permission.

Hicks, Donald. Account of the Olympia sailors in action based on the article "Bluejackets vs. Bolsheviks" by Robert L. Willett in *Naval History Magazine*, August 2016. Accessed online at https://www.usni.org /magazines/navalhistory/2016-08/bluejackets-vs-bolsheviks.

Hogan, Freeman. The story "Hero of 10 Years Ago Just a Sandwich 'Ad'" is from the *Detroit Free Press*, July 12, 1929. Hogan's opinion of the Bolsheviks from the article "Doughboys Tell of Doings of 'Bolos'" in the *Kinston (NC) Daily Free Press*, July 7, 1919.

Hunt, Frazier. Correspondent Hunt's article "Americans Glad to Bid Russia Goodbye" is from the *Nebraska State Journal*, May 14, 1919.

Ironside, Edmund. See *Archangel: 1918–1919*.

Ketcham, Harry. Ketcham's unpublished manuscript "On the Onega Front" is from Manuscripts and Publications, 1918–1919, Wisconsin Historical Society, Main Stacks, Madison, WI. Series 1704 MAD 3/43B7.

Kooyers, Fred. Kooyers's diary found in the "George Albers Papers," BHL. Used with permission.

Laursen, Jens. Laursen's quotes about the Bolsheviks found in the *Tyrone (PA) Daily Herald*, July 7, 1919.

Leitzell, Glenn. Leitzell's account of capture and imprisonment from *The History of the American Expedition Fighting the Bolsheviki* and the article "Doughboys Tell of Doings of 'Bolos'" in the *Kinston (NC) Daily Free Press*, July 7, 1919.

Lyttle, Alfred. The account of Lyttle's wounding and subsequent death is from "The Alfred E. Lyttle Papers, 1918–1919," BHL. Used with permission.

Macalla, Michael. Macalla's account of the recovery of American bodies from Russia is from his report, "The Michigan Commission to Russia," in "The Michael J. Macalla Papers," BHL. Used with permission. The account of the death of Sgt. Edward Young and Macalla's hauling his body to Archangel is from the *Detroit Free Press*, November 17, 1929.

Malm, Clarence. Account of Malm's death from *Quartered in Hell*. Biographical information from the *Pere Marquette Magazine*, February 19, 1919.

Martin, Hugh S. Martin's report "Mutinies in North Russia" from the U.S. National Archives' Historical Files of the American Expeditionary Force, North Russia, 1918–1919 (hereafter AEFNR), File Number 23-36.1, Microfilm M924, Roll 2. Also August 20, 1919, "Memorandum for Colonel Ruggles," File 23-11.4, Microfilm M924, Roll 1. Accessed via https://www.fold3.com.

May, Albert. May's account of the Polar Bear Expedition found in the *Star Tribune* (Minneapolis, MN) of September 28 and October 5, 1919; and the *New York Tribune* of September 28, 1919.

McPhail, Hugh. McPhail's quotes from *Quartered in Hell*. Used with permission.

Mead, Harry. See *The History of the American Expedition Fighting the Bolsheviki* and *The Romance of Company "A"*. His account of the action at Ust Padenga from the story "Inch from Death—Memory of Russia" from the *Detroit News*, February 1959.

Moore, Joel. See *"M" Company 339th Infantry in North Russia* and *The History of the American Expedition Fighting the Bolsheviki*. His reminiscences about his coaching days from the *Great Falls (MT) Tribune*, September 26, 1947; account of removal from his teaching job from the *Great Falls Tribune*, June 8, 1911. Other biographical information from the Ancestry website.

Mylon, James. Mylon's letter found in the *Detroit Free Press*, March 9, 1919.

Odjard, Otto. His letter describing privations at the front ran in the *Detroit Free Press*, December 25, 1918.

Parrish, Silver. "Silver Parrish Diary" found in BHL. Used with permission.

Phillips, Clifford. Accounts of his debating activities from the *Omaha (NE) Daily Bee*, December 10, 1905; and the *Nebraska State Journal*, June 4, 1909. Account of his lingering death from Harry Ketcham (see listing on page 290). Telegrams from Capt. Richard Ballensinger and Phillips to Phillips's wife provided by his grandson William Phillips Reich.

Poole, DeWitt. See *The History of the American Expedition Fighting the Bolsheviki*.

Powers, Ralph. Biographical information from the *Cincinnati (OH) Enquirer*, May 11, 1915. Account of his service and his wounding and death from *The Romance of Company "A"* and *The History of the American Expedition Fighting the Bolsheviki*. Account of his grave tender from the article "Return of Soldier's Corpse Bares Tale of Russian Love," *Akron Beacon Journal*, November 30, 1929.

Prince, Arthur. Accounts of Prince's capture and release found in the *Detroit Free Press* of August 5, August 6, and October 29, 1920. Account of his arrival home found in the *Detroit Free Press* of October 29, 1920.

Richardson, Wilds. His "Notes on the War and on the North Russia Expedition" from AEFNR, File Number 23-11.4, Microfilm M924, Roll 1.

Ryan, Charles. Ryan's diary and letters home from "The Charles Brady Ryan Papers, 1916–1919," BHL. Used with permission.

Sapp, Frank. Entries from Sapp's diary found in the article "Frank Sapp Diary Is Saga of Young American Soldier" in the *Fairmount (IN) News*, June 9, 1938.

Scheu, Clarence. "Clarence G. Scheu Diary" found in BHL. Used with permission.

Schroeder, Herbert. Account of Schroeder's disappearance is from the *Detroit Free Press*, February 8, 1920. Also see *The History of the American Expedition Fighting the Bolsheviki* in the bibliography. Account of Schroeder's having been seen by Jens Laursen in Moscow from U.S. State Department Records, American Prisoners of War, Document Number 763.72114A. Accessed via https://www.fold3.com.

Smith, Gordon. "The Gordon W. Smith Diary" and the story "The Forgotten Regiment" by Odessa Ruth Smith in the May 25, 1930, *Detroit Free Press* found in BHL. Used with permission.

Stewart, George. November 14, 1918, cablegram suggesting withdrawal from Russia found in AEFNR, File Number 23-33.2, Microfilm M924, Roll 2. His February 13, 1919, cable to the War Department from AEFNR, File Number 23-11.1, Microfilm M924, Roll 1. Accessed via https://www.fold3.com.

Surran, Harry. Background on Surran's mother found in the Huntington (IN) *Daily Democrat* of March 23, 1894. Biographical material on John Surran from *History of Huntington County, Indiana* and the

Huntington Herald, March 25, 1904. Account of Harry Surran's funeral from the November 24, 1919, *Huntington Herald*.

Toornman, John. Toornman's account of his experience on the Pinega River front from *Quartered in Hell*. Used with permission.

Weeks, Glen L. Weeks's diary found in Manuscripts and Publications, Wisconsin Historical Society, Main Stacks, Madison, WI. Series 1704 MAD 3/43/B7.

Young, Edward. See entry for Michael Macalla above. Account of Young's funeral from the November 18, 1919, *Wilkes-Barre (PA) Record*.

BIBLIOGRAPHY

BOOKS

Anderson, Godfrey J. *A Michigan Polar Bear Confronts the Bolsheviks.* Edited by Gordon L. Olson. Grand Rapids, MI: William B. Eerdmans, 2010.

Carey, Donald E. *Fighting the Bolsheviks: The Russian War Memoirs of Private First Class Donald E. Carey, U.S. Army, 1918–1919.* Edited by Neil G. Carey. Novato, CA: Presidio Press, 1997.

Costello, Harry J. *Why Did We Go to Russia?* Detroit, MI: Harry J. Costello, 1922.

Cudahy, John. *Archangel: The American War with Russia.* Chicago: A. C. McClurg, 1924.

Francis, David R. *Russia from the American Embassy: April, 1916–November, 1918.* New York: Charles Scribner's Sons, 1921.

Gilbert, Martin. *The First World War: A Complete History.* New York: Henry Holt, 1994.

Gordon, Dennis, and Hayes Otoupalik. *Quartered in Hell: The Story of the American North Russia Expeditionary Force, 1918–1919.* Missoula, MT: Doughboy Historical Society and G.O.S., 1982.

History of Huntington County, Indiana. Chicago, IL: Brant & Fuller, 1887.

Ironside, Edmund. *Archangel: 1918–1919.* Uckfield, East Sussex, UK: Naval & Military Press, 2007.

Kotkin, Stephen. *Stalin: Volume I; Paradoxes of Power, 1878–1928.* New York: Penguin Press, 2014.

Kuzmarov, Jeremy, and John Marciano. *The Russians Are Coming, Again: The First Cold War as Tragedy, the Second as Farce.* New York: Monthly Review Press, 2018.

Moffat, Ian C. D. *The Allied Intervention in Russia, 1918–1920: The Diplomacy of Chaos.* London: Palgrave MacMillan, 2015.

Moore, Joel R. *"M" Company 339th Infantry in North Russia*. Jackson, MI: Central City Book Company, 1920.

Moore, Joel R., Harry H. Mead, and Lewis E. Jahns. *The History of the American Expedition Fighting the Bolsheviki: Campaigning in North Russia, 1918–1919*. Detroit, MI: Polar Bear Publishing, 1920.

Rhodes, Benjamin D. *The Anglo-American Winter War with Russia, 1918–1919: A Diplomatic and Military Tragicomedy*. Westport, CT: Greenwood Press, 1988.

York, Dorothea. *The Romance of Company "A," 339th Infantry, A.N.R.E.F.* Detroit, MI: McIntyre Printing, 1923.

PERIODICALS

Chew, Dr. Allen F. "Fighting the Russians in Winter: Three Case Studies." Leavenworth Papers No. 5. Combat Studies Institute, U.S. Army Command and General Staff College, December 1981.

Lukacs, John. "America and Russia, Americans and Russians." *American Heritage*, vol. 43, no. 1, February-March 1992.

Rhodes, Benjamin D. "Wisconsin's War Against Russia, 1918–1919." *Transactions of the Wisconsin Academy of Sciences, Arts and Letters* 72 (1984): 65–78.

Richardson, Wilds P. "America's War in North Russia." *Current History: A Monthly Magazine of The New York Times*, vol. 13, October 1920–March 1921.

Steele, Daniel H. "The Defense of Ust Padenga." *The American Legion Weekly*, October 20, 1922.

———. "The Evacuation of Shenkursk." *The American Legion Weekly*, November 30, 1923.

———. "Armistice? Never Heard of It." *The American Legion*, October 1938.

Strakhovsky, Leonid I. "The Canadian Artillery Brigade in North Russia, 1918–1919." *Canadian Historical Review* 39, no. 2 (June 1958): 125–46.

OTHER SOURCES

"Report of Expedition to the Murman Coast, Sept. 1918–Apr. 1, 1919, compiled by Lt. Charles E. Lewis." AEFNR, File Number 23-33.2, Microfilm M924, Roll 2.

"Report of Operations of the 339th Infantry Regiment in North Russia from Sept. 4, 1918 to Apr. 1, 1919, compiled by Lt. Charles E. Lewis." AEFNR, File Number 23-33.2, Microfilm M924, Roll 2.

United States National Archives: Record Group 391, Entry 2133, *Records of Regular Mobile Army Units*. Boxes 3677–3701.

ONLINE SOURCES

https://www.ancestry.com

https://www.fold3.com

https://www.newspapers.com

INDEX

U.S. Graves Registration Service, 279, 280
USS *Olympia*, 32–34
Ust Padenga (village), vii, 66, 69, 126,
134–137, 140–142, 182–190, 198,
256, 269

Vaga River, 1, 64–66, 69, 71, 93, 110,
134–136, 139, 141, 181–184, 191–
195, 199, 204–213, 228, 236,
247–251, 256
VanDerMeer, John, 58
Vanis, Anton, 204, 261, 265–266
Versailles, 17
Veterans of Foreign Wars, 279
Viatka (town, now called Kirov), 35, 273–274
Vistafka (village), vii, 201–213, 227
Vladivostok (Russian port), viii, 8, 10–11,
14, 28
Vojta, John, 96
Vologda (village), 35, 39, 54, 61, 93, 96, 170,
216, 259, 261–262, 271

Wagner, Harold, 161
Wallace, Floyd, 121
Washington Times, 19, 20
Weapons
bayonets/bayonet charge, 37, 44, 59, 102,
156, 164, 169–170, 187, 189, 259
Bolo swords, 219, 242, 253
Browning rifles, 106
Colt pistols, 106
eighteen-pound gun, 134, 183, 211
Lee-Enfield rifles, 29–30, 105–106
Lewis machine guns, 46, 72, 85,
100, 114, 118–119, 130, 145, 149,
151, 156, 159–160, 164, 169, 219,
241, 273
Mosin-Nagant 7.62 rifles, 29–30, 106
one-pound guns, 173, 183
"pom-poms," 53, 173, 183
75mm guns, 173, 241
twelve-pound artillery, 66
Very pistol, 72
Vickers machine guns, 30, 72, 98,
100–101, 119, 130, 149, 219
Weeks, Glen, 17, 135, 197, 203
Weimeister, Harold, 141
Weitzel, Henry, 136
Welstead, Walter, 212
Wenger, Irvin, 136

Wetershof, John, 55
Whiskey. *See* Alcohol and drunkenness
White Army/Whites (loyal to the Czar)
attempting to undo the Revolution, 7, 81,
90–91, 275–277
civil war with Red Army, 45, 121, 129
fighting with Allied forces, 169, 250–253,
272–273
fighting with U.S. forces, 173–177,
209–210, 236, 238–241
mutiny and refusal to fight, 226–227, 249,
273–274
reestablishment of Eastern Front, 54
removal of Allied support, 230, 248, 275
victory of Red Army over, 277
White Chapel Memorial Cemetery, 280
White Sea, viii, 37, 84, 88, 249, 253, 255. *See
also* Kola Peninsula
Why Did We Go to Russia? (Costello), 73, 283
Wieczorek, Robert, 103–104
Wierenga, Peter, 189
Wilczewski, Kasmir, 85
Williams, Charles Turner, 11
Wilson, Sir Henry, 90
Wilson, Woodrow
opposition to U.S. intervention, 9
ordering U.S. intervention, 13–14, 28, 32,
45, 126, 275–276
peace talks, 104–105, 150–151, 231
questioning expedition goals, 228–229
support of the Czech Legion, 11
withdrawal of troops from Russia,
229–230, 248
Winslow, Douglas, 190
Women
interactions with U.S. soldiers, 65–66, 175
marriages to U.S. soldiers, 270–271
peasant living conditions, 42, 139
Red Army soldiers/nurses, 61, 117,
262–263
"snaffled" by officers, 202–203
suffering the horrors of war, 106, 124–125
sympathizing with wounded soldiers, 259
tending American graves, 269–270, 280
World War I
1914–1917 war on the Western Front, 3–5
1914–1917 war on the Eastern Front, 6–7
1917 U.S. declaration of war, 5
1918 entry of U.S. into combat, 8
1918 German expansion into Finland, 7

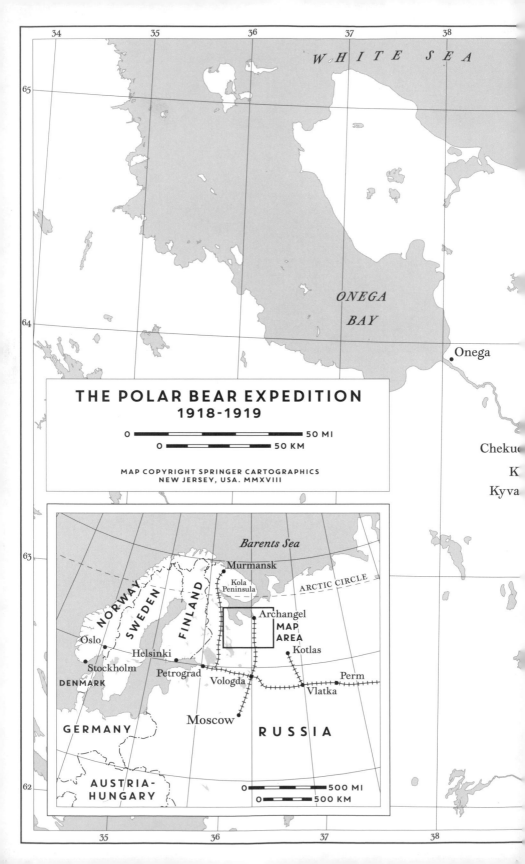

THE POLAR BEAR EXPEDITION
1918-1919

0   50 MI
0   50 KM

MAP COPYRIGHT SPRINGER CARTOGRAPHICS
NEW JERSEY, USA. MMXVIII

WHITE SEA

ONEGA BAY

Onega

Chekue

K

Kyva

Barents Sea

Murmansk

Kola Peninsula

ARCTIC CIRCLE

NORWAY

SWEDEN

FINLAND

Archangel

MAP AREA

Kotlas

Oslo

Helsinki

Stockholm

Petrograd

Vologda

Perm

Vlatka

DENMARK

Moscow

RUSSIA

GERMANY

AUSTRIA-HUNGARY

0   500 MI
0   500 KM